By the same author

SOMERVILLE AND ROSS
(Bucknell University Press)

GERALD GRIFFIN 1803-1840:
A CRITICAL BIOGRAPHY
(Cambridge University Press)

ST JOHN ERVINE:
SELECTED PLAYS
(Colin Smythe)

THE ANGLO-IRISH NOVEL
VOLUME ONE: THE NINETEENTH CENTURY

Volume Two

1900-1940

Appletree Press
Belfast

Barnes & Noble Books
Savage, Maryland

First published and printed by
The Appletree Press Ltd
7 James Street South
Belfast BT2 8DL
1990

The publisher acknowledges the financial
assistance of the Arts Council of Northern
Ireland in the publication of this volume.

British Library Cataloguing in Publication Data
Cronin, John, *1928-*
The Anglo-Irish novel.
Vol. 2, 1900-1940
1. Fiction in English. Irish Writers – Critical studies
I. Title
823.0099415
ISBN 0-904651-34-7

First published in the United States of America
1990 by
Barnes & Noble Books
8705 Bollman Place
Savage, Maryland 20763

Library of Congress Cataloging in Publication Data
(Revised for vol. 2)
Cronin, John. 1928-
The Anglo-Irish novel.

Vol. 2 published in Savage, Md.
Includes bibliographies and index.
Contents: v. 1. The nineteenth century – v. 2.
1990-1940.
1. English fiction – Irish authors – History and
criticism. 2. Ireland in literature. I. Title.
PR8797.C7 1980   823'.009'9415.   80-124317
ISBN 0-389-20014-X (v. 1)
ISBN 0-389-20918-X (v. 2)

9 8 7 6 5 4 3 2 1

CONTENTS

PREFACE

The present volume, like its predecessor, is no more than a necessarily sketchy attempt at the filling out of a literary landscape. Considerations of space, as always, prevail as an unavoidable limitation. Since the publication of Vol. 1 (*The Nineteenth Century*), many valuable studies relevant to Irish writing at the beginning of the present century have appeared and most of these are detailed in the Reading List at the end of the book. In addition, the last decade has seen the resuscitation in a new or newish guise of many of the old critical acrimonies. The debate has been vigorous and the cognoscenti already familiar with the broil will need no guidance from me. Those few others who have been sleeping the while with the Fianna in a deep cave on some Celtic hillside will find a witty and entertaining guide to the matter in Dr W. J. McCormack's *The Battle of the Books* (1986).

Benedict Kiely, who published a valuable general study of Irish fiction in 1950, expressed his own sense of the problems of coverage in that volume. He grouped his writers under thematic chapter headings but, in his *Postscript*, voiced the view that 'it might be possible that six long essays on the six most notable writers of any period would better reveal that period'. My only justification of my own necessarily limited approach is that the individual major works so often seem to confound the weightier critical *dicta*. Daniel Corkery, for instance, is now safely pigeon-holed for all time, it would seem, as a 'cultural nationalist' and he is either ikon or Aunt Sally according to your atavistic bent. Yet, such simplicities seem to have no relevance whatever to his only novel, *The Threshold of Quiet* (1917). The book simply refuses the label of 'cultural nationalism'. The stock phrase has nothing to offer to our reading. The novel is, in fact, marked by a bleak integrity which suggests Beckett rather than Pearse. At the other end of the ethnic spectrum, much critical impatience has been voiced about the curious persistence of the 'Big House' genre of Irish fiction. This sense of critical tedium has been neatly incorporated by Seamus Deane into his vigorous and, I believe, salutary revisionism in regard to our greatest poet and poseur, W. B. Yeats. Yeats's poetry, Deane suggests, is the real link between the fiction of the nineteenth century and that of the twentieth century. The assertion has the neat attraction of the aphorism, yet it clearly does much less than justice to the best of the Big House novels, works which unfailingly function as exposures of the system of privilege they recount. It may well be that the weakest of them rest on a boring and historically unjustified nostalgia but the better ones bring sparkling resources of wit and irony to bear on targets which might have been specially chosen by a select committee of the Gaelic League. A critical viewpoint which fails to rejoice in the appearance of an Elizabeth Bowen or a Molly Keane is, surely, somewhat askew? In general, the fiction, of whatever sort, often confounds the critical generalisations and we need occasionally to remind ourselves of that.

As with Vol. 1, the present work offers some suggestions for further reading on the works discussed. These brief lists are, as in Vol. 1, merely intended as points of departure. As was pointed out before, some of the source works mentioned will direct the interested reader to other valuable bibliographical aids. Those who instinctively lust after saturation in this area must already be well aware that the entire Anglo-Irish literary field is immeasurably better served in these respects than it was even a decade ago. Apart from the sterling work done in volume form by professional bibliographers of the calibre of Professor Maurice Harmon or Professor Richard Finneran, this area of study is well served by the helpful lists published by such bodies as the Committee for the Study of Anglo-Irish Literature at the Royal Irish Academy, the IASAIL Bibliography Sub-Committee and the varius energetic transatlantic and European associations (e.g. ACIS, CAIS and CERIUL). There is no suggestion that a work as necessarily limited as the present one should aspire to bibliographical completeness. On Beckett, on Joyce? The mind boggles. Mention of Joyce necessarily reminds also of the deliberate omission of the single most important novel of the period. Well, *Ulysses* has, after all, not suffered from critical neglect and, in any case, it remains in its time something to be wondered at rather than imitated. It must be saluted as the one Irish novel which really transcends the pressures which had for so long haunted Irish writers of fiction. As Seamus Deane has aptly said, 'after it, the tremendous prestige of the English novel was never again so oppressive for Irish writers'. Whatever *Ulysses* is, it is certainly not the typical Irish novel of its period.

It may be that the fiction of this period serves yet again to indicate only that Irish writers are not particularly happy with the novel as a form. Certainly, many of the writers discussed seemed to work more confidently in the short story. Some of the most interesting of the novels are subversive of the form itself. A plethora of energy is accompanied by a deficiency of serenity. The writers certainly display greater sophistication and skill than their nineteenth-century predecessors but one can discern just as much creative uncertainty and unease as before. Fantasy, history, satire, social criticism, verbal pyro-technics – the troubled variety of styles perhaps reflects the turbulence of the times, as modern Ireland dragged itself from a colonial condition into a partial independence. Yet, in their determined struggles with the form and despite uncertainties which range from the formation of an idiom to the definition of an audience, the Irish writers of these four troubled decades subject the novel to a rigorous examination which often yields startlingly impressive results even if sometimes, also, it causes the practitioners themselves to find their true métier elsewhere.

INTRODUCTION

It is a commonplace that the Irish Literary Revival produced notable poets and dramatists but few significant novelists. When Ernest Boyd published his survey of the period, *Ireland's Literary Renaissance* (1916), he devoted only one short chapter, the last in the book, to 'Fiction and Narrative Prose' and gave it the revealing sub-title, 'The Weak Point of the Revival', contending that:

> Anglo-Irish Literature has been rich in poetry and drama but the absence of good prose fiction is noticeable . . . Of novelists in the proper sense of the word we have very few and they do not appear so intimately related to the Revival as the poets and dramatists.

In the following year, the American Lloyd Morris, in his 'survey of the Renascence in Ireland', entitled *The Celtic Dawn* (1917), was similarly severe:

> The novel has been the one literary form in the manipulation of which Irish writers have been conspicuously deficient . . . This is all the more remarkable since, at the outset of the Romantic Revival, it was an Irish novelist, Maria Edgeworth, who taught English writers to find a social as well as an artistic interest in peasant life, and who first brought the humanitarian motive, destined in the Victorian period to occupy the chief attention of English writers, into English fiction.

Morris treated George Moore as a bird of passage 'whose effect upon the Celtic revival has been slight' and singled out for commendation instead St John Ervine and James Stephens, 'two novelists who stand in the front rank of contemporary English writing'. He also praised Patrick MacGill's *Children of the Dead End* (1914) and *The Rat Pit* (1915) for their power as social documents.

When the Belfast novelist, Forrest Reid, contributed a brief essay to *The Voice of Ireland* (a curious volume issued in 1924 to celebrate various aspects of the recently established Irish Free State) he reiterated the familiar judgement on the paucity of prose fiction during the early part of the century:

> At the beginning of the revival, prose was sporadic and inclined to be

overlooked, criticism concentrating almost exclusively upon poetry and drama . . . after Standish O'Grady, John Eglinton was regarded as almost the only prose writer.

Reid roundly condemned Joyce's recently published *Ulysses*, wrote warmly of Seumas O'Kelly's *The Lady of Deerpark* (1917) and, looking to his own corner of the island, found little to enthuse about there apart from Shan Bullock, St John Ervine and Seumas MacManus.

Looking back to the close of the nineteenth century, Ernest Boyd noted with only qualified approval the work of Emily Lawless and Jane Barlow, finding both women a trifle condescending in their approach to Irish material. He was severe on Lawless's best-known novel, *Hurrish* (1886), in which 'the agrarian movement is seen in the darkness of anti-national prejudice, not in the light of understanding' and he found in most of Barlow's works 'a suggestion of patronage'. He was able to summon up more enthusiasm for Seumas MacManus and Shan Bullock, finding the latter, in particular, to be possessed of a commendable gravity, but he reserved his only real enthusiasm for George Moore's collection of short stories, *The Untilled Field* (1903), and his novel, *The Lake* (1905), describing these as 'until recently, the only works of the first class in Irish fiction'. He separated the novels and stories of James Stephens and Lord Dunsany from the main line of the tradition and voiced unease about the mixture of realism and fantasy in the work of the former:

> Neither Lord Dunsany nor James Stephens has carried on the tradition of William Carleton or George Moore, and it is impossible to associate them with any other writers of the Revival. They form a class in themselves although the only trait uniting them is an exuberance of fancy, and their independence of the traditional forms of fiction. James Stephens began by making a slight concession to the accepted convention of the novel, but before *The Charwoman's Daughter* had reached many chapters that convention was abandoned. Lord Dunsany, on the other hand, has conceded only so much in his short stories as to suggest their ancestry in the fairy tale.

Otherwise, Boyd could only fall back on the usual contention that Irish writers seemed to incline naturally towards the writing of short stories and prose essays rather than novels. His view of the situation had, in fact, been recently anticipated by one of the few Irish writers he singled out for approval. In a lecture to the Irish Literary Society in 1912, the Fermanagh novelist, Shan Bullock, had conducted a survey of the Irish fiction of the nineteenth century and had concluded his remarks by glancing at the state of the Irish novel in his own day. The report of this occasion by *The Irish Booklover* of April 1912, outlines a general view every bit as gloomy as Boyd's:

> He concluded by considering the status of the novel in Ireland, finding that
> it was not worthy of the country and its people. We had the material and
> the writers; but somehow we never got beyond the parochial and the racial,
> and only in 'The Real Charlotte' had we attained a glimpse through a
> whole book of the universal as it is attained by the great masters. He
> deplored this and said it was caused by the indifference of the Irish read-
> ing public and the tendency of the Irish Literary movement to develop
> entirely in the direction of the drama and poetry. So that whilst all over the
> world we found the novelist nowadays expressing the spirit of his age and
> country to the biggest audience and to his own renown and reward, in
> Ireland the novelist had to fight for the chance of a hearing. And, nine times
> out of ten, he can only get published by the benevolence of an English
> house. It is a tremendous pity that whilst elsewhere nationalities are being
> voiced in fiction – Ireland is being voiced only by politicians and a school
> of dramatists which often distorts. But until the artist is sure of the reward
> even of recognition in his own country no school of novelists can arise.

In Bullock's remark about 'distortion' by dramatists one hears an echo of the
hectic days of the 'Playboy' riots at the Abbey Theatre – in 1912, such events
would have been still fresh in the minds of Bullock's audience. More
interesting, however, is Bullock's irritation at 'the indifference of the Irish
reading public', since this raises the perhaps unanswerable quesion as to the
exact nature of that audience and its appetite for fiction. The point has often
been made that the novel as a form originated from and flourished most
strongly in an urbanised middle-class and that Ireland with its largely rural
population proved an uncongenial setting for the form. The creative dilemma
of many Irish writers of the nineteenth century, troubled as they were by
linguistic unease and uncertainty as to their proper audience, has often been
noted. The strong oral strain in the Irish tradition is frequently linked with this
to explain the Irish preference for short stories, often for tales addressed to a
particular rustic audience and with a strong emphasis on the personality of
the narrator. Bullock's brief reference to the difficulties which Irish novelists
experienced in getting their work published is also worth noting. The Irish
novelist, he tells us, is at the mercy of 'the benevolence of an English house'.
Nearly a century earlier, Gerald Griffin had complained resentfully to a
nephew about his annual chore of having to visit London to make what he
called his 'winter bargains' with his publishers there. William Carleton had
been the first Irish writer of importance to publish in Dublin. Maunsel and
Company founded their publishing house in Dublin in 1905 but they closed

down in 1925 and, as Tim Pat Coogan indicates in *Ireland Since the Rising* (1966), 'from then until 1951, when the Dolmen Press was set up, there was no Irish publishing company devoted to issuing imaginative literature on a commercial scale'. As a result, most Irish writers at this time had to seek publication either in London or New York.

When Ernest Boyd published a second edition of his work in 1922, the chapter on prose fiction was the one which he revised most fully. The half dozen years between the Easter Rising and the establishment of the Irish Free State had greatly altered his view of the state of Irish fiction and he now outlined new developments which make Forrest Reid's opinions, published two years later, seem more than a little grudging. It would be easy to suggest that what had happened in the meantime was the emergence of James Joyce but this would be nothing like the whole truth. In fact, in 1922, Boyd was able to identify a large number of other able writers who had made a significant contribution to the novel form. Among these, Forrest Reid himself was an important find, as was also Daniel Corkery with *The Threshold of Quiet* (1917), a novel which Boyd linked with Joyce's *A Portrait of the Artist as a Young Man*, expressing the view that 'dissimilar as they are in every respect, Daniel Corkery and James Joyce have brought the Irish novel back into literature'. Other important figures now noted by Boyd were Brinsley MacNamara and Eimar O'Duffy, two writers who seemed to be introducing into Irish realistic fiction a new note of caustic bitterness, with novels such as *The Valley of the Squinting Windows* (1918), *The Clanking of Chains* (1920) and *The Wasted Island* (1919). Boyd's revised estimate of the situation and his remarking of a spurt of novelistic activity in the period after 1916 was to be echoed, much later, by Sean O'Faolain in a *Bell* editorial of February 1942, in which that most experienced monitor of the Irish literary scene interestingly identified what seemed like a complete reversal of the balance of genres as first remarked by Boyd. O'Faolain, writing in the middle of the war years, cast a cold eye on the development of poetry since the days of the Revival, but found Irish prose to be in an aggressively healthy state:

> From about 1915 onwards novels, histories, biographies, literary studies and bibliographies poured from the presses, thus completing all the categories of the literary revival. How much of these will remain? We may be moderately certain of Joyce and Moore . . . and of most of the scholarly works. But the general standard has been honourably high, and if Irish prose has accomplished nothing else it has courageously explored a far wider and far more difficult spiritual geography than any Irish writers have ever done before.

Boyd's revised summary appeared in the very year of the publication of *Ulysses*, while O'Faolain's comments were made some twenty years later in a period when Irish writing was still subject to the corrosive irritations of the Censorship Board. The tone of O'Faolain's remarks here is noticeably more genial than usual and it should, perhaps, be borne in mind that his main emphasis in this editorial was on the decline of Irish poetry in the period after Yeats. As a general rule, his view of the state of Irish prose fiction and of Ireland as a base for novelists was altogether bleaker. Writing for an English readership in *The Month* of December 1949, he outlined fully his strong convictions about the inadequacy of the Ireland of the day to the novel genre. The basis of this oft-quoted analysis is Henry James's *Nathaniel Hawthorne*. O'Faolain uses James's interpretation of American culture and society as an analogy for the Ireland of his own day. He quotes, with evident approval, James's assertion that 'the flower of art blooms only where the soil is deep', that 'it takes a great deal of history to produce a little literature' and that 'it needs a complex social machinery to set a writer in motion'. O'Faolain sees in Ireland another 'thinly composed' society of the kind James identified in America. In the new Ireland, he says

> ... the stratified, and fairly complex social life which a writer of 1915, say, could have known in Dublin has given way to a far more simple and uncomplex, a much 'thinner' social life. The life now known, or knowable, to any modern Irish writer is either the traditional, entirely simple life of the farm (simple, intellectually speaking); or the groping, ambiguous, rather artless urban life of these same farmers' sons and daughters who have, this last twenty-five years, been taking over the towns and cities from the Anglo-Irish.

A 'thinly composed' society, in O'Faolain's view, offers the novelist inadequate subjects for novels of the kind which Trollope or Balzac wrote. The novel as social document cannot thrive in the new Ireland and O'Faolain enumerates a group of Irish novelists all of whom 'got one novel each out of the social picture in Ireland, and no more'. The writers he lists are Elizabeth Bowen, George Moore, Somerville and Ross, Lennox Robinson, Daniel Corkery and James Joyce. He proceeds to draw the logical conclusion that Irish writers are necessarily driven back on the short story:

> In such an unshaped society there are many subjects for little pieces, that is for the short-story writer; the novelist or the dramatist loses himself in the general amorphism, unthinkingness, brainlessness and general unsophistication.

O'Faolain himself managed to complete not one but three novels before reverting to his natural métier in the short story but, almost four decades after the third novel, as he approached his eightieth birthday, he made an unexpected return to the longer form which had so tantalised him, publishing *And Again?* as recently as 1979. Frank O'Connor wrote two novels before he too devoted himself to the short story and the essay. In an essay in *The Irish Novel in Our Time* (1976), Maurice Harmon concurs with O'Faolain's judgement and draws attention to the many Irish novelists who tended to abandon the realistic novel in favour of other forms of fiction. He instances Austin Clarke, who set stories in the pre-Norman period; Mervyn Wall, whose whimsical tales of the monk, Fursey, are set in medieval times; and, even, Kate O'Brien who, after a brave beginning in *Without My Cloak* (1931) and *The Ante-Room* (1934), later abandoned Irish settings and placed the action of novels such as *Mary Lavelle* (1936) and *That Lady* (1946) in Spain.

The most recent commentator on the fiction of the early part of the century, John Wilson Foster, in his *Fictions of the Irish Literary Revival* (1987), echoes the sentiments expressed by all his distant predecessors about the rather cavalier attitude of the revivalists to the novel:

> Because the revival encouraged other literary forms at its expense, the novel as a recognizable and autonomous form received a setback at the hands of the revival and its aims and aspirations. True, one of the greatest achievements of the revival years was a novel, but *Ulysses* was not a novel in the current accepted sense, nor was it written by a supporter of the revival. For several decades after the movement expired, a debate was waged as to whether we could refer honorifically to 'the Irish novel' at all!

Foster suggests that critics may have neglected the movement's achievements in fiction because 'the fiction of the revival represents a highly diverse and uncooperative body of work'. Because, as he acknowledges, his real subject is the revival and its underlying ideology and because he sees the prose written from the 1890s onwards as having been written 'in furtherance of or *in conscious reaction against* the Irish literary revival', Foster finds it necessary to extend the scope of his enquiry to include, in addition to novels and short stories, such works as autobiographies and translations, as well as collections and adaptations of folktales or ancient sagas and romances. Consequently, he devotes only one of his book's five sections to the realistic novelists. Nevertheless, he continues to speculate throughout the work about possible reasons for the absence from the Irish literary scene of a convincing tradition of mainstream, bourgeois fiction. His musings on this topic sometimes lead him to rather dubious speculations, as when he strays into the hazardous regions of ethnic generalisation to tell us that

> The past and the future are the dimensions in which the Irish tend to live, which might explain a certain lack of enthusiasm for realism in art and explain (or be explained by) there having been no important middle-class dedicated to the present with all its immediate fulfilments.

This rose-tinted view of the Irish as a people torn between incessant nostalgia and perpetual prognostication scarcely convinces and, as a diagnosis of the absence of an 'important middle-class' seems to pay too little attention to the grim realities of the history of Ireland since the seventeenth century. Foster achieves a more convincing formulation elsewhere when speculating about the absence of the family from much Irish fiction of the revival period. In this connection, he suggests that

> One answer may be that the ideological and philosophical business of the revival precluded more mundane concerns, which may be, indeed, one reason why the revival did not produce a body of fiction recognizably novelistic.

Even after the revival period, novelists like Kate O'Brien had to work pretty hard to establish their fictional families in their readers' consciousness – hence such chronicle novels as O'Brien's own *Without My Cloak* and O'Faolain's *A Nest of Simple Folk*.

While O'Faolain's 'thinly-composed' society was coming to birth, the Anglo-Irish world which it was displacing continued to produce its occasional talented elegist, and the well-established 'Big House' type of novel, untroubled by the task of new social definition, continued instead to mourn the passing of the older order. Violet Martin's death in 1915 had terminated the partnership made famous under the pseudonym of 'Somerville and Ross' but the surviving cousin, Edith Somerville, continued to write, producing five further novels after her partner's death. Two of these (*Mount Music*, 1919 and *The Big House of Inver*, 1925) had, in fact, been planned by the two together before Violet Martin's death, but had been temporarily set aside because the writers feared that the topic of inter-marriage at Big House level between Protestant and Catholic was likely to prove an unduly sensitive one. Edith later pressed on by herself and, in *The Big House of Inver*, achieved one of the best of modern Irish historical novels. Her younger contemporary, Elizabeth Bowen, produced a stylish addition to the genre when, in 1929, she published what was to be her own favourite among her many novels, *The Last September*. The resilience of this kind of novel has continued to surprise critics (and to irritate some). In the hands of recent writers like Jennifer Johnston,

Caroline Blackwood, Helen Wykham, Aidan Higgins, Molly Keane and others, Big House novels have continued to prove commercially and critically successful long after, in the opinion of some observers, the genre should have had the historical decency to lie down and die. The suggestion that the surprising durability of such novels is proof of the parlous state of Irish fiction in the modern era may leave out of account the curious flexibility of this kind of novel in properly talented hands. How very well, for example, the supposedly creaky old form has withstood the brutal cross-examination of that most navel-gazing of the contemporary Irish writers, John Banville, in *Birchwood* (1973) and *The Newton Letter* (1982).

On the whole, and in spite of *Ulysses*, the novels of the newly independent Irish Free State were not experimental or adventurous in form. They partook of the tentative and embryonic nature of the emergent society itself. O'Faolain is only one of many commentators who have been at pains to point out that the new Ireland was conservative and cautious in all its aspects, economic, political and cultural. George Russell ('A.E.') wrote to the American author, Van Wyck Brooks, in 1925:

> We in Ireland are reacting against the idealism which led us to war and civil war and I fear we are in for an era of materialism. Our new government is however honest and energetic and from a romantic conception of Ireland is being evolved the idea of the highly efficient modern state. I would like to live for fifteen years more because I think we will react again to the imaginative and spiritual and we shall probably begin a fight for spiritual freedom.

Just four years later, the new State signified its official attitude to the imaginative and spiritual by enacting the Censorship of Publications Act of 1929. Yeats's 'terrible beauty' remained unrealised and, instead, the rough beast of puritanical mediocrity slouched towards Leinster House to be born. Cynics were later to assert that the published lists of banned books served a useful purpose in identifying for the discerning reader the worthwhile publications of the day but, in truth, the full extent of the damage done then and during several subsequent decades by the censorship has never been fully estimated and perhaps never will be. It seems safe to say that the Censorship Board, by banning many of the best works by Irish writers and others, disastrously delayed the emergence in Ireland of a genuinely discriminating public for fiction. Benedict Kiely, in his *Modern Irish Fiction: A Critique* (1950) sums this up in what is for this genial critic an unusually acerbic passage:

The Dublin literary censorship has been since its foundation a group of men sitting in the clouds and responding to spasmodic Puritan appeals on behalf of decency. The main results of the labours of this remarkable body have been to penalise serious readers in Ireland, to make the country look ludicrous to the eyes of any interested foreigners, to label the majority of Irish writers as lecherous and improper persons . . . A parochial puritanism does to a certain extent bear the burden of blame for the actions of the censorship, but as much or more to blame is our general inability to realise the exact relation of the writer to the society in which he lives, to see clearly that, in relation to the nationalism or creed in which he was reared, a writer may as readily be an apostate as an apostle. As a people we have only a very limited understanding of the necessities of literature.

In *Ireland: A Social and Cultural History 1922-1979*, Terence Brown has remarked the striking contrast between this sad state of things and the part played by writers during the earlier pre-revolutionary period at the beginning of the century. Then, writers believed that they had an important role to play in revivifying the national psyche. Yeats could ask, and mean it, 'Did that play of mine send out /Certain men the English shot?' and three poets, MacDonagh, Plunkett and Pearse were executed after the Rising. The infant Free State had, however, come to painful birth after the agonising travail of the Civil War and it would have been too much to hope for that the new administration might be possessed of the kind of confidence on which a genuinely liberal society could have been based. To begin with, the Cumann na nGaedheal administration of President Cosgrave had to stabilise an uncertain new regime in a partitioned island, devising a new police force, a new army, new policies on education and the economy. A mere decade later, de Valera came to power in 1932 and soon embarked on the nationalistic protectionism of the tariff war with Britain. Then, in 1939, Europe plunged into an appalling war from which a neutral Irish Free State stood aloof. Now, in Patrick Kavanagh's phrase, 'Ireland froze for want of Europe'.

Broadly speaking, then, the four decades between 1900 and 1940 fall conveniently into two near halves, with the dividing point at 1922, the year of *Ulysses* and of independence. In the early part of the first half, prose fiction either draws on a mythical past, as in Stephens and Dunsany, or proclaims patterns of rejection or resignation, as in Moore, Joyce, O'Donovan, O'Duffy or Corkery. In the main, as Maurice Harmon has noted, the fiction writers (those born around 1900) who had to cope with the novelistic treatment of the new Ireland had to take as their material for fiction an emergent Catholic bourgeois class, with the decline of the Anglo-Irish squirearchy which had sustained an important strand of Irish fiction in the previous century. The sense of embittered anti-climax is strong, as the hoped-for terrible beauty gives way to the grocers' republic and as writers become subject to the philistine intrusions of the Censorship Board. *Ulysses*, though it startles the entire literary world, will exert little real influence on Irish fiction for a long time to come. O'Connor and O'Faolain, having paid their respects to the novel form in a number of works which fall short of complete success, revert to the more congenial form of the short story. Even O'Flaherty, who perseveres longer as a novelist, writes in the main romances rather than realistic novels and significantly achieves his greatest success with his historical novel, *The Famine* (1937). The Irish novel of our chosen period only begins to shake off its traditional forms and its embittered attitudes just as the war clouds begin to gather over Europe. At that time, two highly experimental novels appear which make all that has gone before, with the exception of Joyce, look dated. Both, however, fail to win immediately the attention which they will receive many years later. Samuel Beckett's *Murphy* (1938) got a warm reception from his Irish fellow-novelist, Kate O'Brien and a cool one from a surprisingly uncomprehending Dylan Thomas, but Beckett would wait another fifteen years or so to win world attention with *Waiting for Godot*. In any case, his mature development would take him far beyond the narrow world of Anglo-Saxon realistic fiction, even away from the English language itself into a kind of creative oscillation between two languages. Soon after *Murphy*, Beckett, quite literally, translated himself to a culture and a language through which he would control the Hibernian logorrhoea which almost swamps his striking first novel.

Flann O'Brien's *At Swim-Two-Birds*, appearing in the very year which saw the outbreak of war, at first won him only a small cult following among his Dublin contemporaries. It had to wait some twenty years before the English literary establishment of the Sixties would excitedly rediscover it. Kingsley Amis, John Wain and Philip Larkin were to chortle delightedly over the weird doings of Trellis, Finn MacCool and the Pooka MacPhellimey long after Niall Sheridan and John Garvin had done likewise in Dublin. Even allowing for the six years of the war, that long hiatus of anonymity for O'Brien says something about the experience of the Irish novelist who does not fit conveniently into the established pattern of Joycean exile. When John Wain published a lengthy and enthusiastic article on *At Swim-Two-Birds* in *Encounter* of July 1967, some six years after its author's death, he proclaimed his honest puzzlement about the book even in the title of his article, 'To Write For My Own Race'. This intelligent, sympathetic English critic could grasp the structural anarchy of O'Brien's anti-novel and respond delightedly to its frenetic comedy, yet concede that there was an entire 'Irish' dimension of the work which he could sense but not inhabit. There is, one feels, a certain appropriateness about that. Place *At Swim* beside *Lucky Jim* or *Strike the Father Dead* and the contrast elicits an immediate awareness of the fundamental differences between the two traditions of the novel involved. English satirical comedy inhabits a reassuringly familiar middle-class world or begins to explore a little further down the social scale, while the Irish novel rages in several kinds of historical dark, deriding the while its own very existence. Wain's warmly responsive article comes some thirty-three years after the first publication of O'Brien's novel, yet the book has for him, as he himself is quick to admit, an essentially alien charm. In an Ireland where, according to O'Faolain, the novel cannot flourish, it seems oddly appropriate that the most exciting book to appear before the outbreak of the war should have been a derisively mocking anti-novel.

I

Canon Sheehan (1852–1913)

LUKE DELMEGE

Patrick Augustine Sheehan was born in Mallow, Co. Cork, the third child and first son of Patrick Sheehan and Joanna Regan. Two more sons followed, Denis who became a Civil Servant and John who died at the age of five. The future novelist got his early education at the National School in Mallow. Tragedy struck the family with the death of the father in 1863 and the mother's death a few months later, at the beginning of 1864. The orphaned children were placed under the guardianship of the Parish Priest of Mallow, Fr John McCarthy, and when they were of a suitable age the girls were despatched to the Loreto Convent school in Fermoy while the boys went to the diocesan seminary, St Coleman's College in the same town. The two girls later entered the Order of Mercy and died young. Patrick remained at St Coleman's College from 1866 to 1869 and seems to have enjoyed his time at the school, developing a fondness for Greek and, in general, doing well in his studies. The Fenian Rising of 1867 took place while he was at the school and the political turbulence of the period made an impression on the boy's mind and surfaced later in his last novel, *The Graves at Kilmorna,* which was published posthumously in 1915. He entered Maynooth in August 1869, the year of the Irish Church Disestablishment Act, under which Maynooth ceased to be an endowed college, with its management passing from the hands of lay trustees to a Committee selected by the Irish bishops. The change had consequences of a financial kind for the college , which lost its annual grant and received instead a lump sum for investment by way of compensation. More significant for new entrants were the substantial changes now made in the rules and curriculum of studies. The Maynooth authorities implemented a syllabus received from Pope Pius IX in 1864 and the curriculum now laid heavy emphasis on scholasticism and the teaching of philosophy in the Latin language. The young Sheehan found this rather heavy going but seems to have acquitted himself reasonably well, without achieving any startling scholastic success. His literary interests, as he later reveals, had to be indulged surreptitiously since 'it was a serious thing to be detected in such clandestine studies'. His health was never robust and he had to take a break from Maynooth during most of 1872. He returned there in 1873 and was ordained priest in 1874. His first appointment was to the diocese of Plymouth and he later served as curate at Exeter, replacing the regular priest who had fallen ill. After two years, he was recalled to Ireland and appointed curate in his native Mallow. He was an active and conscientious cleric, busying himself about his parochial duties and also finding time to set up a literary and debating society in the parish. In 1881, he was transferred to Queenstown (now Cobh). He developed a strong interest in the furthering of religious education in schools and began to write articles on this subject for the Irish Ecclesiastical Record. He suffered another breakdown in health in 1888 and was moved back to a curacy in Mallow. In 1895, he was appointed Parish Priest of Doneraile in north County Cork, where he was to spend the rest of his life.

He embarked on the writing of fiction with a general didactic purpose, realising that essays and lectures were a comparatively ineffective means for communicating his ideas on education and other topics. His first novel, *Geoffrey Austin, Student* (1895), reflects this educational interest and its sequel, *The Triumph of Failure* had a similar purpose. The first novel was accorded a fairly hostile critical reception and its sequel would hardly have been accepted for publication had it not been for the very favourable reception accorded to what was to prove Sheehan's first real success, *My New Curate*. This appeared first as a serial in the *American Ecclesiastical Review* and was published in book form at the end of 1899. Sheehan continued to publish steadily during the next decade, alternating between novels and works of a non-fictional, academic nature, such as *Under the Cedars and the Stars* (1903), *Parerga* (1908) and *The Intellectuals* (1911). *Glenanaar* (1905), an historical novel about the 'Doneraile Conspiracy' of 1829, achieved considerable popularity in Ireland, as did also *The Queen's Fillet*, a novel of the French Revolution. In *The Blindness of Dr Gray* (1909), a portrait of an austere parish priest who first alienates his flock by his severity but later wins their hearts by revealing his affection for them in a farewell sermon, he developed the themes he had begun to sound in *My New Curate*. There was much of Dr Gray in Sheehan himself. He was an intensely conscientious clergyman, devoted to his parish and to the ideal of developing and improving the moral fibre of the Irish people. In manner, he was reserved and shy, fully at ease only among his beloved schoolchildren and cherishing his contacts with a group of literary friends such as Fr Matthew Russell, editor of *The Irish Monthly*, and Justice Oliver Wendell Holmes, son of the celebrated author of *The Autocrat of the Breakfast Table*. Canon Sheehan died in Doneraile, after a lengthy illness, in 1913. A statue to his memory was erected there in 1913.

LUKE DELMEGE (1901)

Sheehan's eventual biographer, the Rev Dr Herman J. Heuser, was also responsible for his first popular success. Heuser, editor of the *American Ecclesiastical Review*, read Sheehan's first novel, *Geoffrey Austin*, shortly after its appearance in 1895. Despite the generally severe critical reaction to this overtly didactic novel, Heuser suggested to Sheehan that he might provide for his journal a series of clerical sketches in which he would depict a Catholic priest at work in his parish. The result was *My New Curate*, first published serially in Heuser's journal and put into book form at the end of 1899. Its success was considerable and *My New Curate* remains to this day the book which most people readily associate with the name of Canon Sheehan. The original serial form of the work imparts to it an episodic quality which is at odds with the novelist's obligation to provide some kind of controlling plot for the work. The structure is simple – the elderly Fr Dan, known affectionately to his loving parishioners as 'Daddy Dan', recounts the varied adventures and misadventures of his vigorous new curate, the young Fr Letheby, lately arrived from the English mission, filled with energy and a naive determination to stir things up in sleepy Kilronan. From long experience, Fr Dan knows well how such early enthusiasms are likely to flounder when they come up against the realities of life in a poor Irish parish. It is easy to see why the work appealed particularly to its first readers in America. It offers a genial and gentle picture of the daily doings of the sort of parish from which many of the Irish- American clergy themselves would have come. The developing relationship between the old priest and the young one is charted with a kind of affectionate paternalism. There is a judicious mixture of gravity and gaiety. At times, the work can recall the humorous high jinks of Sheehan's more famous contemporaries, Somerville and Ross. Fr Letheby's encounter with the redoubtable Mrs Darcy, the 'chapel woman' with only a scant regard for cleanliness, could have formed the basis for an 'R.M.' story and the same is true of the stratagem by which Jem Deady defeats the visiting bailiffs in Chapter xxx. In general, though, the tone of the writing is purposefully serious. Whereas Somerville and Ross tend to see the ordinary Irish people as engaging rogues, Sheehan wants, eventually, to present them as instinctively moral and deeply devout. Despite the occasional lively moments, it is Kickham rather than the ladies of Castletownshend who comes most frequently to mind. Knocknagow and Kilronan have much in common and both Kickham and Sheehan have an obvious liking for the more sentimental moments of Dickens. Thus, we must endure yet again in *My New Curate* the

Little Nell figure whom Kickham turned into Norah Lahey. Sheehan comes near to canonising her in the person of Allua, a young village beauty who is scarred by disease and eventually (and altogether unconvincingly) turns into an impossibly saintly stigmatic. At its weakest, this most celebrated of Sheehan's early works is spoilt by a pervasive and cloying sentimentality and by a tone of paternalistic clerical condescension which requires of a modern reader a tolerance which even the most conscientious of historical adjustments will scarcely enable him to make. As Francis MacManus has pointed out, Sheehan was artistically adrift in a period which provided him with no suitable models for his fictions :

> There was nothing great in Irish fiction to give him a mould, or to clarify his vision, or to teach him artistic honesty. He had little time between school and college, and between college and arduous Maynooth, for reading – even if he had found mentors. He might have learned from, say, the Russians, but he did not know the Russians. He did not learn from any tradition of the novel – if one except the sentimentalities and the Stage Irishisms of Victorian writers. Instead, he found out, fumblingly, awkwardly, though with a native vigour.

That native vigour eventually salvages the work and the novelist manages to hold the reader's attention with lively clerical dinners and debates, with Fr Letheby's ups and downs in his efforts at reforming the village and its inhabitants and, in the main, through the character of the narrator, Fr Dan, who somehow escapes from Sheehan's moralistic strait-jacket often enough to suggest a kind of larger wisdom. Having thus established his parochial territory, Sheehan next came up with a much longer and more ambitious novel, in *Luke Delmege*. Fr Delmege is another version of the earlier Fr Letheby but the new novel abandons the painting of village genre pictures and the episodic recounting of village rumours and accidents in favour of a much more robust and interesting exploration of Irish character and of Anglo-Irish racial tensions. The hero moves in the opposite direction to that taken by Fr Letheby and, instead of the new curate's returning home to have his veneer of English decorum erased by Irish serendipity, young Luke Delmege is sent to be tested in the larger field of the English mission. His tormented responses to his new environment turn him into a kind of clerical Larry Doyle, torn between his growing admiration for all things English and his fading loyalties to his Irish origins. In a scene reminiscent of encounters between Tom Broadbent and Larry Doyle in the first act of *John Bull's Other Island*, Fr Delmege is set to arguing passionately with his English colleague, Fr Sheldon, about his wish to settle in England permanently. Sheldon has quietly urged upon him the advisability of returning to his native land but Luke will have none of it:

> You see, everything in Ireland is fixed in a cast-iron mould. They don't understand change, which is progress. Everything is judged by age. You buy a bottle of wine – the first question is: How old is it? You buy a horse: How old? Everything is old, and feeble, and decrepit; and no matter how distinguished a man may be in England or in America, you sink down to a cipher the moment you touch the Irish shore; and a Newman or a Lacordaire takes his place at the end of the queue. No one asks: What can you do? or, What have you done? But, How old are you? How long have you been on the mission? Result: After a few spasmodic efforts, which become convulsive, you sink into a lethargy, from which there is no awakening. You become aged, not by years, but by despair.'

Luke's disenchantment with Ireland begins the moment he leaves Maynooth. He has been the most brilliant scholar of his year there and has been designated 'First of First' in his finals but his bishop assigns to a much less successful student the teaching post which Luke covets and despatches Luke to the English mission. Even before he leaves for England, he is made unhappily aware of his social inadequacy during an uneasy dinner at the house of the local Canon where he is treated with insulting condescension by the Canon's nephew, a young medical student who plays the man of the world and causes poor Luke to lose his temper during an argument. Thus, Luke emerges quickly as a young man of considerable natural ability and great ambitions who is not really at home either in his own country or in England. Even this early in the novel, though, Sheehan's blurring of the important issues which he sounds is evident. The Canon, for instance, is potentially one of the book's more interesting characters, a clerical snob who anticipates the Canon Skerritt of Paul Vincent Carroll's best-known play, *Shadow and Substance*. He is intensely loyal to the Crown and maintains a careful relationship with the gentry of the neighbourhood, with resultant benefits for his parishioners. His parish is fortunate in its material well-being and owes this to the Canon's carefully cultivated friendship with the landlord. Yet, Sheehan cannot refrain from patriotically sentimentalising this figure so that, when Luke unexpectedly sings a rebelly ballad after dinner, the Canon, while disapproving of his choice of song, is nevertheless seen to be himself affected by its revolutionary message. The author seems to want to have things both ways but, in trying for such complexities, simply makes the Canon a less credibly consistent figure. This is all the more regrettable, one feels, because Canon Maurice Murray must surely have reflected something of Sheehan's own experience as a conscientious and hardworking pastor of an Irish town during politically uneasy days. Much later in the novel, in Chapter XXXVI, Sheehan's unrealised potential as a genuine realist is revealed when the Canon is humiliated at the Dublin offices of the land agent who is foreclosing on the tenants for arrears of rent. The Canon has unwittingly revealed to a visiting Government official the prosperity of his parish and is, therefore, himself the source of his people's disaster but, on this occasion, his much vaunted capacity for influencing the gentry in favour of his parishioners is found sadly wanting and the Canon's cultivation of his influential gentry friends is exposed as the craven kow-towing which it really is. One constantly has, with Sheehan, the sense that a powerfully realistic writer is straining to break through the veils of prudery and melodramatic improbability with which he shrouds his most important themes.

The novel expands interestingly when Luke goes to England, to work in various curacies. He finds himself torn between admiration for England's wealth and good order and an instinctive shrinking from the undemonstrative coldness of his new clerical colleagues. He works hard to impress them and his congregation with carefully prepared, elaborate sermons, involves himself with dangerously liberal discussion groups and, in general, does a kind of violence to his own nature which is fundamentally that of a devout and conservative Irish Catholic. He is plunged into agonies of guilt when one of his favourite converts appears to stray from the Church and blames Luke's fashionably liberal views for his apostasy. These issues are rather blurred and, in a long novel which looks too many ways at once, this strand of the narrative gets lost in the general confusion.

With *Great Expectations* in mind, Sheehan might well have profited from Dickens's subtle employment of varying narrative perspectives for the development of his vainglorious hero, Pip. Indeed, in fairness to Sheehan, he does try hard to control his narrative within several frames. The elaborate opening chapter offers us a highly self-conscious clerical narrator who presents himself as having met Fr Luke Delmege as a result of the accident which causes the death of Fr Luke. Curious about this austere and retiring figure, who preserves his solitude from the curiosities of his fellow clerics, the narrator proposes to tell Fr Luke's story and, to this end, prevails on the executor of his estate to vet his tale, so that justice may be done to the truth of the life under review:

> And so, with bits and scraps of frayed yellow paper, torn and tattered letters, sermons half-written and diaries badly kept, I have clothed in living language the skeleton form of this human life . . . now and again, an angle of the skeleton – some irregularity – will push forward and declare itelf. Sometimes it is an anachronism I cannot account for . . . Sometimes there

is a curious dislocation of places . . . and sometimes I have found it difficult to draw the seams of some rent together . . . And if 'the tear and smile' of Ireland alternate in these pages, it is withal a solemn history; and many, perhaps, will find in it deeper meanings than we have been able to interpret or convey.

In the main, however, the narration is of a direct, third person nature which proves less than entirely satisfactory for the presentation of the very pensive central figure. It is a relief when we get, in Chapter xxii, some effective diary entries which manage to transmit to us the direct thoughts and experiences of Fr Delmege at a crucial moment in his career in England. About half way in the novel, Luke returns to Ireland and then, from the beginning of Book iv (at Chapter xxv), the novel deteriorates into regrettably sentimental melo-drama which involves the saccharine heroine in an absurd vow which incarcerates her in a convent for ten years. The genuinely interesting conflicts and tensions of Books i to iii are lost sight of and meaningful probings and questionings disappear from view in a welter of sanctimonious silliness.

Nevertheless, Sheehan's fictional world is often a varied and interesting one. Even if he never finally managed to reconcile his two vocations of priest and novelist in a coherent aesthetic, his achievements remain real. Where Gerald O'Donovan, a little later, was to spoil a good case in *Father Ralph* by obvious kinds of special pleading, Sheehan convinces us of the truth of many of his clerical characterisations by virtue of an essential geniality and by the variety of types he puts before us. His priests may be given to a mixture of excessively learned argument and moralistic simplesse but we encounter them in convincing settings, men who are going about their daily work with real people in lovingly observed surroundings. Luke Delmege has something in common with George Moore's Fr Gogarty, even if the elaborately gauche crafting of Sheehan's novel never matches up to the melodious subtleties of *The Lake*. The literary predecessor whom Sheehan most persistently recalls, however, is, without question, Gerald Griffin. Both men were gentle, pacific souls, intensely Catholic and filled with a passionate desire to improve the lot of their poorer fellow-countrymen through education and moral fervour. Both spent a period working in England, acquiring thereby a valuable ampli-fication of their Irish perspectives which imparts to much of their writing a new largeness and insight. Neither succeeded entirely in reconciling in himself the Levite and the novelist and both, at the end of their lives, destroyed large quantities of their writings. Griffin's brother, Daniel Griffin, arrived too late to prevent the holocaust of Gerald's manuscripts in 1838, but Sheehan's brother, Denis, was present when the Canon destroyed his unpublished memoirs just before his death in 1913. If, in many ways, Sheehan looks back to the often fumbling novelistic experiments of early nineteenth-century predecessors, he also looks forward to such later novelists as Francis MacManus, Michael McLaverty and the Richard Power of *The Hungry Grass* (1969). The few short book-length studies which have been published do not adventure beyond conventional hagiography and Sheehan deserves more careful extended study.

SELECTED BIBLIOGRAPHY

RELATED WORKS

My New Curate, Boston, 1899.
The Blindness of Dr Gray, London, 1909.

BIOGRAPHY

H. J. Heuser, *Canon Sheehan of Doneraile*, New York, 1917.
Francis Boyle, *Canon Sheehan: A Sketch of His Life and Works*, Dublin, 1927.

CRITICAL STUDIES

M. P. Linehan, *Canon Sheehan of Doneraile,* Dublin, 1952.

CRITICAL ARTICLES

Francis MacManus, 'The Fate of Canon Sheehan', *The Bell*, xv, (November 1947), 6-27.
Benedict Kiely, 'Canon Sheehan: The Reluctant Novelist', *Irish Writing*, 37 (Autumn 1957), 35-45.
Terence Brown, 'Canon Sheehan and the Catholic Intellectual', *Ireland's Literature: Selected Essays,* Mullingar & New Jersey, 1988, 65-76.

II

George Moore (1852–1933)

THE LAKE

Moore had recorded his judgement on the older Ireland of his youth, the Ireland of declining landlords and increasingly recalcitrant tenants, in *A Drama in Muslin* (1886) and *Parnell and His Island* (1887). He began his flirtation with the Literary Revival movement at the turn of the century. The opening chapters of *Ave*, the first volume of his celebrated autobiographical trilogy, gives a typically entertaining account of how Edward Martyn first and Yeats, a little later, attracted him to the work of the Irish Literary Theatre. Moore, the cosmopolitan familiar of the French Impressionists, the celebrated author of *Esther Waters* (1894), began to toy with the idea of restoring his talents to his native land:

> 'The talent I brought into the world might have produced rarer fruit if it had been cultivated less sedulously. Ballinrobe or the Nouvelle Athènes – which ?'
> The bitterness of my meditation was relieved, somewhat, on remembering that those who had remained in Ireland had written nothing of any worth – miserable stuff, no novel of any seriousness, only prose farce. Lever and Lover and a rudiment, a peasant whose works I had once looked into, and whose name it was impossible to remember. 'Strange that Ireland should have produced so little literature, for there is a pathos in Ireland, in its people, in its landscapes, in its ruins.'

In spite of his many reservations about Ireland, he was tempted into assisting the theatrically inexperienced Edward Martyn and W.B.Yeats with the rehearsals of their plays, *The Heather Field* and *The Countess Cathleen* and, in May 1899, he travelled to Dublin to attend the performance of *The Countess Cathleen* in the Antient Concert Rooms. He was established now as the third director of the Irish Literary Theatre, along with Yeats and Martyn. Soon he was collaborating with Yeats in rewriting Martyn's unsatisfactory play, *The Tale of a Town* which, under its new title of *The Bending of the Bough*, had a success at the Gaiety Theatre early in 1900. Moore now became enamoured of the Irish language revival movement and the work of

the Gaelic League and this enthusiasm, combined with a certain disenchantment with the British Empire and its war against the Boers, was to involve him
more and more in Irish affairs. He amused Dublin by announcing that,
although too old to learn the Irish language himself, he would persuade his
brother and sister-in-law to educate their children through the medium of
Irish. He settled into a house at No. 4 Ely Place, just off Stephen's Green, and
became part of the lively literary ferment of Dublin. His friend, John Eglinton
(W. K. Magee), suggested that Moore should make his contribution to the
Revival movement by writing stories of Irish life in the manner of Turgenev's
Tales of a Sportsman and this prompting produced Moore's collection of Irish
tales, *The Untilled Field*. The work made its first appearance in 1902, in an
Irish language version entitled *An T-úr-Ghort*. Moore had had the stories
translated into Irish so that they might serve as literary models for the pupils
of Irish primary schools but, much to his disappointment, little notice was
taken of the Irish volume and the Gaelic League did not even display it in their
window. Moore then got T. S. Rolleston to render the stories back into
English once again and, working from these versions and adding other stories,
he produced *The Untilled Field* (1903), commenting that the stories which
had undergone the translation process had been 'much improved by their bath
in Irish'.

With the appearance on the scene of the brothers Fay and their Irish
National Dramatic Company, Moore gradually lost contact with the dramatic movement which had first brought him back to Ireland. His work on
The Lake absorbed him and in it he embodied in muted form many of his
complex and contradictory responses to Ireland, her people and her religion.
As his earlier enthusiasms for the revival of Irish and the furtherance of the
dramatic movement began to wane, he became increasingly disenchanted
with his native country once again. He provided considerable entertainment
for the Dublin gossips when he publicly declared himself a convert to
Protestantism and was disappointed when the Archbishop, Dr Peacocke, sent
a mere curate to call at Ely Place to confer with the new recruit to Anglicanism.
Moore turned the entire incident, as he did so many of his experiences, into
rich anecdotal comedy. He soon began to re-establish his contacts with
England and with his friends there and stopped in London for long periods
on his trips to and from Paris. As his biographer, Joseph Hone, remarks, *The
Lake* marked a turning point in Moore's career in that it was 'the first of his
books of which the complaint was made that he seemed to be more interested
in manner than in content'. In its slow, controlled lyricism it foreshadowed
the work of his later period. In 1906, *Memoirs of My Dead Life*, which had
already appeared in the form of articles in the magazine, *Dana*, came out in

book form, In 1906, also, he informed his brother, Colonel Maurice Moore, that he had begun work on what he called his 'Farewell to Ireland':

> It is to be called Ave Hibernia! Atque Vale and the theme is that Catholicism has not produced a book since the Reformation. I want to be quite fair and if you like you can supply the arguments on the other side. This will be very easy to do as it takes the form of dialogue.

Ave, the first volume of the trilogy known as *Hail and Farewell*, was published in 1911, the year in which Moore left Dublin for London, explaining that 'it would be in bad taste to remain in Dublin meeting my friends and acquaintances, my models, in the street'. In London, he settled into a house at 121 Ebury Street, in which he was to live until his death in 1933. The closing decades of his life were devoted to new works in his celebrated 'melodic' style such as *The Brook Kerith* (1916), *Heloise and Abelard* (1921), and *Aphrodite in Aulis* (1930), and to numerous revisions and dramatisations of earlier works.

THE LAKE (1905)

Moore had originally intended to include *The Lake* as one of the stories in *The Untilled Field* (1903) but finally decided to reserve it for separate publication. Judging by the Preface which he wrote for the extensively revised and much improved edition of the novel in 1921, he would seem to have regretted his decision and to have come to the conclusion that the book of short stories and the novel had both suffered by the separation. He writes in 1921:

> The concern of this Preface is with the mistake that was made when 'The Lake' was excluded from the volume entitled 'The Untilled Field', reducing it to too slight dimensions, for bulk counts; and 'The Lake', too, in being published in a separate volume lost a great deal in range and power, and criticism was baffled by the division of stories written at the same time, and coming out of the same happy inspiration, one that could hardly fail to beget stories in the mind of anybody prone to narrative – the return of a man to his native land, to its people, to memories hidden for years, forgotten, but which rose suddenly out of the darkness, like water out of the earth when a spring is tapped.

Like almost everything Moore writes about his own work, this comment is at once illuminating and tantalising. On the one hand, his view that 'bulk counts' and that *The Lake* 'lost a great deal in range and power' by being published separately may well confirm some readers in the view that *The Lake* somehow lacks substance, that it is altogether too thin and vaporous to be a really satisfactory novel in its own right. On the other hand, however, what are we to make of his seemingly careless association of *The Lake* with stories about 'the return of a man to his native land' when the novel is, in fact, about precisely the opposite, the decision of Fr Gogarty to abandon his priestly calling and exile himself permanently from his native land? Moore was often, of course, outrageously casual in his pronouncements and to search for precision in his *obiter dicta* is often to court frustration, but this seemingly paradoxical account of *The Lake* may ultimately prove illuminating if we attend to his insistence that the novel came 'out of the same happy inspiration' as the short stories of *The Untilled Field*. Quite obviously inaccurate as an account of the novel's plot, these remarks in the 1921 Preface may nevertheless guide us to a fruitful association of *The Lake* with the underlying spirit of such stories as 'Home Sickness', so that we may be thus enabled to probe beyond the story-line to important levels of meaning which underlie the work's narrative surface. By associating *The Lake*'s fundamental concerns with the carefully structured fluctuations of such stories as 'Home Sickness' and 'So On He Fares', we may attain to a reading of the novel which pushes beyond transitory issues of a querulously dogmatic kind and achieves a more enduring significance. Seen in this light, the novel, while remaining intensely Irish, becomes also a document of universal validity in relation to man's experience in general. Throughout *The Lake* Moore is concerned with the puzzle of causation, the problem which torments Fr Gogarty's retrospective survey of his experience from the very beginning:

> No doubt there is a moment in everyone's life when something happens to turn him into the road which he is destined to follow; for all that it would be superficial to think that the fate of one's life is dependent upon accident. The accident that turns one into the road is only the means which Providence takes to procure the working out of certain ends. Accidents are many: life is as full of accidents as a fire is full of sparks, and any spark will suffice to set fire to the train. The train escapes a thousand, but at last a spark lights it, and this spark always seems to us the only one that could have done it . . .

So muses Fr Gogarty as he thinks back over his early decision to become a priest, a decision to which he is prompted by his forceful sister, Eliza. These broodings about the reasons for his having become a priest in the first place are a necessary part of the careful unravelling of the pattern of his life which Gogarty will be made to undergo. The perfervid ardours of his early enthusiasms, the hectic impulses which made him wear pebbles in his shoes and bare his back to the cruel lash of his brutal fellow-student at Maynooth, must be subjected to the calm gaze of rational enquiry so that the pattern may be re-arranged, choice exercised, the man differentiated from the priest and the personal conscience separated from the impersonal conscience. All of Oliver Gogarty's fluctuations of mood, his long agonising over the woman he has wrongly banished from his parish, his tangle of inherited obscurantisms and occasional hard-won insights, all stem back to the tormenting curiosity about the nature of human choice itself. Moore had already engaged with the subject in the finest of his short stories, 'Home Sickness', where, as in *The Lake*, he subjects a thoughtful Irish protagonist to the pestering irritations of a puritanical, 'unwashed' Ireland but finally raises his story clear of the pettiness of local issues and succeeds in turning it into a profoundly moving illustration of the agony of choice itself. In considering this central concern of *The Lake* one finds oneself associating Moore's novel with Jane Austen's *Persuasion* where we are told about the heroine, Anne Elliott:

> She had been forced into prudence in her youth, she learned romance as she grew older – the natural sequel of an unnatural beginning.

The Lake, like *Persuasion*, is a novel about 'the natural sequel of an unnatural beginning', about someone who is given a second chance by life, and we may even feel entitled to suggest that Moore comes well out of this demanding comparison, since he offers his protagonist no neat romantic solution. Moore's resolution of Oliver Gogarty's struggles, as of the problems of James Bryden in 'Home Sickness', involves the loss of the woman who is at the heart of the matter and the clear-eyed acceptance of alternative solutions which admit of no romantic ardours. Moore's chosen figures are mature men who cannot permit themselves the bravura which Joyce assigns to the youthful Stephen at the climax of *A Portrait of the Artist as a Young Man*. Neither Gogarty nor Bryden will do any forging in the smithies of their souls. They will settle for mundane and ordinary alternatives to the spiritual claustrophobia of the Ireland from which they have succeeded in painfully freeing themselves. The preoccupation with tormenting speculation about the nature of human decisions and their consequences is what *The Lake* has in common with the better stories in *The Untilled Field* and this is why Moore can so ignore the surface narrative of the novel when he associates it with notions of returned exiles and says that it comes 'out of the same happy inspiration'. The very extent of his apparent error is the measure of his genuinely felt conviction about the fundamental similarity between the works and about *The Lake*'s intimate associations with the book of short stories. Many of the issues raised in *The Untilled Field* and canvassed there from a wide variety of viewpoints are reassembled in *The Lake* and filtered through the single, controlling consciousness of Fr Gogarty. Where the short stories are a bustle of differing characters and a theatre for the debating of conflicting opinions, with the sculptor, Rodney, and the painter, Harding, providing an intellectual framework for the whole, in *The Lake* all the issues considered are pondered in the mind of Oliver Gogarty, so that the material which provided in *The Untilled Field* a wide range of conflicting characters and issues produces in the novel a serene, subdued pattern of reflection. When Joyce refashioned *Stephen Hero* into *A Portrait of the Artist as a Young Man* he achieved a somewhat similar effect, with monologue and soliloquy taking the place of more general dialogue and a single figure occupying the centre of the stage, so that the other characters are pushed towards the periphery of the action, into the shadows. The central change is tonal, from the conflict of many voices to the pensiveness of one, from debate to reflection, from mockery and satire to painful psychological self-analysis. Moore makes the same sacrifices as did Joyce, in abandoning drama for monologue, placing control of the entire matter in Fr Gogarty's soul:

> The drama passes within the priest's soul; it is tied and untied by the flux and reflux of sentiments, inherent in and proper to his nature; and the weaving of a story out of the soul substance without ever seeking the aid of external circumstances seems to me a little triumph.

Elsewhere in the 1921 Preface he makes it clear that he viewed the novel as an important artistic challenge and that he conceived of it as a book in which he would transmute materials which had previously provided him with transitory effects into some sort of artistic permanence:

> . . . my reason for liking 'The Lake' is related to the very great difficulty of the telling, for the one vital event in the priest's life befell him before the story opens, and to keep the story in the key in which it was conceived, it was necessary to recount the priest's life during the course of his walk by the shore of a lake, weaving his memories continually, without losing sight, however, of the long, winding, mere-like lake, wooded to its shores, with hills appearing and disappearing into mist and distance. The difficulty overcome is a joy to the artist, for in his conquest over the material he draws nigh to his idea, and in this book mine was the essential rather than the daily life of the priest.

Thus, the echoes from the book of short stories to the novel are many, but they are deliberately muted. In *The Untilled Field*, Irish philistinism in relation to the arts is the subject of vigorous debate between Rodney and Harding in such stories as 'The Way Back', and the sculptor is made to voice the most forthright attack on Ireland's cultural decline. The Gael is presented as a cultural yokel. 'Since Cormac's chapel he has built nothing but mud cabins', Rodney informs us. In response to his friend Harding's mild protests he advances a characteristic piece of polemic:

> 'You know as well as I do, Harding, that the art and literature of the 15th and 16th centuries were due to a sudden dispersal, a sudden shedding of the prejudices and conventions of the middle ages; the renaissance was a joyous returning to Hellenism, the source of all beauty. There is as little free love in Ireland as there is free thought; men have ceased to care for women and women to care for men. Nothing thrives in Ireland, but the celibate, the priest, the nun and the ox. There is no unfaith and the violence of the priest is against any sensual transgression. A girl marries at once or becomes a nun – a free girl is a danger. There is no courtship, there is no walking out, and the passion which is the direct inspiration of all the world's music and art is reduced to the mere act of begetting children.

Fr Gogarty's thoughts are given a somewhat different slant:

> His thoughts lingered in the seventh and eighth centuries, when Ireland had given herself to the wise guidance of the priests, and the arts were fostered in monasteries – the arts of gold-work and illuminated missals. These were Ireland's halcyon days; a deep peace brooded, and under the guidance of the monks Ireland was a centre of learning when all the rest of Europe was struggling in barbarism. There had been a renaissance in Ireland centuries before a gleam of light had appeared in Italy or in France.

The incident which forms the mainspring of *The Lake* is anticipated in one of the stories, 'Julia Cahill's Curse', in which the beautiful and independently-minded Julia refuses to conform to the matrimonial mores of her village and flaunts her sexual independence in the face of the domineering Fr Madden:

> 'It is said that he went down to speak to her a second time and again a third time; it is said that she laughed at him. After that there was nothing for him to do but to speak against her from the altar. The old people say there were some terrible things in the sermon. I have heard it said that the priest called her the evil spirit that sets men mad. I don't suppose Fr Madden intended to say so much, but once he is started the words come pouring out.'

Julia Cahill's response, however, is notably different from Rose Leicester's when she finds herself similarly anathematised. Where Rose quietly withdraws to the safe haven of London to carve out her own life in quiet independence, Julia Cahill dramatically calls down a curse upon the village so that 'since that curse was spoken, every year a roof has fallen in'. Julia Cahill's story is put into the mouth of a credulous village boy and made the stuff of local legend and fireside gossip. The listening narrator, agent for the Irish Industrial Society, is made to pronounce the judgement of the man of the world:

> 'He has sent away Life,' I said to myself, 'and now they are following Life. It is Life they are seeking.' . . . 'When,' I said, 'will a ray from the antique sun break forth and light up this country again ?'

The material which, in *The Untilled Field*, is thus conveyed through melodramatic hearsay, becomes in *The Lake* the source of much more convincing and realistic characterisation. Rose Leicester's letters to Fr Gogarty make clear her cool contempt for the standards by which she was judged and banished and Fr Gogarty himself is gradually made to grope his way convincingly towards an understanding of the significance of his ritualistic cruelty to Rose. Most impressive is Moore's refusal to allow his character in the novel to take refuge, as the earlier narrator had done, in vague generalities about 'Life'. When Fr Gogarty confronts the significance of his decision to abandon his country and his priestly calling, what we hear very clearly is the voice of the realist who wrote *Esther Waters* as some sort of counterblast to Hardy's more metaphysically conceived *Tess of the D'Urbervilles*:

> If he were going away to join Rose in America he could understand his going. But he would never see her again – at least, it was not probable that he would. He was not following her, but an idea, an abstraction, an opinion; he was separating himself, and for ever, from his native land and his past life, and his quest was, alas! not her, but – he was following what? Life? Yes; but what is life ? Do we find life in adventure or by our own fireside? For all he knew he might be flying from the very thing he thought he was following.

This is, once again, the clear-eyed refusal to romanticise his situation which also distinguishes the James Bryden of 'Home Sickness' as he makes his choice between Ireland with Margaret Dirken on the one hand and the brutal freedom of the Bowery on the other. The refusal of Bryden and Gogarty to clothe their decisions in a rosy haze of romantic self-delusion evokes for us all the more vividly the special poignancy of their dilemmas. Throughout *The Lake* we are made to experience Gogarty's intense love for the land he must leave. He has grown up in this Ireland, his youthful imagination has been fired by its legends, he has walked and pondered by this lake and has made his garden beautiful with shrubs and flowers. He is not allowed to suggest that life as a journalist in the dreariness of some anonymous modern city will be an attractive alternative to the dreamy solitude he has known in Ireland. The self-inflicted exiles of Ireland's most celebrated fictional heroes have almost always been vulgarly oversimplified by commentators, in a manner which does insufficient credit to the profounder insights of their creators. Oliver Gogarty's mood, as he swims his lake and takes ship for America, is one of quiet hope rather than brazen confidence. He even finds time to laugh at himself when he contemplates the possibility that some countryman may have found the bundle of clothes he has hidden on the other side of the lake and that he may find himself sitting 'naked in Kearney's cottage hour after hour':

> 'If anyone comes to the cabin I shall have to hold the door to. There is a comic side to every adventure,' he said, 'and a more absurd one it would be difficult to imagine.'
> The day had begun in ridiculous adventure – the baptism of the poor child, baptised first a Protestant, then a Catholic. And he laughed a little, and then he sighed.
> 'Is the whole thing a fairy-tale, a piece of midsummer madness, I wonder? In America I shall be living a life in agreement with God's instincts. My quest is life.'

He has come a long way from his early, pompous moralisings about Rose to this wryly amused speculation about his flight and his future.

The Lake, then, develops and refines the central themes of *The Untilled Field*, offering us the painful re-education of a sensibility in place of the clamour of conflicting opinions. The novel also employs a similar landscape but integrates it more into the essential pattern of the work. Where scenery is used as background in the earlier work, in *The Lake* it is part of the very fabric of the priest's experience. His first spiritual ardours are related to the hermit, Marban. His youthful imagination is inflamed by stories about this holy and learned man who lived a solitary life on Church Island. Significantly, however, Marban's island refuge is ten miles away, at the farther end of the lake, and too far for Oliver Gogarty to reach by rowing boat. He is evidently not destined to a life of solitary spirituality far from the eyes of men. Gradually, his youthful ideals are brought down to earth by the stern practicality of his sister, Eliza, and the sensible advice of his Maynooth teachers. In his first parish of Garranard, he tries to adopt Eliza's practical approach to life and strives to get a bridge built across the strait to link the western side of the lake with the town of Tinnick. He fails in this and also fails in his efforts to have the Abbey of Kilronan re-roofed. His successor, Fr Moran, is now struggling to bring both schemes to fruition but Gogarty has long since lost interest in these projects. His attempt to turn himself into a public benefactor and leader of his people has failed since it is quite contrary to his real nature:

Without doubt a public meeting should be held; and in some little indignation Father Oliver began to think that public opinion should be roused and organised. It was for him to do this; he was the people's natural leader; but for many months he had done nothing in the matter. Why, he didn't know himself. Perhaps he needed a holiday; perhaps he no longer believed the government susceptible to public opinion; perhaps he had lost faith in the people themselves! The people were the same always; the people never change, only individuals change.

Tormented by his fear that he may have driven Rose Leicester to suicide, he takes refuge from the turmoil of his thoughts in the contemplation of Nature's recurring pattern:

> He could not think of her any more for the moment, and it relieved his mind to examine the green pips that were beginning to appear among the leaves. 'The hawthorns will be in flower in another week,' he said; and he began to wonder at the beautiful order of the spring. The pear and the cherry were the first; these were followed by the apple, and after the apple came the lilac, the chestnut, and the laburnum. The forest trees, too, had their order.

When the first letter comes from the London priest, telling him that Rose is safe, he flees to the wood to relish his relief and joy in solitary communion with the trees and the birds:

> Trees always interested him, and he began to think of their great roots seeking the darkness, and of their light branches lifting themselves towards the sky. But he and these trees were one, for there is but one life, one mother, one elemental substance out of which all has come. That was it, and his thoughts paused. Only in union is there happiness, and for many weary months he had been isolated, thrown out; but today he had been drafted suddenly into the general life, he had become again part of the general harmony, and that was why he was so happy.

One need not strain unduly to grasp the significance of Fr Gogarty's interest in those mighty trees. His own roots are sunk deep in the traditions of his Church and the new tendrils of his awakened consciousness are struggling towards the sunny warmth of Rose Leicester. Yet, Moore does not press the point too hard. Gogarty is not made to define here any merely personal aspiration towards freedom but is, rather, made to feel part of a general harmony of nature, now that his fears for Rose's safety are allayed. Moore's use of natural imagery to reflect Gogarty's developing viewpoint has been most exhaustively explored by Eileen Kennedy in her very detailed article, 'Design in George Moore's *The Lake*'. Professor Kennedy's main object there is to demonstrate a clear symbolic pattern in which Derrinrush wood and Fr Gogarty's carefully tended garden are the main ingredients:

Moore, as critics have noted often but have not elaborated upon, uses the lake as an important symbol in the novel, but no one, so far as I have been able to ascertain, has examined Derrinrush wood near the lake and the rectory garden the priest cultivates as equally important symbols in shedding light on the priest's quest. Neither has anyone scrutinised the bird images scattered throughout the novel and used to underline the theme.

Professor Kennedy then constructs an elaborate argument to demonstrate that Fr Gogarty's wanderings in Derrinrush wood represent his journey into the unconscious and that the flowers in his garden are symbolic of the clash between celibacy and sensuousness, while images of caged birds and the curlew with its feet cruelly bound with string make their obvious points in relation to Fr Gogarty's struggles to free himself from all that binds him to the past in Ireland and the Church. There is much in Professor Kennedy's argument which is helpful in illuminating the novel's design, but she tends occasionally to push her conclusions a little far, imposing precise correspondences where, one feels, Moore scarcely had them in mind. She seems not to share Moore's own regrets about the separate publication of the novel, expressing the view that 'the theme of *The Lake* needed an elaborate orchestration incompatible with the simple melodic structure of *The Untilled Field*.' Curiously enough, Moore had, in his 1921 Preface, voiced a view which runs directly counter to this. He there uses the same image of the orchestra but firmly rejects the idea that his new novel will call for anything in the way of elaborate orchestration. Addressing Dujardin in the Prefatory letter and discussing their shared memories of Mallarmé at Valvins, he writes:

> To explain the sadness of this beautiful country strewn with empty castles, haunted by the memory of long-lost festivities, a whole orchestra would be needed. I hear it first on the violins, later they add other instruments, certainly the horns, but to render the sadness of my poor country all that would not be needed. I can hear it very well on a lone flute placed on an island surrounded by the waters of a lake, the player seated on the jumbled ruins of a Welsh or Norman retreat.

In this passage, Moore seems to be quite clearly dismissing the notion of elaborate orchestration as a requisite part of the design of his novel, emphasising rather the poignant isolation of the central figure. Professor Kennedy, when she explores the significance of the various plants which are to be found in Fr Gogarty's garden, succeeds in making some interesting suggestions about the novel's development and Fr Gogarty's changing moods. Here again, however, she seems to offer conclusions of an unduly specific kind. In discussing a short passage about sweetbriar, for example, she writes:

> The Latin name for sweetbriar, *rosa eglanteria*, and its pink colouring suggest Rose, whose warmth and sympathy have invaded the priest's chaste life. The 'apple-like smell' recalls Eve and the primal temptation in the Garden of Paradise. Even in the rectory garden, despite the priest's sternest efforts, sensuous odours conflict with the celibate ideal.

This ascribes to Moore a symbolic precision which is hardly his habit. Joyce may often work in that tightly disciplined manner, but it is hardly characteristic of Moore. Furthermore, if the name 'Rose' is of such significance in this passage, one wonders why Moore should have been content to change the heroine's name to the distinctly un-floral 'Nora Glynn' when he revised the book later. Moore's use of nature symbolism throughout has its evident importance but it strikes one as being rather more episodic and casual than Professor Kennedy suggests.

One of the charges most commonly levelled against Moore is that he incessantly revised his novels as a substitute for new creative activity, but this is not a charge which can be made to stick in relation to his revision of *The Lake*. The extensive changes he made in the later version of the work improve the novel considerably and conduce to the better implementation of Moore's desire to make Oliver Gogarty the sole focus of his artistic purposes. In the 1905 version, Moore employs the epistolary method in a rather hum-drum fashion, assigning letters to Gogarty and to Rose almost on a basis of equality. This allowed Rose to play a dominant part in the novel and to do so in a manner which conflicted seriously with the role which Moore wished to assign to Gogarty. The Rose of the 1905 version of *The Lake* is a schoolmarmish, self-satisfied creature who never hesitates to reprimand Oliver Gogarty for what he did to her and all too often sounds like a vehicle for the expression of overtly anti-clerical, anti-Irish sentiments of a fairly threadbare kind. As Gettmann notes, Moore was at this point using Rose as a mouthpiece for some of his own more tiresome attitudes:

> The revision of Rose's letters is a capital example of what Morgan means by the 'exorcism' of the unregenerate Moore, for the deleted passages are obviously expressions of Moore's egotism and sentimentality. All this authorial egotism has been removed in *The Lake*.

As an example of the sort of top-heavy material which Moore finally expunged from the novel, here is Rose in full admonitory flood, at an early stage of the correspondence with Fr Gogarty in the early version of *The Lake*:

> The real injury you did was not, as I have said, a material, but a sentimental one; your callous silence disheartened me. Not one letter to inquire whether I was alive or dead! I didn't know then why you didn't write,

though more than once I suspected you were a victim of habit and prejudice; your personal intelligence and sympathies were overruled, and during
those months you were the typical priest who looks upon women as the
deadly peril and the difficulty of temporal life. After a while your intelligence began to assert itself, and the natural man to suspect the humanity
of the code which orders that the infected sheep shall be driven out of the
fold lest the rest of the flock become contaminated. This is the usual jargon,
and I have heard so much of it from Father O'Grady that it comes to my
tongue quite easily.

Much else, too, comes to her tongue quite easily, in the first edition, including
an intolerable Cook's-tour of a letter on the arts and European travel, which
occupies the whole of Chapter IX, almost thirty dreary pages in all. The result
is a serious imbalance in the novel and a disruption of its main purpose in that
sympathy for this bossy, emancipated female rapidly dwindles and one finds
it increasingly difficult to accept her in the role of victim in which she was first
cast. It also becomes more and more difficult to believe that Oliver Gogarty
actually loves this gabby specimen of a human Baedeker. In the early version
of the novel, the heroine is made far too obviously a mouthpiece for the more
querulous, more strident aspect of Moore's Hibernian antipathies. The later
version rectifies all that, cutting severely into the fat of Rose's correspondence
and restoring to Oliver Gogarty his proper role as the novel's central figure.
The awful Chapter IX is excised in full and much else of a tedious nature is also
removed. This effects a notable improvement in the work by restoring to
Gogarty his real importance and also by making Rose, who is later renamed
'Nora', a more appealing figure in her own right. Gettmann sums up the
position perceptively:

> In 1906 Moore simply assumed that the epistolary technique demanded
> equal space for each correspondent. By 1921 he had learned that, subject
> matter and theme permitting, a restricted point of view yields a heightened
> intensity and a closer sympathy between the reader and the characters of
> the novel. Therefore he deleted long passages in which Rose described Mr
> Ellis, expounded his theory of poetry, and chattered about his manor
> house. He also left out her long account of her travels, with the detailed
> notations, navigation, the topography and art galleries of Holland, Wagner,
> and the florid architecture of Germany. This compression of Rose's letters
> is altogether an improvement, for *The Lake*, in theme and situation, is Fr
> Gogarty's novel.

Another consequence of the revisions which Gettmann remarks is that Ralph
Ellis (later renamed Walter Poole) almost disappears from Nora's letters
whereas he had loomed large in Rose's. This removes him to his proper place

in the work, what Gettmann dubs 'a place in Fr Gogarty's thought and feeling'. Altogether, the reworking of the material makes *The Lake* a much better novel than it had been on its first appearance. Artistic control and selection have taken over from self-indulgent stridency. Moore was, in the long run, the best critic of his own characteristic defects.

It has sometimes been objected against the novel that the central character is quite simply unacceptable as a portrait of an Irish country parish priest. Desmond Shawe-Taylor voiced this view in a chapter which he contributed to Joseph Hone's biography of Moore:

> So intoxicated was Moore with his discovery of the imaginative reverie that he did not sufficiently differentiate the priest's musings from his own: often Father Gogarty is nearly absorbed in the personality of his creator, and the background of the priest's daily life is so lightly sketched in that we are left with the somewhat irritating impression that he had nothing to do all day but dream of Nora Glynn and the forms of the mountains across the lake.

This, as Gettmann points out, is hardly fair to the actual events of the novel, since we see a good deal, in fact, of the working life of Fr Gogarty. He entertains the visiting London priest, rescues his curate, Fr Moran, from his alcoholic tribulations, endures the venomous visits of the village gossip, discusses the building of the bridge and the re-roofing of the Abbey, mediates in the comic quarrel between the two grandmothers before the hilarious double-baptism of the Rean baby, and negotiates Pat Kearney's matrimonial arrangements. In addition, of course, we also learn a great deal of a factual nature about Fr Gogarty's youth, his near-marriage to Annie McGrath, his detestation of his father's shop-keeping life, his studies at Maynooth and his formative relationship with his masterful sister, Eliza. The novel is by no means devoid of workaday detail but it is certainly true that the impression which abides with us is one of the reflective working-out of the destiny of a solitary soul which has to devise its own escape from the prison-house of Irish convention. All attempts made by Fr Gogarty at accommodating his nature to the requirements of his position in the community leave him dissatisfied and unhappy and it takes the shock of his encounter with Rose Leicester to startle him into a decisive pattern of revaluation of his entire experience. At thirty-four he is asked by life to cast aside the accumulated trappings of a ritualised lifetime, to discard the inherited assumptions of his class and creed and to adventure into the unknown territory of individualism. It is, indeed, a form of rebirth which he is required to undergo and his symbolic baptism in the lake as he swims out of the old experience into the new sets the appropriate seal on his decision.

Ernest A. Boyd, in *Ireland's Literary Renaissance* (1916), pays tribute to Moore for having, in *The Lake*, given the Revival 'its first and only novel of distinction'. It is a large claim, but probably justified. In this translucent, pensive work, Moore enshrined themes and characters which were of abiding interest to himself and also prophetic of much with which the Irish novel would concern itself in modern times. Throughout *The Lake*, Oliver Gogarty's reflections and experiences prefigure much that will be representative in the Irish *bildungsroman* in the twentieth century. Early on, we learn of Oliver Gogarty that he embarks on his clerical studies filled with a passionate idealism:

> . . . no sooner had he begun his studies for the priesthood, than he found himself overtaken and overpowered by an extraordinary religious fervour and by a desire for prayer and discipline. Never had a boy left home more zealous, more desirous to excel in piety and to strive for the honour and glory of the Church.

Versions of the type will become familiar in later works by other writers, from the Ralph O'Brien of Gerald O'Donovan's *Father Ralph* (1913) to Joyce's Dedalus and McGahern's young Mahoney in *The Dark* (1965). Gogarty's soul-journey from repressive asceticism to lonely self-realisation establishes the emotional gamut for one important type of Irish fictional hero. Many of the details deployed by Moore will prove a staple part of other related novels later on. When Fr Moran insists to Fr Gogarty that 'he who betrays his religion betrays his country' we seem to hear also the voices of Davin and Cranly and Lynch as they debate issues of nationality and religion with the supercilious Stephen Dedalus. Fr Gogarty's mortifications of his flesh during his early days in the seminary prepare us for the corresponding activities of Daniel Corkery's young Finnbarr Bresnan and for Dedalus's sterile penitential practices. The pragmatic Eliza in her convent at Tinnick, the gossiping villagers, the alcoholic Fr Moran, we shall meet them all again and again, from Brinsley MacNamara's *Valley of the Squinting Windows* (1918) to Richard Power's *The Hungry Grass* (1969).

Perhaps the essential triumph which Moore achieved in *The Lake* was the important artistic one of fashioning a style and a technique to gentle and control themes of a potentially polemical and querulous nature. Something of the creative, evolutionary process which effected this has already been suggested in the comparison of the two versions of the novel. More and more, as he reconsidered his material, Moore refined away from his original everything of a distractingly contentious nature, working always to fashion an enduring commentary on man's continuing isolation rather than to make debating points about a particular place and time. Ernest A. Boyd has remarked this valuable aspect of the work:

> With delicate art Moore has outlined this drama of revolt against celibacy and belief, so that the banal theme is invested with a charm absent from the traditional rendering of the conflict. He avoids the querulous didacticism of the familiar novel of proselytism or agnosticism, just as he eliminates all suggestion of merely physical temptation. Oliver Gogarty's relation towards Rose is a profound piece of psychological analysis, in which the material factor is diminished to such a point that the woman becomes, as it were, a symbol.

Herbert Howarth, in his essay 'Dublin 1899-1911: The Enthusiasms of a Prodigal', takes a similar line:

> *The Lake* is a work of polemic. Yet on a modern reader the impression it leaves is of composition: material worked to coherence; a deliberate harmony; a paradigm of the unity of body and mind . . . I may have lost sight of the realist touches and the occasional brutalities in *The Lake* . . . The very success of Moore's technique in merging the details of *The Lake* in a delicate haze means that in retrospect we do lose sight of these incidents.

Moore himself had an obvious fondness for the work and clearly felt that he had achieved his artistic purpose, though he also evidently feared that the novel's deliberately muted tone might not appeal to all readers equally:

> It may be that I heard what none other will hear, not through his own fault but through mine, and it may be that all ears are not tuned, or are too indifferent or indolent to listen; it is easier to hear 'Esther Waters' and to watch her struggles for her child's life than to hear the mysterious warble, soft as lake water, that abides in the heart. But I think there will always be a few who will agree with me that there is as much life in 'The Lake,' as there is in 'Esther Waters' – a different kind of life, not so wide a life, perhaps, but what counts in art is not width but depth.

He adjudged the novel, on balance, 'a little triumph' and one would not wish to quarrel with that characteristically subtle piece of self-congratulation.

SELECTED BIBLIOGRAPHY

RELATED WORKS

The Untilled Field, London, 1903.
The Brook Kerith, London, 1916.

BIOGRAPHY

John Freeman, *A Portrait of George Moore in a Study of his Work*, London 1922.
Joseph Hone, *The Life of George Moore*, London, 1936.
Helmut E. Gerber, *George Moore in Transition: Letters to Fisher Unwin and Lena Milman*, Detroit, 1968.

CRITICAL STUDIES

Malcolm Brown, *George Moore: A Reconsideration*, Seattle, 1955.
Graham Owens (ed.), *George Moore's Mind and Art*, Edinburgh, 1968.
Janet Eagleson Dunleavy, *George Moore: The Artist's Vision, the Story-teller's Art,* Lewisburg, 1973.
Richard Allen Cave, *A Study of the Novels of George Moore,* Gerrards Cross, 1978 (see also Cave's 'Afterword' to his edition of *The Lake*, Gerrards Cross, 1980).
Robert Welch (ed.), *The Way Back: George Moore's 'The Untilled Field' and 'The Lake'* Dublin, 1982.

CRITICAL ARTICLES

Royal A. Gettmann, 'George Moore's Revisions of *The Lake, The Wild Goose* and *Esther Waters*', P.M.L.A., LIX (June 1944), 540-555.
Max Cordonnier, 'George Moore's *The Lake* and Literary Wagnerism', *The Dublin Magazine*, 6, 1 (Spring 1967), 3-12.
Eileen Kennedy, 'Design in George Moore's *The Lake*', *Modern Irish Literature: Essays in Honor of William York Tindall*, ed. R. J. Porter & J. D. Brophy, New York, 1972, 53-66.
Jean C. Noel, 'Rambling Round *The Lake* with George Moore', *Cahiers du Centre d'Etudes Irlandaises*, Rennes, 5, 1980, 71-88.
Elizabeth Grubgeld, 'George Moore's *The Lake* and the Geography of Consciousness', *English Studies*, 67, 4 (August 1986), 331-344.

III

James Stephens (1880?-1950)

THE CROCK OF GOLD

James Stephens was born to poor, Protestant parents in Dublin and, towards the end of his career, graduated to being a familiar figure in the literary salons of London and a much-loved broadcaster for the BBC. His date of birth and, indeed, his entire background are shrouded in mystery. There is even some suggestion that the very name, James Stephens, may itself have been an invention. His biographer, Hilary Pyle, favours 1880 as his date of birth but some commentators have been captivated, as Stephens was, by the idea of his sharing a birthday with James Joyce and have accordingly preferred the date, 1882. In a useful Appendix to his edition of *Letters of James Stephens* (1974), Professor Richard Finneran has reviewed the problem thoroughly and concludes that 'there is not enough evidence to make a firm choice' of the various possible dates. It appears that the boy's father died when James was only two and that he later lived in various Dublin slums with his mother until he was about six. He was then committed to the Meath Protestant Industrial School for Boys and soon lost contact with his mother. He left the Meath School in 1896 and began work as a clerk in various solicitors' offices. Although of tiny stature, less than five feet in height, he seems to have been a skilled gymnast and was a member of the Dawson Street Gymnastic Club team which won the Irish Shield in 1901.

His first work to appear in print was an essay in *The United Irishman*, in 1905. He met Arthur Griffith and began to contribute regularly to *Sinn Fein* and *The United Irishman* from 1907. He was 'discovered' by 'AE', George Russell, and began to frequent the literary gatherings which took place in the houses of various well-known Dublin writers. In 1908 he set up house with a Mrs Millicent Kavanagh, who had been deserted by her husband (Stephens married his 'Cynthia', as he called her, in 1919, when her husband's death made this possible). Their son, James Naoise, was born in 1909. Stephens's first novel ran as a serial in *The Irish Review* in 1911 under the title *Mary, Mary* and appeared in book form as *The Charwoman's Daughter* in the following year. In 1912, also, he published a book of poems, *The Hill of Vision*, and his best-known novel, *The Crock of Gold*. He now gave up his

47

employment as a clerk and became a full-time writer. In 1913, *The Crock of Gold* won him the Edmund Polignac Prize of £100. In that year also, he took an apartment in Paris and for some years moved between Dublin and Paris. His novel, *The Demi-Gods*, appeared in 1914. In 1915 he was appointed Registrar to the National Gallery of Ireland and settled into a flat in Fitzwilliam Place in Dublin. He published his account of the Easter Rising, *The Insurrection in Dublin*, in 1916. An enthusiastic supporter of the movement for the revival of the Irish language, he went to the Kerry Gaeltacht to practise speaking Irish and he also attended Gaelic League classes. Early in his career he had come under the influence of William Blake and was later, like many of his contemporaries, interested in Madame Blavatsky's cult of Theosophy. He subsequently turned to the study of Indian mystic writings. He published *Irish Fairy Tales* in 1920 and, in 1924, his novel *Deirdre* (1923) was awarded the Tailteann Gold Medal. In 1924, he resigned from his post in the National Gallery and went to live in London.

From this time on, although he paid visits to Ireland, Stephens was effectively an exile from his own country, frequenting the literary salons of London and enchanting them with the brilliance of his conversation, but writing little. At Lady Ottoline Morrell's house he met most of the artistic celebrities of the period, among them Augustus John, Lytton Strachey, Middleton Murry and Leonard Woolf. He formed a particularly close friendships with Stephen MacKenna, the celebrated translator of Plotinus, and with the critic and litterateur, Samuel Koteliansky. His *Collected Poems* appeared in 1926 and the short stories, *Etched in Moonlight*, in 1928. He travelled and lectured in America and, in 1932, was a founder member of the Irish Academy of Letters. He was profoundly saddened by the death of his only son in an accident in 1937. When war broke out, Stephens and his wife went to live near Cirencester in Gloucestershire and from there Stephens would travel to London to record his broadcasts for the BBC. In 1942 he was granted a British Civil List pension and, in 1947, he was awarded an honorary D. Litt. by Trinity College, Dublin. His final years in London seem to have been rather sad and lonely ones. He was dogged by ill-health, suffering severely from gastric ulcers which often prevented him from eating over long periods. He underwent an operation for this condition in July, 1950 and died, with a certain chronological felicity, on St Stephen's Day, 26 December 1950 at his home in Kingsbury, North London. A gentle and lovable little man and a great talker, James Stephens enjoyed a considerable literary reputation during his lifetime. He was highly thought of by W.B. Yeats and James Joyce was said to have paid him the horrendous compliment of suggesting that he might undertake the completion of *Finnegans Wake* if Joyce himself did not survive to finish it. After his death, perhaps because his best work had all been achieved a generation before, his reputation as a writer dwindled and he came to be remembered as an engagingly whimsical personality and brilliant entertainer. Happily, in recent years, serious critics have begun to redress the balance and to resuscitate the reputation of a notable writer who, it must be admitted, was himself mainly to blame for creating the leprechaun-ish legend which has tended to obscure the true nature of his achievement.

THE CROCK OF GOLD (1912)

The kind of amiable disservice done to James Stephens's reputation by his most ardent admirers is well illustrated by a comment of Walter De La Mare's which appeared as part of his generally eulogistic preface to a paperback edition of *The Crock of Gold* in 1953. Beginning by recalling the excitement engendered in him by his discovery of the novel on its first appearance in 1912, de la Mare continues:

> . . . it is not a book at all, but a crazy patchwork, stitched zigzag loosely together – a kind of motley overall in which one may sit in one's bones on the verge of time and space and contemplate everything and nothing, the high gods, the ninety-six Graces and Man and Pan and Innocence . . .

This left-handed commendation highlights the modern reader's principal problem in relation to the work, the difficulty of deciding the degree of James Stephens's success in integrating the effervescent and disparate elements of his novel into some sort of coherent whole. Is it, in De La Mare's terms, a book or a crazy patchwork? Stephens himself, in a short account of it which he wrote on the flyleaf of a first edition, seems to indicate that his own conception of the work implied some sort of over-all unity, though he is characteristically modest about the degree of success he may have achieved in carrying out his design:

> In this book there is only one character – Man – Pan is his sensual nature, Caitilin his emotional nature, the Philosopher his intellect at play, Angus Og his intellect spiritualised, the policemen his conventions and his logics, the leprecauns (sic) his elemental side, the children his innocence, and the idea is not too rigidly carried out, but that is how I conceived the story.

Stephens's high regard for the novel form and his sense of the prose-writer's responsibility to his material is evident from a passage in the Preface which he wrote for his *Collected Poems* in 1926:

The matter under description is, for the prosewriter, a complete interest. He cannot depart from it; nor treat it disrespectfully; nor overlook any of its parts. To observe his matter, to analyse it, and, if he can, to ornament it, is his whole duty. Like the scientist, he can refuse to be interested in God, or in any abstract matter whatever, on condition that he is thoroughly interested in matter and its modes. And, in this sphere, the perfection that he can arrive at, or aim at, is as splendid as is that of any other artist.

Neither of these passages suggests that we are entitled to assume that any prose work by Stephens is 'a crazy patchwork'. By his own account, he appears to apply the same perfectionist standards to his prose works as to his poems. He is, clearly, a prose writer with a real ambition to match form and content in his novels as cogently as possible. A criticism which offers merely enthusiastic approval of an implied incoherence is clearly inappropriate.

As has been pointed out by Barton Friedman in his detailed and helpful article, 'William Blake to James Stephens: The Crooked Road', the novelist's own account of the genesis of the work and his assertion that 'there is only one character – Man' implies the novel's essential nature as an effort 'to achieve unity of being in an act of Divine Imagination'. Stephens's formidable task as novelist was to deploy the various personages of his story, who are by his own account all only parts of the one ideal being, Man, in a plot which will convincingly effect his purpose of bringing them all to a realisation of their essential selves and of their essential unity. The novel depicts the spiritual and imaginative education of its imperfect beings, who are almost 'humours' in the Jonsonian sense of the term. As with all such characters, the danger is that the particular propensity of the individual figure, its special 'humour', may be in danger of dominating a scene, to the exclusion of all else, with a consequent imbalance and a diminution of human interest. The writer's principal weapon against this eventuality, with Stephens as with Jonson, is comedy and this ranges in tone all the way from the hilarious brilliance of the opening section on the two Philosophers and their wives to the corrosively reductive treatment of the policemen later in the action. Stephens's imagination may well have been specially attuned to this form of characterisation. As Augustine Martin points out:

Stephens is by nature not a realist but a fabulist. He is not attracted by the patient elaboration and annotation of human relationships within the social context . . . we see him transform his juvenilia in the realist short story into fictional patterns wherein characters are transformed into active human principles, dominant and often obsessive states of mind.

Martin is here discussing Stephens as a writer of short stories, but the remarks have an evident application to his practice as a novelist in *The Crock of Gold*. He moves from the comparatively naturalistic treatment of place in *The Charwoman's Daughter* to the idyllic fantasy of his second novel and on to the profound comedy of the tinkers and the angelic host in *The Demi-Gods*. 'The patient elaboration and annotation of human relationships within the social context' are less and less his concern and, as his novels develop, they become increasingly involved with the delineation of 'active principles', both human and divine, in an Irish landscape which is made to do service as a universal stage, so that Ireland is transformed from a geographical location into a psychic landscape.

Not surprisingly, just as there has been some tendency among unthinking devotees to present Stephens as a delightful but incoherent zany, there has also been a contrasting tendency among more serious commentators to oversystematise his work in relation to powerful influences which he himself acknowledged and which are evident everywhere, both in his prose and in his poetry. Clearly, the single most powerful influence on Stephens was William Blake and Stephens made a characteristically wry acknowledgement of his debt to the great Romantic in 'An Essay in Cubes', published some two years after *The Crock of Gold*:

> I make no mountainous claim for Blake as a poet . . . but he is still (as Fuseli said of him long ago) very good to steal from; and let it be conceded that theft is the first duty of man.

Hilary Pyle discusses Blake's influence on Stephens in some detail in Chapters 3 and 4 of her biography, indicating that he had not been the first of the Irish writers to come under the powerful sway of Blake's philosophy. W. B. Yeats and William Ellis had produced their celebrated edition of the works of Blake in 1893 and Yeats and many of his brilliant contemporaries clearly found Blake's passionate conviction of the poet's religious significance of great importance as they confronted the various brands of Irish conservatism and puritanism. As Pyle indicates, however, Stephens's devotion to Blake was lifelong and he went on quoting from Blake and referring to his works all through his career. Pyle details the numerous respects in which Stephens found Blake a congenial exemplar. Both men share a clear view of the infinite which frequently leads to an impressively natural quality in their accounts of things immortal. In Stephens, of course, this produces his deceptively casual handling of the Gods in *The Crock of Gold* and his amusing account of the hereafter in *The Demi-Gods*. Like Blake, he moves between heaven and earth with enviable ease. Like Blake also, he has a fondness for direct expression in his verse, though Stephens was critical of Blake's casual attitude to the craft of poetry and was later to argue that Blake 'committed every artistic crime in the calendar' and had hardly ever spent the necessary time and effort on perfecting his work. In spite of all his reservations about Blake's imperfections, however, he was of the firm opinion that 'He is a genius, and there is no one like him, and he is the beloved, and there is no one better worth loving.' Both men, Pyle points out, had an instinctive understanding of a child's mind and used the powerful innocence of the child's point of view to devastating effect. Both mourned the advance of what modernity calls civilisation, a process which enslaves mankind for gain and perverts Nature. Both also, in their respective ways, rejected conventional Christian doctrine on a wide range of issues, seeing it as the enemy of spontaneity and the creator of oppressive forces. The official enunciators of the various 'Thou Shalt Nots' produce in their turn the oppressive forces of a punitive system of law and order and Stephens reserves a special derision for policemen. The comedy he lavishes on them, however, never quite obscures their continuing capacity for genuine menace and, although the policemen who arrest the Philosopher are led a merry dance through the darkness at the opening of Book v, the actual imprisonment of the Philosopher proves sadly effective in dashing the victim's spirits and robbing him of his capacity for intellectual independence:

> 'Can one's mind go to prison as well as one's body?' said he. He strove desperately to regain his intellectual freedom, but he could not. He could conjure up no visions but those of fear. The creatures of the dark invaded him, fantastic terrors were thronging on every side: they came from the darkness into his eyes and beyond into himself, so that his mind as well as his fancy was captured, and he knew he was, indeed, in gaol.

The cruelty which inspires this incarceration of the mind and body stems back to an oppressive doctrine presided over by Blake's Nobodaddy, the alternative God whom men have fashioned as a kind of divine bogey-man. Pyle notes how, in the very year of the publication of *The Crock of Gold*, Stephens was discussing Blake's theology in an article which he wrote for the *Irish Review* under the title 'The Wisdom of the West'. She quotes from this a passage which is of considerable relevance to the novel's effort at creating unity of being:

> Blake does not postulate a Trinity but a quaternity, in his Republic. His battlefield is the human body; the protagonists under the titles of Urizen, Luvah, Tharmas and Urthona, are Powers, Intellect, Love, Spirit and Matter, and each of these had further its female, its emanation, its spectre, metal, space, and physical function . . . At some time one of these states is in the dominant, and again a different one takes the sway, and the battle

cannot be ended until Imagination, or the Redeemer, has fused them into the peace of the Universal Brotherhood, which is his objective.

Stephens would have approved of Wordsworth's injunction:

> Give all thou canst; high Heaven rejects the lore
> Of nicely-calculated less or more.

In *The Insurrection in Dublin* (1916) he roundly condemned any literal interpretation of Justice of an even-handed kind:

> After a certain point I dislike and despise Justice. It is an attribute of God, and is adequately managed by him alone; but between man and man no other ethics save that of kindness can give results.

In place of conventional Christian rulings on morality Stephens preached a Blakean counter-creed of energetic response to the interplay in the universe of Good and Evil, basing his ideas on Blake's celebrated doctrine that 'without contraries is no progression'. At the beginning of Book IV of *The Crock of Gold* he tells us that 'All would be very well if Thought would but continue to frolic' and goes on to regret that

> . . . there has been no matrimony of minds, but only an hermaphroditic propagation of automatic ideas, which in their due rotation assume dominance, and reign severely. To the world this system of thought, because it is consecutive, is known as Logic, but Eternity has written it down in the Book of Errors as Mechanism, for life may not be consecutive, but explosive and variable, else it is a shackled and timorous slave.

Like Louis MacNeice later, he took an intense delight in 'the drunkenness of things being various'. This impulse leads on inevitably to his ardent desire for gaiety and *joie de vivre* to express themselves in a dance of spontaneous delight, and the entire strategy of his novel is geared to the apocalyptic dance which climaxes it. Stephens shared Yeats's conviction that

> . . . the good are always the merry
> Save by an evil chance,
> And the merry love to fiddle,
> And the merry love to dance.

In the light of so many echoes, direct and indirect, Hilary Pyle feels entitled to claim that 'In *The Crock of Gold*, Stephens was to attempt a full exposition of Blake's philosophy', though she modifies this view slightly a little later when she says instead that '*The Crock of Gold* is important in that it contains the basis of his somewhat confused philosophy and owes a considerable debt to William Blake.' She links the central deity of Stephens's novel, Angus Óg, with the lonely God of Blake's *Jerusalem*, who needs the companionship of man. Man has been cut off from God by the undue development of his ego and has become lost in regions of sterile rationalism. Just as Blake had condemned in *Jerusalem* 'abstract philosophy warring in enmity against Imagination', Stephens satirises in his novel the Philosopher's fruitless dedication to the accumulation of mere knowledge which has not had cast upon it the warming rays of Imagination. The education of the Philosopher's sensibility, the thawing of his frozen mind, is one of the novel's main concerns. Furthermore, as Pyle indicates, Caitilin, in choosing Angus Óg over Pan in the brief but important Book III, is exercising a Blakean Pity:

> ... and she did not go with him because she had understood his words, nor because he was naked and unashamed, but only because his need of her was very great, and, therefore, she loved him, and stayed his feet in the way, and was concerned lest he should stumble.

The other principal female character in the novel, the Thin Woman, wife of the Philosopher, must also undergo a Blakean process, in her case 'the performance of that sacrifice which is called the Forgiveness of Enemies'. She forgives the leprechauns and this generosity leads, in turn, to the children's returning of the Crock of Gold to the leprechauns and to the leprechauns' repentance which is soon transformed into a dance of joy. The Thin Woman is now free to set out upon her journey and to encounter those most Blakean of figures, the Three Absolutes. Hilary Pyle and other commentators have traced these awesome personages without too much difficulty to Blake's *Descriptive Catalogue* of 1809. According to the account of the Ancient Britons, only three Britons survived the last battle of King Arthur. These were the strongest man, the most beautiful man and the ugliest man. They will rise again when Arthur wakes from sleep to resume his dominion. The legend is reminiscent of the Irish tale of the sleeping heroes of the Fianna who are said to be sleeping in a cave somewhere in Ireland, in full armour, awaiting their hour. The significance of the three Britons is specified in terms which Stephens subsequently modified for his own purposes:

> The Strong Man represents the human sublime. The Beautiful Man represents the human pathetic, which was in the wars of Eden divided into male and female. The Ugly Man represents the human reason. They were originally one man, who was fourfold; he was self-divided, and his real humanity slain on the stems of generation, and the form of the fourth was like the son of God.

As Pyle indicates, Stephens differed clearly from Blake in his treatment of the third figure, the Ugliest Man. In *The Crock of Gold*, though the Ugliest Man is given an appropriately hideous description, we are also told that 'from his little eyes there glinted a horrible intelligence' and that this power exerted great influence over the Thin Woman, so that she was saved from the vile attractions of the Ugliest Man only by having the arms of the children about her. Blake would not allow his Ugliest Man to possess such impressive intelligence, so that, as Pyle remarks, we have here a clear example of Stephens's necessarily eclectic use of his sources. This aspect of the matter is usefully developed by Barton Friedman in his detailed article published in the year after the appearance of Hilary Pyle's biography. While Friedman agrees that Stephens's best-known novel is clearly a fictional representation of Blakean philosophy, he takes the matter several necessary steps further, in that he identifies many points where the Irish writer can be seen to have diverged from his Romantic source and, more importantly perhaps, he also highlights the peculiar hazards of an undue stressing of a critical approach which depends too heavily on the tracing of direct influences. Much of Friedman's commentary has to do with the poetry and he is particularly good at conveying the wide range of influences which were brought to bear on Stephens during the first decade of the century, so that one must take account of what Friedman calls 'several reservoirs of esoterica underlying Stephens' art':

> Stephens may have begun by reading Blake; but he sought and found in theosophy confirmation of what the Prophetic Books had told him. Little of the symbolism in 'Psychometrist', or, say, in his most Blakean romance, *The Crock of Gold*, could not have been fished from *Isis Unveiled* and *The Secret Doctrine*. The tree of life on which stones will hang to sing the joy of resurrection, and to which Caitilin ni Murrachu aspires in *The Crock*, is an emblem familiar to all occultists. Even the characteristic Blakean mode of distinguishing the enlightened being from the benighted one, the living from the living dead, as a difference between the free and the unfree is a way of seeing Stephens could have learned from AE, from Madame Blavatsky, from Yeats.

The joyously carefree use which Stephens was soon to make of theosophical concepts in his next novel, *The Demi-Gods*, is indeed sufficient warning to the source-hunter that, like all great borrowers, Stephens takes what suits him and does with it what he will. Thus, we can eventually see that, in *The Crock of Gold*, he is most deeply indebted to Blake for the novel's thrust of energy, its inmost assertion that man's proper development is intimately related to his creative, imaginative, poetic development. His broad sympathy with the generous impulses of his great predecessor does not require niggling fidelity in matters of detail.

In any case, when all debts have been acknowledged, there remains the critical duty of assessing the degree of the writer's success in the use of his materials. Whether it be fictionalised Blake or borrowed Blavatsky, has it, in the end, cohered into a good novel? The critic who has most capably confronted this question recently is Augustine Martin, in Chapter 3 of his useful study. Martin approaches the novel in a variety of ways, all of them revealing of certain aspects of Stephens's creative effort, and he bases himself on the assertion that the novel can be read perfectly well without any reference to Blake at all:

> . . . the fable can be perfectly enjoyed without any reference to the English poet. The use of prose narrative frees Stephens from the intrusion of Blake's style; the comic idiom, the Irish setting and *dramatis personae* give free play to the originality of Stephens's genius. And the relevant areas of Blake's thought have been so thoroughly absorbed by Stephens that they merge easily into the elaborate narrative pattern of the fantasy.

Martin, in fact, singles out the most obviously Blakean borrowing, the Thin Woman's encounter with the Three Absolutes, as 'the least successful phase of the novel', though he suggests various ways in which even these massive intruders can be integrated into the book's emotional and psychological patterns. He is properly eager to rescue *The Crock of Gold* from trivialising associations with the prose fantasies of writers such as Kenneth Grahame and Walter De La Mare, so that attention may be directed to the novel's more serious purposes in the areas of satire, allegory and prophecy. Martin sees Stephens as deriving his apocalyptic structure from AE's writings about an Irish Golden Age in *The Irish Theosophist* and from Yeats's *The Secret Rose* (1897). He notes, of course, that Stephens imparts to his tale of the return of the ancient Gods an amiably parodic tinge, in that, where Yeats's treatment of such matters tends to be noble and solemn, Stephens's version is 'exultant, humorous and optimistic'. Stephens was, as Martin indicates, the first of the Irish writers to write with comic irreverence about the ancient gods and heroes of the Celts and pagans, thereby initiating a tradition of comic burlesque which was later to include such notable figures as James Joyce and Flann O'Brien. Eimar O'Duffy, whose *King Goshawk and the Birds* appeared in 1926, was another such writer and when Macmillans sent O'Duffy's novel to Stephens on its first appearance, the older writer appeared to recognise his own part in it when he acknowledged the book and praised it:

> I think it is exceedingly clever, & shows that Mr O'Duffy has a much greater talent than I had suspected . . . There are parts of this book that no one could better; an ease & clearness of expression and a generous rage and

humour that is unusual. He will, of course, outgrow his models . . .

Dublin readers had already recognised a certain amount of amiable parody of contemporaries in Stephens's previous novel, *The Charwoman's Daughter*. They had delightedly identified the 'tall man with a brown beard, whose heavy overcoat looked as though it had been put on with a shovel' as A.E. Others whom Mary Makebelieve encountered on her walks through the Dublin streets were equally unmistakeable. The long thin black man who smiled his secret smile and whom Mary heard 'buzzing like a great bee' could only be Yeats, while 'the tiredest man in the world' who 'looked at people as if they reminded him of other people who were dead a long time and whom he thought of but did not regret' was clearly none other than George Moore. Thus, while Stephens was prepared to respect his great contemporaries and elders, he was not prepared to be solemn about either them or their beliefs, and where Yeats's heroes tend to stalk the stage Stephens's have a distinct tendency to romp a bit. His satire against society and its punitive practices is equally good-humoured on the surface, though there is, in the sombre stories told by the Philosopher's companions in prison, a grimness which recalls Stephens's darker short stories. Irish prudery and distrust of the passions and of sexuality are gently but firmly mocked through the figure of Pan, who is 'very lonely in this strange country', where nobody has done him reverence. Satire, whether of Yeatsian mumbo-jumbo or Irish prudery, is not so much blurred as gently absorbed into the never-never land of the novel's comic landscape. In a country where aged Philosophers spin themselves to death like humming-tops, where leprechauns seem as natural as squirrels and classical deities chat learnedly with their Celtic counterparts, a golden haze of happy improbability seems to hang over everything. For, *The Crock of Gold* is, as Augustine Martin insists, 'above all a comic novel':

> Though all of its fictive characters may stand for separate human faculties they must also put on flesh and bone and become believable human personalities. To achieve this verisimilitude Stephens had to find a narrative idiom which would suspend disbelief and persuade the reader of a lived reality while, at the same time, making sure that the doctrinal implications of the fable would not drop altogether from sight.

In maintaining this necessary balance between delight and instruction, one of Stephens's principal tactics is, as Martin shows, the alternation of grave and gay in his narrative. A passage such as Pan's instruction of Caitilin in the delights of human sexuality will be followed by her father's hilarious embassy to the Philosopher when he tries to get his daughter back but comes up against the Philosopher's deadly determination to utter mantic generalities without apparent end. Stephens undoubtedly achieves many comic triumphs through-out his novel, but principally, one feels, in the early part of it where he manages to blend his comedy and his more serious purposes with masterly skill. His confidence is manifested in the boldness with which he undercuts his own effects. No sooner does a didactic note sound than it is counterpointed by a matching mockery. Thus, for example, when the Philosopher who is bent on ending his life announces his intentions to his friend, the latter, though he grants the other's right to his decision, nevertheless proceeds to recount the numerous aspects of knowledge which the would-be suicide has not yet mas-tered. His friend, he says, has not yet learned to smoke strong tobacco or dance in the moonlight with a woman of the Shee. He does not know how to play the tambourine or how to be nice to his wife or get up first thing in the morning and cook the breakfast. The other treats all this with proper scorn:

> 'Brother,' replied the other Philosopher, 'your voice is like the droning of a bee in a dark cell. If in my latter days I am reduced to playing on the tambourine and running after a hag in the moonlight and cooking your breakfast in the grey morning, then it is indeed time that I should die.'

And he promptly sets about doing exactly that. The point is that the surviving Philosopher has, in fact, been enunciating a central tenet of the novel, namely that 'the ultimate end is gaiety and music and a dance of joy' but his slightly prosy preaching is given its conversational come-uppance at once by his doomed partner. This argues a confidence on the part of the author in his ability to sustain his comic narrative in fruitful independence of the novel's more solemn didactic purposes. Early on, this kind of happy clash of opinions is often evident. When Pan informs Caitilin that 'every person who is hungry is a good person, and every person who is not hungry is a bad person' she quite simply refuses to let him get away with such simplicities. She has, she says, often been hungry, and it was never good. Even the stolid Meehawl MacMur-rachu is allowed to silence the Philosopher when the latter tries to tutor him on the proper approach to death:

> 'We must acquiesce in all logical progressions. The merging of opposites is completion. Life runs to death as to its goal, and we should go towards the next stage of experience either carelessly as to what must be, or with a good, honest curiosity as to what may be.'
> 'There's not much fun in being dead, sir,' said Meehawl.
> 'How do you know?' said the Philosopher.
> 'I know well enough,' replied Meehawl.

Again and again, balloons of fine sentiment are exploded by the barbs of commonsense, without regard to whether the sentiments are true or false. It is a technique which was later to be freely imitated by Flann O'Brien. Stephens maintains his comic momentum for a considerable stretch of his novel and achieves some wonderfully funny moments. The clash between the Philosopher and his wife, the Philosopher's various crazily irrelevant answers, the occasional parody of Synge-song; the whole thing is for a long time a sheer delight. The first bad break in the comic continuum comes at the very beginning of Chapter XIII, the opening passage of Book IV. Here, for the very first time, Stephens hectors us in his own person for several pages in a distressing lapse from his earlier masterly control of his complex narrative, and it would be idle to pretend that the novel ever fully recovers its first fine careless rapture, though there are many incidental felicities later. Augustine Martin, as has been remarked, dislikes the intrusion of the Three Absolutes, and it might also be possible to fault the introduction of the gloomy prison tales told in the last chapter of Book V. In general, however, it may be said that the Thin Woman is not too bad a substitute for her husband in carrying the narrative successfully enough from the opening of the final chapter to the climax of the Happy March at the end. The finale is achieved by a bold thrust of sheer assertive energy rather than by any fictional logic, but it would be churlish to fault this most genial piece of anarchic escapism because it does not quite sustain its superb early tonal consistency throughout its entire length. Its remarkable combination of many diverse materials and many different modes, the sheer exuberance in which it clothes its fundamentally serious concerns, its powerful yea-saying against the odds, all entitle it to the enduring affection which it undoubtedly earns and also to the genuine critical appreciation which, perhaps, it receives more rarely. Reading it nowadays, in an age when the gombeen-men would seem finally to have triumphed, in an Ireland riven by hideous dissensions, it fills one with sad wonder, but the brilliantly variegated tale itself makes it seem almost logical that Joyce might have conceived of James Stephens as his collaborator on the most daringly experimental of all his works.

SELECTED BIBLIOGRAPHY

RELATED WORKS

The Charwoman's Daughter, London, 1912.
The Demi-Gods, London, 1914.
Deirdre, London 1923.

BIOGRAPHY

Birgit Bramsback, *James Stephens: A Literary and Bibliographical Study*, Upsala, 1959.

Hilary Pyle, *James Stephens: His Work and an Account of his Life*, London, 1965.

CRITICAL STUDIES

Augustine Martin, *James Stephens: A Critical Study*, Dublin, 1977.

Patricia McFate, *The Writings of James Stephens: Variations on a Theme of Love*, London, 1979.

CRITICAL ARTICLES

Vivian Mercier, 'James Stephens: His Version of Pastoral', *Irish Writing*, 14 (March 1951), 48-57.

Barton R. Friedman, 'William Blake to James Stephens: The Crooked Road', *Eire-Ireland*, I, 3 (1966), 29-57.

Werner Huber, 'James Stephens: His Philosophy of Composition', *Studies in Anglo-Irish Literature* ed. Heinz Kosok, Bonn, 1982, 182-189.

Birgit Bramsback, 'The Philosophical Quest in *The Crock of Gold*', *Studies in Anglo-Irish Literature*, ed. Heinz Kosok, Bonn, 1982, 190-197.

IV

Gerald O'Donovan (1871-1942)

FATHER RALPH

He was born Jeremiah O'Donovan in Co. Down. His father's family came from Cork and the boy attended schools in Cork, Sligo and Galway. He entered Maynooth in 1889, was ordained in 1895 and served as curate in various towns in the west of Ireland before being appointed to Loughrea in 1896. His superior was Bishop Healy of Clonfert and, under his administration, O'Donovan worked energetically as a forward-looking, socially active priest. He interested himself in a wide variety of activities and causes, including workhouse reform, education, village libraries and the Irish Literary Revival. He was a contributor to the Jesuit-run journal, *The New Ireland Review* and also became associated with the Irish Agricultural Organisation Society which, under Sir Horace Plunkett and George Russell, was working for the establishment of agricultural cooperatives in Ireland. As Administrator in Loughrea, he became involved in the building and decorating of the new cathedral of St Brendan, designed by William Scott. He persuaded Dr Healy to commission Irish artists to work on the cathedral and, as a result, Sarah Purser created the stained glass windows and other notable Irish artists such as Jack Yeats and John Hughes also produced important works for the new building. O'Donovan worked hard to stimulate the cultural life of his parish, bringing the youthful John McCormack to sing in the new cathedral choir and persuading the Irish National Theatre Company to undertake their one and only provincial tour, to Loughrea in 1901. All in all, he brings to mind one kind of priest depicted in the stories of George Moore, the kind who battles like Fr James McTurnan of 'A Playhouse in the Waste' to bring something of the cultural vigour of the metropolis to deprived rural areas. Indeed, Fr McCabe, the priest in Moore's story, 'Fugitives', is said to have been based on O'Donovan.

The decisive crisis of O'Donovan's life came in 1903, with the death of the Bishop of Tuam. O'Donovan's patron, Dr Healy, was appointed to the newly vacant bishopric and this left the See of Clonfert vacant in its turn. Although O'Donovan, at the age of thirty-one, would have been very young for so senior an office, there was considerable support for his appointment among

61

the diocesan clergy. In the event, he lost out to Dr Thomas O'Dea, who was appointed Bishop of Clonfert in place of Bishop Healy and took up residence in Loughrea. Relations between O'Donovan and his new bishop seem to have been strained from the beginning. At the end of 1903, O'Donovan travelled to the United States to lecture on the Irish Literary Revival and on the cooperative movement but, on his return, his differences with his bishop reached a crisis and, towards the end of 1904, O'Donovan withdrew from both Loughrea and the priesthood. George Moore supplied him with letters of introduction to various London publishers and he embarked on his new life as a writer under the name of Gerald O'Donovan. In 1910, he was appointed warden of Toynbee Hall and in the same year he married Beryl Verschoyle. There were three children of the marriage, a boy and two girls. Macmillan published his first novel, *Father Ralph*, in 1913. The book was largely autobiographical, though the priest in the novel breaks with his Church because of his refusal to submit to the requirements of the papal encyclical condemning modernism, rather than as a result of a personal conflict with his bishop. *Father Ralph* remains the work by which O'Donovan is best known, but other novels followed. *Waiting* (1914) took as its theme the problems caused for a young couple by the papal decree of *Ne Temere* concerning marriage between Catholics and non-Catholics. Later novels were *Conquest* (1920), *Vocations* (1921) and *The Holy Tree* (1922). During the First World War, O'Donovan worked in the Italian section of the British Department of Propaganda and became its Head in 1918. Through this, he met and became the intimate friend of the novelist, Rose Macaulay. His creative impulse seems to have died away during the last two decades of his life. In the summer of 1939, while on a holiday in the Lake District with Rose Macaulay, he and Macaulay were both involved in an accident in which he suffered a fractured skull. This brought about a protracted illness and he died of cancer in July, 1942.

FATHER RALPH (1913)

This is a novel which does not so much travel hopefully as arrive – and at a preconceived destination. It is a polemical book in which barely concealed anger leads to the employment of stereotypes and argumentative simplesse. Alternatively, one might suggest that the considerable measure of autobiography which it contains is insufficiently absorbed in the fiction. Clearly, the story derives directly from O'Donovan's own troubled experiences as a liberal cleric in a conservative Church at a crucial time when, within that Church, the struggle against modernism was reaching a climax. Whether O'Donovan would have been prepared to accommodate himself to the clerical conservatism outlined in the papal encyclical *Pascendi Dominici Gregis* if he had achieved appointment to the bishopric of Clonfert in succession to Dr Healy in 1903 is, in the absence of any definitive biography, impossible to establish. That is an unanswered question of the life rather than the work and, in this, his first and best-known novel, he is careful to make the priest's final, crucial decision hinge on a point of moral conviction rather than professional advancement. The climactic scenes towards the end of the novel when news comes through of the papal decision to condemn the modernists are, in their way, quite tense and gripping. The decisive moment when Fr Ralph refuses to submit to the bishop's demand for conformity is ably recounted and there are even effective moments of earthy clerical humour in the sardonic comments of some of the older priests present at the gathering who realise how the entire situation is being manipulated against Fr Ralph by the unscrupulous parish priest, Fr Molloy. The mental torment of Ralph himself is convincingly presented, often in a manner which suggests that O'Donovan may have Moore's Fr Gogarty very much in mind. Not that O'Donovan's dissident priest at all resembles Moore's – whereas Gogarty gradually moves towards a realisation that he cannot continue a priest if he is to be true to his essential nature, Ralph O'Brien is poignantly aware that he most certainly wishes to remain a priest but is being forced out of his sacred vocation by oppressive forces whose demands on his intellect he cannot tolerate. When he first contemplates the possibility that he may have to abandon his priesthood, he is appalled by the prospect:

> Panic seized him. He lost all power of thought. He felt a passionate longing for the ritual and practices of the Church. He clung desperately to something vague that was being forcibly taken from his grasp . . . A succession of detached memories made him calm: the little blue and white altar of the Virgin in his nursery; his first rosary beads, with Ann Carty explaining how he was to say the prayers. Of course Ann was somewhere in the house now. He was safe. Then, kaleidoscopically: Clarendon Street Church, the smell of incense, the priest saying mass at the altar, the lay brother lighting and quenching candles, a hill with the sea at his feet, and his father, his kind face set sternly, saying that the O'Briens had always been Catholics . . .

Furthermore, unlike Moore's peripatetic Fr Gogarty, Fr Ralph is depicted as a hard-working, practical parish worker who thrives on the daily challenges of a difficult working life. When the machiavellian bishop arrives back from

Rome with his plans laid for the assault on Fr Ralph, his victim-to-be is not at the station to meet him because he is, instead, helping to nurse the victims of a typhus epidemic which has recently broken out in the neighbourhood. The craven sycophancy with which the bishop is greeted ·by others is portrayed with comic relish:

> The bishop arrived home, and was received at the railway station by the brass band. Darcy read an address written by Fr Molloy. The bishop in reply made a glowing speech on the wisdom of the Pope, whose unceasing care of his people would be manifest when the great encyclical, a copy of which he had the happiness to have in his pocket, was read in the churches. It would gladden the Pope's heart to hear that the bearer of his encyclical had received such a magnificent welcome, worthy alike of the great occasion and of the holiness of the people.
>
> Ralph, who had spent the night in one of the fever houses, heard all this next day from Father Dempsey.
>
> 'Your absence was remarked on by his lordship. I said you were on a sick call, but he was none too pleased. He said it showed a lack of zeal, not to be present to welcome one's bishop after a long absence.'

Painful as Ralph finds it to abandon his priestly calling, O'Donovan allows him a Gogarty-like sense of relief when he faces up to the ultimate necessity for action. He tells his journalist friend, Boyle, how he feels:

> 'I shall go out like a shivering deserter. I feel at this moment as if everything that bound me to life was about to snap. My whole life has been built up on illusions, and they have left their mark on me. I have to face reality at last. Religion, duty, honesty force me to it, but I shall feel in doing it as if I were committing some unthinkable crime.'

Later again, he talks with the sympathetic nun who has, until recently, been Reverend Mother of the local convent. She is concerned when he tells her of his impending departure but Ralph is allowed a moment of release which, in its reflection in the beauty of the autumn day, recalls *The Lake*:

> The nun sat absorbed in thought, or prayer, for she fingered her beads rapidly. Ralph's eyes wandered over the grounds in front. Sound and sight were no longer painful. He drank in the beauty of the wonderful autumn colouring, brown and gold against the light green of the well-mown grass and the harsher green of the evergreens gleaming in the sun. The autumn day had all the freshness of spring and the genial warmth of early summer. A weight seemed to have fallen from his spirit . . .

There are clear signs early on in the novel that O'Donovan's generally polemical purpose will betray him into regrettable oversimplifications in the regions of character and plot. The first stereotype to be wheeled into position is Ralph's improbable mother who is depicted as being a Catholic so devout as to border on the farcical. Much later, she will be duped by the canny bishop (another wooden piece of oversimplification) into parting with large sums of money and, eventually, even her house. The mother's improbable dottiness is compensated for somewhat by her husband's common-sense in his approach to Ralph as a child and as he grows to manhood. Mrs O'Brien wants the boy to enter the Carmelite Order and is not at all pleased when he eventually opts for becoming a secular clergyman. One recalls the brand of Irish religious snobbery which had Mr Dedalus inveighing against the Christian Brothers and commending the Jesuits by comparison. For O'Donovan's novelistic purposes, it is vital that Ralph should prefer the secular clerical vocation because this sends him to Maynooth, a place which O'Donovan is keen to describe and explore in his novel. Ralph first attends the bishop's seminary in Bunnahone, where he encounters many of the clerical students who will accompany him to Maynooth. The seminary is a wretched place, with dreadfully low academic standards and peopled by uncouth rustics whose gross manners jar on the sensitive Ralph. The students cheat in their exams, with some covert assistance from their teacher, Fr Doyle, and one of them, Magan, thus gains an entirely undeserved exhibition. Maynooth, to begin with, proves to be a kind of larger extension of Bunnahone. Duncan, a new arrival who has already spent three years at the Dublin seminary of Clonliffe, comments critically on his first experiences of Maynooth:

> 'Bad as I thought Maynooth would be, I never dreamt it would be anything like this. Look at the dirt on that table, and these filthy bowls. You can see the marks of the dirt of the trays on the bread. This isn't a bad-looking place on the outside, I admit. But inside! The boards of my room weren't washed since the place was built, and I don't believe, 'pon my word I don't, that that servant lounging against the wall over there washed since he came into the house. Do you see his hands?'
>
> Ralph was amused. His experience at Bunnahone had inured him to dirt and coarse food; and he had long since decided that it was part of his religious duty to put up with disagreeable things.

The college teachers prove, on the whole, an undistinguished and unexciting lot and the libraries are poorly stocked:

> During the few free days before the arrival of the general body of students Ralph, accompanied by Devine, explored the College: the poky ill-supplied divisional libraries, without catalogue, order, or classification, or any book that one wanted to read; the rather fine College library, not quite as despicable as the admirer of Marie Corelli found it, but still pitifully unrepresentative of any general culture.

And 'pitifully unrepresentative of any general culture' Maynooth is to prove for Ralph during his entire period there. Ralph's impatience with the dreary classes he has to endure leads him into the kind of reading which will eventually prove his undoing:

> Year followed year at Maynooth. The gloom of winter yielded to the fresh joy of spring, and Ralph experienced frequent alternations of hope and feelings that were almost akin to despair. Father Hay's lifeless abstractions and the crude legalism of moral theology left his heart cold and repelled his mind. He spent many hours during retreats trying to reconcile the futilities of the classes with the claims of the Church to learning. He read widely round every subject, and was relieved to discover Catholic writers who felt as dissatisfied as he did with the modern teaching of the Church. He read again and again Blondel's Sorbonne thesis, maintaining the possibility of religious certainty independently of the schools.

He discusses his difficulties with the sympathetic and cultured Fr Sheldon, an older man who is a kindred spirit, and Fr Sheldon urges him to put up with the backwardness of Maynooth in the conviction that better times lie ahead for Ireland and the Catholic Church:

> 'For years I have been hoping for better things, which are slow in coming. But,' his face brightened, 'they are coming. France and Italy and Germany are showing the way. Some day Ireland will move too. Who knows but you may have a part in the great work? Don't mind the quibbles of the schools. Try to get to the kernel inside the husk. Live your life as closely as you can on the pattern of Christ's. You'll never convert a soul from evil nor help it to heaven by a syllogism.'

Later, when the bishop returns from his visit to Rome and confronts the parochial clergy with a demand for submission to the terms of the decree, *Lamentabili Sane*, which is a precursor to the anti-modernist papal encyclical, Sheldon will give way. He explains his dilemma to Ralph and Boyle:

> 'My own conscience is my worst accuser, but I cannot leave my parish. For the first time in my life I am going to temporize. It's not all selfishness,' he said appealingly. 'It is impossible to explain, yet I owe you both an explanation. I encouraged you and now I hold back.' He did not lift his eyes. After a short pause he went on: 'I have been in my parish thirty years. Most of the people I meet on the roads and at their firesides, I baptised, or married, sometimes both. I promised many a mother and father on their deathbeds to look after their children. My heart is chained to the place. You are young and can make new ties. You may be too young to understand, but God knows an old man's weakness.'

Fr Sheldon is too old to go and Fr Ralph too young to stay. He and Boyle make clear to Fr Sheldon that they fully understand his predicament and do not hold it against him that he feels he must temporize. The relationships between Ralph and those few people in the parish who are at all of his mind are well depicted. Ralph's efforts to sink himself in hard work and to find spiritual consolation in the ardent piety of the poor of Bunnahone are convincingly rendered. We are made to experience a genuine sense of his mental anguish. O'Donovan's clear demonstration of his novelistic competence in these matters makes one regret all the more that he should so often fall back on such cardboard villains as the bishop and Fr Molloy for the furtherance of his plot. At its best, the novel not only probes Ralph's personal anguish sympatheti-cally but also manages to provide an excellent sense of the conflicting social and political interests of the period. We encounter Irish language enthusiasts, workers in the cooperative movement, Land Leaguers, and acquire a real feeling for the trough of Irish time between the fall of Parnell and the explosion of the Insurrection of 1916. There is, however, a central flaw in the conception of the main character, one which derives from O'Donovan's regrettably oversimplified depiction of the demented piety of Ralph's mother. This has the unfortunate effect of making Ralph himself seem, for a long time, almost unacceptably naive. He takes far too long to awaken to the one-sidedness of the forces which have conspired to make a priest of him in the first place and this weakness undercuts, to some extent, the conviction we need to feel at the close about his grand gesture in giving up his priesthood. Nevertheless, the novel repays re-reading today and a reprint might be of considerable interest to the less monolithic Irish Catholicism which has emerged in the period following the second Vatican Council.

SELECTED BIBLIOGRAPHY

RELATED WORKS

Waiting, London, 1914.
Conquest, London, 1920.
Vocations, London, 1921.
The Holy Tree, London, 1922.

CRITICAL STUDIES

Peter Costello, *The Heart Grown Brutal*, Dublin, 1977, 58-64.

CRITICAL ARTICLES

Sean McMahon, 'Turbulent Priest: A Reappraisal of *Father Ralph*', *Ulster Tatler* (Sept. 1982), 49-52.

V

James Joyce (1882-1941)

A PORTRAIT OF THE ARTIST AS A YOUNG MAN

James Augustine Joyce was born at 41 Brighton Square in the respectable Dublin suburb of Rathgar on 2 February 1882. He was to be the eldest of ten children. His father, John Stanislaus Joyce, prototype of the convivial Simon Dedalus, was from Cork and his mother, Mary Jane Murray, from Longford. John Stanislaus had inherited property in Cork, which he progressively mortgaged to meet the needs of his growing family. At the time of his first son's birth, he held a post in the office of the Collector of Rates and was reasonably prosperous. Ambitious for his clever son, he sent the boy at the age of six and a half to the Jesuit boarding-school, Clongowes Wood College. In 1891, however, the post in the Rates Office was abolished and Joyce senior was left with only a small pension. James was withdrawn from Clongowes with his school bill still unpaid and, after he and his younger brother Stanislaus had spent a couple of terms with the less fashionable Christian Brothers at the O'Connell Schools in North Richmond Street, the two boys were sent to the Jesuit day-school at Belvedere College. As the father's fortunes declined the family made a series of moves to ever less fashionable neighbourhoods, forsaking the more elegant south side of the city for drabber suburbs north of the river Liffey.

James entered University College in 1898 and graduated BA in 1902, his degree subjects being French, English and Italian. He had made his mark as a literary controversialist and debater among his fellow students at university and had attracted considerable attention when the influential *Fortnightly Review* published his appreciation of Ibsen's *When We Dead Awaken* in April 1900. After graduating, Joyce decided to become a doctor and briefly embarked on courses of medical studies, first in Dublin and later in Paris but he soon gave up the idea of a medical career. His mother's final illness recalled him from Paris in April 1903. She died of cancer in the following August and the prominent part she plays in most of his fiction indicates the importance to the young Joyce of her pain-racked final illness and death. Joyce's first extended literary effort was an essay with the significant title, 'A Portrait of the Artist' which he offered unsuccessfully to the magazine *Dana*. He now began work on a lengthy autobiographical novel which was to be called *Stephen Hero*, but he abandoned this after writing some 600 pages of it. In 1904, the first three of the *Dubliners* stories, *The Sisters, Eveline* and *After the Race*, appeared in George Russell's *Irish Homestead* but it was then made clear to the author that his stories were uncongenial to the journal's readers and that no more of them would be accepted for publication. In 1904, also, Joyce met his future wife, Nora Barnacle, for the first time. They walked out together on 16 June 1904, the day which was subsequently to be immortalised as Bloomsday in *Ulysses*. In October, they left together for Trieste. When they got there it emerged that the local Berlitz school to which Joyce had applied for a job knew nothing about him but he got a post at Pola, some fifty miles away. Joyce and Nora moved back to Trieste in 1905 and their son, Giorgio, was born there in July of that year.

Joyce was now working on *Dubliners* and embarking on the heartbreaking battle with publishers and printers chronicled in such agonising detail by the first of his biographers, Herbert Gorman. In 1906, he moved to Rome to take a post in a bank but moved back to Trieste in the following year. His first work to achieve publication was *Chamber Music*, a book of poems brought out in London by Elkin Matthews in 1907. In the same year his daughter, Lucia, was born. In 1909, Joyce travelled back to Dublin with his son and made a second trip to Ireland later that year with the intention of opening cinemas in Dublin, Belfast and Cork. The project had a certain amount of success in its early stages and the Volta Cinema opened in Mary Street, Dublin to favourable reviews just before Christmas 1909. When Joyce returned to Trieste, however, the venture failed and the new cinema had to be sold. In 1912, Nora travelled to Ireland with little Lucia to visit her family in Galway and James followed soon after with Giorgio. The visit was a great success on the family level but was spoilt for Joyce by Maunsel's persistent refusal to bring out *Dubliners*. Their managing director, George Roberts, and the printers finally wrecked his hopes by destroying the sheets of the proposed new publication in September 1912. Furiously angry and bitterly disappointed, Joyce left Ireland for the last time. In 1913, he began work on his only play, *Exiles*, and in the following year made the first drafts of sections of *Ulysses*. Through the good offices of Ezra Pound, the revised version of the abandoned *Stephen Hero, A Portrait of the Artist as a Young Man*, began to appear in serial form in the *Egoist* early in 1914 and in June of that year *Dubliners* was at last published by Grant Richards.

At the outbreak of war in 1914, the Joyces went to live in Zurich and in

1916 Joyce received a Civil List pension of £100 from the British treasury. He completed *Exiles* but failed to get it staged. In 1916, *A Portrait of the Artist as a Young Man* was published in New York and a British edition appeared in 1917 and was favourably reviewed. About this time, also, Joyce's chronic financial difficulties were eased by the first of a series of generous grants of money from an English benefactor, Harriet Shaw Weaver, who had been business manager of the *Egoist* and was later its editor. She was to give the Joyces unstinting financial assistance over many years. In Zurich, Joyce met many of the artists and political refugees who had been forced by the war to take up residence there and he struck up a friendship with the English painter, Frank Budgen, who was to write one of the first books about *Ulysses*. In 1917, Joyce had to undergo the first of a series of painful eye operations undertaken in an attempt to save his failing sight.

Ulysses began to be serialised in *The Little Review* in New York in 1918 and the *Egoist* began to publish episodes from the novel in the following year but in 1920 a court injunction stopped the serialisation in *The Little Review* and it was clear that publication in volume form would be fraught with difficulty. After the war, the Joyces returned to Trieste but they finally settled in Paris in 1920 and were to remain there for twenty years, until the next great European cataclysm disturbed them again. *Ulysses* was published in Paris on Joyce's fortieth birthday in 1922 and the troubled history of its turbulent public reception had begun. Several printings of the Paris edition sold out rapidly but some five hundred copies of the first edition were seized and burnt by the British Customs officials at Folkestone. It was to be another decade before Judge Woolsey's celebrated decision that *Ulysses* was not a pornographic work made possible the publication by Random House in New York of the complete text of the novel.

Joyce began work on his last major work in 1923. The eventual title, *Finnegans Wake,* was kept secret and the strange new venture was known simply as 'Work in Progress'. Its first fragments appeared in the *Transatlantic Review* and Eugene Jolas published the work almost continuously in *transition* from 1927 to 1938. From 1920 onwards, the Joyces lived in various Paris flats and also made frequent trips to holiday resorts and watering places from time to time. The closing decade of Joyce's life was to be profoundly saddened by the ever-worsening schizophrenic illness of his daughter, Lucia, who underwent her first serious mental breakdown in 1932 and finally had to be permanently hospitalised. Joyce's eyesight also caused him constant distress and he was fortunate in having the assistance of various devoted friends such as Paul Leon and the young Samuel Beckett. The new book was brought to a close in 1938 and published in 1939. In that year, the

Joyces gave up their Paris flat in April and visited Entretat, Berne and Zurich. They returned to France when war was declared. It was a matter of grave concern to them that Lucia was still in a mental institution in Occupied France but Joyce's efforts to get her out came to nothing and she spent the entire period of the war there. James and Nora, with Giorgio and their grandson, Stephen, got to Zurich in December 1940 after many financial complications and various difficulties with passports. In January 1941, Joyce was taken ill with agonising stomach pains caused, as subsequent medical investigations were to show, by a perforated ulcer. An operation was performed with apparent success but his serious condition had been misunderstood and tackled too late. He died on 13 January 1941 and two days later was buried, after a simple ceremony, in the Fluntern cemetery.

A PORTRAIT OF THE ARTIST AS A YOUNG MAN (1916)

Joyce said to me in Zurich:
'Some people who read my book, *A Portrait of the Artist*, forget that it is called *A Portrait of the Artist as a Young Man.*'
He underlined with his voice the last four words of the title. At first I thought I understood what he meant, but later on it occurred to me that he may have meant one of two things, or both. The emphasis may have indicated that he who wrote the book is no longer that young man, that through time and experience he has become a different person. Or it may have meant that he wrote the book looking backwards at the young man across a space of time as the landscape painter paints distant hills, looking at them through a cube of air-filled space, painting, that is to say, not that which is, but that which appears to be. Perhaps he meant both.

Thus Frank Budgen in one of the more readable books about Joyce, *James Joyce and the Making of 'Ulysses'* (1934). In the same work, Budgen recounts how Joyce had lent him a copy of *A Portrait*. Budgen, when returning the book, sent with it a letter in which he recorded his impressions of the novel. Joyce evidently liked what he said:

'That simile of yours, "A young cat sharpening his claws on the tree of life," seems to me to be very just applied to young Stephen.'

One notes the almost paternally affectionate emphasis on Stephen's youth. Budgen also records another comment which Joyce made to him, which again hints at the special kind of distancing of Stephen implied above:

> At about the time of the publication of the *Lestrygonians* episode he said to me:
>> 'I have just got a letter asking me why I don't give Bloom a rest. The writer of it wants more Stephen. But Stephen no longer interests me to the same extent. He has a shape that can't be changed.'

These comments from Joyce himself should warn against the evident temptation to respond to the *Portrait* as though it were no more than a thinly veiled autobiography. The abandoning by Joyce of the more obviously autobiographical *Stephen Hero* should reinforce the warning.

The subtle adjustments of our responses to Stephen throughout *A Portrait* is one of this novel's most impressive achievements. That process had, in fact, been attempted in *Stephen Hero* but had there been much more clumsily handled, mainly through the remonstrances of Stephen's fellows. Thus, in Chapter XXI of the earlier work, Stephen's closest companion, Cranly, is employed rather awkwardly to comment on Stephen's 'ingenuous arrogance':

> They sat sometimes in the pit of a music-hall and one unfolded to the other the tapestry of his poetical aims while the band bawled to the comedian and the comedian bawled to the band. Cranly grew used to having sensations and impressions recorded and analysed before him at the very instant of their apparition. Such concentration upon oneself was unknown to Cranly and he wondered at first with the joy of solitary possession at Stephen's ingenuous arrogance.

There is much more in this rather rambling vein and, a little later, we are told of Cranly's method of dealing with his companion's more tedious lucubrations:

> If a monologue which had set out from a triviality seemed to him likely to run on unduly he would receive it with a silence through which aversion was just discernible and at a lull bring his hammer down brutally on the poor original object. At times Stephen found this ultra-classical habit very unpalatable.

In *A Portrait* this tedious expository method is abandoned in favour of the crisp, sometimes almost stichomythic exchanges of Chapter 5 and there Cranly's probing of Stephen's arrogant intransigence sets up complex and resonant responses in place of the flat, dull statements of the corresponding area of *Stephen Hero*. The radical change from the descriptive third-person style of the early draft to the largely internalised mode of *A Portrait* required Joyce to devise more subtle means of deflation for his egotistical artist-hero.

Broadly speaking, the necessity for such deflation scarcely arises until fairly late in the novel. The young Stephen is physically weak, short-sighted and lonely. He is a target rather than an actor. Dante, Wells, Fr Dolan and Heron all assail him and, as he grows from infancy to adolescence, we either pity him or admire his slowly growing ability to deflect his persecutors. Details of a kind which will later be employed to cut him down to size are, early in the work, used to evoke our sympathy. So, when Mr Tate accuses him of having 'heresy in his essay', Stephen, before submitting to Tate's moral pressure, is made to experience the wretchedness of his own poverty-stricken state:

> Stephen did not look up. It was a raw spring morning and his eyes were still smarting and weak. He was conscious of failure and of detection, of the squalor of his own mind and home, and felt against his neck the raw edge of his turned and jagged collar.

It is only when Stephen has learnt to control the forces which earlier assailed him that the author begins to undercut his crescent pride in a variety of ways. When, early in Chapter 4, the Director of Studies suggests to Stephen that he might consider a priestly vocation, Stephen's vainglorious reflections about himself in the role of 'The Reverend Stephen Dedalus, S.J.' carry their own charge of ironic reduction as we recall how recent has been his own riot of sin and how fragile his repentence.

Later, mundane and sordid details are employed to diminish him in our eyes. His mother scrubs him with an old washing-glove before he leaves for his lectures at the university, as though he were still a grubby child. His vaunted learning is exposed as something of a sham:

> The lore which he was believed to pass his days brooding upon so that it had rapt him from the companionships of youth was only a garner of slender sentences from Aristotle's poetics and psychology and a *Synopsis Philosophiae Scholasticae ad mentem divi Thomae*. His thinking was a dusk of doubt and self-mistrust lit up at moments by the lightning of intuition . . .

He has no money to give the flower-girl he meets on his way to college and, arrived there, is subjected to the most telling of all his humiliations in his celebrated encounter with the Dean of Studies, during which he has cruelly revealed to him that his treasury of words is, by the cruelty of history, a pitiful second-best. The Dean's courteous, donnish interest in Stephen's use of 'tundish' for 'funnel' exposes to Stephen his own linguistic belatedness:

> The language in which we are speaking is his before it is mine. How different are the words *home, Christ, ale, master*, on his lips and on mine! I cannot speak or write these words without unrest of spirit. His language,

so familiar and so foreign, will always be for me an acquired speech. I have not made or accepted its words. My voice holds them at bay. My soul frets in the shadow of his language.

Stephen's high-flown disquisitions are sometimes bluntly crushed by a purposefully coarse response from a companion. Sometimes, too, Joyce allows himself to indulge in a literary in-joke of his own. When Stephen discourses at great length to Lynch on the subject of *claritas*, climaxing his account with Luigi Galvani's phrase, 'the enchantment of the heart', the bubble of his satisfaction is cruelly burst by the author:

Stephen paused and, though his companion did not speak, felt that his words had called up around them a thought-enchanted silence.

This deliberate echoing of Gabriel Conroy's pompous phrase from *The Dead* ('one feels that one is listening to a thought-tormented music') calls into the novel multiple implications from the great short story and Stephen takes his place with Gabriel as a pitiable compound of pretension and insecurity.

As Stephen moves towards his final grand declamation, the deflationary instances multiply. His villanelle is mocked by a reference to the earth as 'an ellipsoidal ball', recalling the bawdy *sotto voce* comments of students at a lecture earlier. As he broods languorously about his inamorata, E. C., a louse crawls over his neck. In the penultimate diary entry at the novel's end, he tells us that his mother 'is putting my new secondhand clothes in order' and we delight in the comic vision of this self-appointed heresiarch prancing off into impressive exile wearing somebody's carefully laundered cast-offs. As the novel develops and Joyce involves us more and more with his hero, his carefully balanced account of his artist-in-the-making tutors us into an ever fuller understanding of his central figure's strange combination of Luciferean arrogance and juvenile uncertainty. The reasons for Joyce's emphasis on the last four words of his book's title become ever clearer.

In abandoning the flabby *Stephen Hero* in favour of the fiery shorthand of its tense and tightly organised successor, Joyce lifted himself clear of the more historically entrapped works of his competent contemporaries. His central themes of language, nationality and religion were the common ones of his era but where novels like *Father Ralph* and *The Wasted Island* seem now to possess, at best, a period interest, *A Portrait* remains a work of startling modernity. The reduction of what must have been a monstrous manuscript (Joyce horrendously described it, in a letter to Grant Richards, as half-finished at around 150,000 words!) to the five chapters of *A Portrait* has been charted by numerous commentators, since Theodore Spencer first made the *Stephen Hero* fragment readily available in his edition of 1944. Given that comparison of a part with a whole is necessarily unsatisfactory and bound to be in many ways unfair, it is still possible to see very clearly why Joyce abandoned the first attempt and may, indeed, have tried to destroy it. The undeniable occasional pleasures of *Stephen Hero* are far outweighed by the tedium of its more extended passages of descriptive narrative. The nature of Joyce's real achievement in *A Portrait* becomes clearer when we relate parts of *Stephen Hero* to worthy but lesser works by other writers of the period. Consider, for example, the extended account, in Chapter XVIII, of Stephen's meeting with Wells, his Clongowes schoolfellow who is now a student for the priesthood at the Clonliffe seminary. This entire passage is interesting enough in itself, with its uneasy exchanges between the two young men and with Stephen failing at first to recognise the other and embarrassingly mistaking Wells's clerical black for mourning garments. Yet, as the scene develops, one feels that it might almost have been lifted in its entirety from Gerald O'Donovan's *Father Ralph*. The account of Stephen's brief visit to the seminary at Wells's invitation recalls, in all its details, O'Donovan's account of the Bunnahone seminary and Maynooth. The ugly buildings, the students who are forbidden to walk in pairs, the general sense of a suppression of individuality by an unimaginative and domineering regime, the sheer inanity of the students' conversation – all this is the stuff of conventional anticlericalism. Even the seminarians' fatuous exchange, which Stephen overhears, about the ladies they have observed at Mass, recalls O'Donovan's ridiculous pair of sexless priest-haunters, the two Miss Hinnisseys of Bunnahone:

> – But did you see Mrs Bergin?
> – O, I saw her . . . with a black and white boa.
> – And the two Miss Kennedys were there.
> – Where?
> – Right behind the Archbishop's Throne.
> – O, I saw her – one of them. Hadn't she a green hat with a bird in it?
> – That was her! She's very ladylike, isn't she?

The entire passage disappears from *A Portrait*. If anything at all of it can be said to survive, it may, perhaps, be found in Stephen's brief encounter with the Christian Brothers on the bridge at Dollymount, at the climax of Chapter 4. That meeting, which symbolises in the crossing of the bridge Stephen's deliberate move away from the Brothers' humble vocation, is, in its dense brevity, both more effective and more imaginatively powerful than the leisurely Clonliffe chapter of the earlier work. It is noticeably more complex, in spite of its brevity, in the light it throws on Stephen's painful soul-searching, managing to indicate not merely the 'uncouth faces' and 'topheavy silk hats, and humble tapelike collars and loosely hanging clothes' of these awkward and lowly clerics but also contriving to contain a reflection on Stephen's awareness of his own moral inferiority to the despised Brothers in matters of spiritual generosity. In the Clonliffe episode, the self-satisfied Stephen is complacently contemptuous of Wells's confinement in his unlovely clerical prison, seeing Wells as envious of his own freedom, the freedom of one 'who had not forsaken the world, the flesh and the devil'. The entire incident is predictable in its emphases and repetitive in its effects, while the *Portrait* passage is vivid, compelling and valuably surprising in its judgement on the arch egoist, Stephen, at a climactic moment of his experience.

The *Portrait*'s strength lies in its stylistic variety and its dense symbolic patterning. Joyce cleverly balances the work's more tenuous connective sections with welcome oases of epiphanic richness. What remain in the memory are the Christmas dinner scene, the terror of the retreat sermon, the astounding bird-girl vision. Such scenes acquire a special value because of the skeletal nature of the general framework. Stephen's climactic moments of triumph or personal elation are invariably quickly undercut. Chapter 1 ends with his gallant triumph over the brutal Fr Dolan and his elevation on high by his schoolfellows but Chapter 2 opens comically with Stephen being trained as an athlete by a ludicrous duo, his uncle Charles and the distinctly unathletic Mike Flynn. The sordidness which descends with the decline in the family fortunes is now imminent. At the climax of Chapter 2, he is enfolded in the arms of the prostitute and the moment is rendered in an undulating, sibilant prose which captures the youth's mixture of moral guilt and physical release. Instantly, the opening words of Chapter 3 firmly place Stephen's grosser appetites, with his gluttonous reverie on his forthcoming dinner of stew ('Stuff it into you, his belly counselled him'). Chapter 3 ends with his repentance and his delightedly rhapsodic taking of communion ('The ciborium had come to him') but, as Chapter 4 opens, we feel the imminence of his fall in the anti-climax of his sterile programme of repentance. Joyce supplies an unmistakeable signal in the mundane image which he applies to Stephen's sense of his heavenly rewards:

> His life seemed to have drawn near to eternity; every thought, word and deed, every instance of consciousness could be made to revibrate radiantly in heaven; and at times his sense of such immediate repercussion was so lively that he seemed to feel his soul in devotion pressing like fingers the keys of a great cash register and to see the amount of his purchase start forth immediately in heaven, not as a number but as a frail column of incense or as a slender flower.

This passage, a marvellous mixture of false reverence and reductive derision, recalls the telling climax to the short story, 'Grace', in which the repellent Fr

Purdon similarly applies the standards of the market-place to salvation and addresses his congregation in the language of the counting-house, admonishing them to check up on their heavenly accounts. There could be no clearer indication of the futility of Stephen's regimen of piety. The most carefully contrived moment of epiphanic joy for Stephen comes at the end of Chapter 4, where the radiant vision of the bird-girl sets the seal on his vocation as secular artist but the opening of Chapter 5 immediately debunks him again, as we find him drinking watery tea at a table covered in bits of fried bread and dripping, with a louse-speckled box of pawn tickets at his elbow. This carefully calculated process of alternation between delight and despair, between sanctity and sin, between arrogant confidence and sordid domesticity, is tellingly echoed in the contrast offered between Stephen as theorist and practitioner of art. He discourses impressively to his undergraduate companions on his ideas about tragedy, epic and the role of the artist as god of creation but his villanelle is an appropriately limp product of a wet dream. Stephen's poem, the only concrete example of his art which we are permitted to see, is as good (and as bad) as it needs to be. Joyce had always delighted in bending mediocre writing to his broader satiric intentions. At the climax of 'Ivy Day in the Committee Room', he has Mr Hynes recite the direly clichéd ballad, 'The Death of Parnell' and Mr Crofton then pronounces it 'a very fine piece of writing', as indeed it is, bad as it is in itself. It is, of course, 'fine' as the ending to a remarkable story in which Joyce has memorably exploited a debased and second-rate literary tradition to expose all that is debased and second-rate in the public life of Dublin at this time. Hugh Kenner, who insists that 'Stephen does not become an artist at all' sums up the book's meticulous process of oscillation and balance when he says that 'by the time he came to rewrite the *Portrait*, Joyce had decided to make its central figure a futile alterego rather than a self-image'. Stephen is undoubtedly a weak vessel but it is altogether appropriate that he should be so. The Ovidian epigraph, after all, warns us in advance that it is to *unknown* arts he will devote himself and the novel is, in the end, an embarkation on a journey to the unknown. Not surprisingly, the complex depiction of Stephen as hero has left even sophisticated readers at odds about how, in the end, we are to respond to him. Conor Cruise O'Brien is put off by 'all this relentless rapture about self' and treasures only those moments in the novel when the shadowy cast of supporting figures are allowed to come briefly into the limelight. When this is allowed to happen, he suggests, we get a foretaste of the kind of thing Joyce would later do so memorably in *Ulysses*. John Gross inclines somewhat to the same point of view, suggesting that 'it is hard not to be repelled, or on occasion, amused by Stephen's moist romanticism'. On balance, though, Gross finally rejects both extremes of response, refusing to see Stephen as either 'a monster of conceit or the hapless product of a blighting environment'. He suggests that *A Portrait* 'is surely meant to leave us with equivocal feelings about its hero's potentialities'. Stephen, he feels, 'has the courage of his immaturity, which means having the capacity to grow and change, not being afraid of a plunge into the unknown'. J. I. M. Stewart, who writes elegant detective stories as 'Michael Innes' and might, therefore, be supposed to fit his own description of the ideal Joyce reader as someone with a taste for 'progressive crypto-graphic idiosyncrasy', has provided (in Vol. XII of the *Oxford History of English Literature*) a warmly appreciative response to Joyce's achievement in *A Portrait*. He places the novel in an historical context which includes such works as Mrs Humphry Ward's *Robert Elsmere*, Samuel Butler's *The Way of All Flesh* and D. H. Lawrence's *Sons and Lovers* (published shortly before *A Portrait*) but goes on to insist on the startling originality of this quintessen-tially Irish *bildungsroman*, as a book which presents its hero to us 'with a hitherto unexampled intimacy'. He senses the difficult balance which Joyce had to strike between Stephen as artist-to-be and Stephen as unjustified poseur:

> There are always two lights at play on Stephen. In the one he is seen as veritably possessing the sanctity and strength he claims . . . In the other he is only the eldest of Simon Dedalus's neglected children . . . In the one light he is an artist. In the other he is an adolescent, subject to emotions which may be comically in excess of their specific precipitating occasion. It is because he must be seen as thus hovering agonizingly between sublimity and absurdity, hysteria and inspiration, that he is regularly represented in his solitude as outrageously sentimentalizing himself, and as prone to clothe his poignantly felt nakedness in the faded splendours of a bygone poetic rhetoric.

Joyce was soon to move from the self-absorbed Stephen to the astonishing emotional generosity of Leopold Bloom. The Stephen who inhabits the early part of *Ulysses* is the familiar one, lonely, arrogant, touchy and sensitive, responding to Mulligan and Haines with the same edgy self-consciousness. His creator was to indicate that he had 'a shape that can't be changed' and that he was, therefore, of less interest to him than his expansive new creation, Bloom. Nevertheless, Stephen's own novel did not merely offer us a portrait of juvenile artistic aspiration. It gathered into itself with impressive economy of style the informing themes of all of modern Irish fiction and makes much which followed it seem both cumbersome and dated.

SELECTED BIBLIOGRAPHY

RELATED WORKS

Dubliners, London, 1914.
Stephen Hero, London, 1944.
Ulysses, Paris, London, 1922.

BIOGRAPHY

Herbert Gorman, *James Joyce*, London, 1940 (rev. ed. 1948).
Richard Ellmann, *James Joyce*, London, 1959 (rev. ed. 1982).

CRITICAL STUDIES

Hugh Kenner, *Dublin's Joyce*, London, 1955, 109-133.
William T. Noon, S. J., *Joyce and Aquinas*, New Haven, 1957, 18-59.
William York Tindall, *A Reader's Guide to James Joyce*, New York & London, 1959, 50-103.
Thomas E. Connolly (ed.), *Joyce's 'Portrait': Criticisms and Critiques*, New York, 1962.
S. L. Goldberg, *Joyce*, Edinburgh, 1962, 47-63
J. I. M. Stewart, *Eight Modern Writers*, Oxford, 1963, 438-450.
R. M. Kain & R. E. Scholes (eds.), *The Workshop of Dedalus: James Joyce and the Raw Materials for 'A Portrait of the Artist as a Young Man'*, Evanston, 1965.
John Gross, *Joyce*, London, 1970.
Harvey Peter Sucksmith, *James Joyce: 'A Portrait of the Artist as a Young Man'*, London, 1973.
John Paul Riquelme, *Teller and Tale in Joyce's Fiction: Oscillating Perspectives*, London, 1983, 48-85.

CRITICAL ARTICLES

Thomas E. Connolly, 'Kinesis and Stasis: Structural Rhythm in Joyce's *Portrait*', *University Review*, III, 10 (1966), 21-30.
Hugh T. Bredin, 'Applied Aquinas: James Joyce's Aesthetics', *Eire-Ireland*, III, 1 (Spring 1968), 61-78.
Richard Kell, 'The Goddess Theme in *A Portrait of the Artist*', *Dublin Magazine*, 9, 3 (1972), 100-108.
Christopher Butler, 'Joyce and the Displaced Author', *James Joyce & Modern Literature* (eds. W. J. McCormack & Alistair Stead), London, 1982, 56-73.
Elliott B. Gose, 'Destruction and Creation in *A Portrait of the Artist as a Young Man*', *James Joyce Quarterly*, 22, 3 (Spring 1985), 259-270.

VI

Seumas O'Kelly (c. 1875-1918)

THE LADY OF DEERPARK

He was born at Mobhill, Loughrea, Co. Galway. No birth or baptismal records survive, so that the precise date of birth is uncertain. He was the youngest of seven children born to Michael and Catherine Kelly whose families had long been involved in the milling and corn-carrying trade in the west of Ireland. The boy got only a sketchy kind of education, first in some sort of local hedge-school and later as a rather unsatisfactory pupil at St Brendan's College, Loughrea and St Joseph's College in Ballinasloe. He picked up a knowledge of Irish by listening to older local people speaking the language. He was destined to spend his working life as a journalist with various newspapers and made a beginning at this by becoming editor of the *Midland Tribune* before the age of eighteen. He became editor of the *Southern Star* in the Co. Cork town of Skibbereen in 1903 and, in 1906, moved on to Naas, Co. Kildare to become editor there of the *Leinster Leader*. He purchased a house called 'Abbeyville' in Naas and brought his father, sister and nephew to live with him. He had already begun to write for *The United Irishman* and *The Irish Packet* and now began to establish contact with various prominent Republican figures. He became friendly with Arthur Griffith, founder of Sinn Fein, and entertained at his house in Naas the Countess Markievicz. A particular friend was the writer Seumas O'Sullivan whose real name was James Starkey. It seems to have been during his period of residence at Naas that he contracted the rheumatic fever which damaged his heart and was to contribute to his early death.

His first book of stories, *By the Stream of Kilmeen*, appeared in 1906 and he also began to write plays for performance by the amateur company, Theatre of Ireland. This company played his *The Matchmakers* at the Abbey Theatre in 1907 and *The Flame on the Hearth* at the same venue the following year. In 1909 he wrote *The Shuiler's Child* for the actress, Maire Nic Shiublaigh, for whom he had a deep affection and admiration, and the play was put on at the Rotunda and later at the Abbey. He was also writing stories for the *Irish Weekly Independent* and for *Sinn Fein*. In 1911, he moved to Dublin to become editor of the *Dublin Saturday Post* but poor health forced him to give up this job in 1915. His best fiction is in the short story form and is to be found in such collections as *Waysiders* (1917), *The Golden Barque and The Weaver's Grave* (1919) and *Hillsiders* (1921). The single work with which his name is most often associated is undoubtedly the grotesquely comic novella, *The Weaver's Grave*, which is generally acclaimed as a classic of the form.

When he resigned as editor of the *Dublin Saturday Post*, O'Kelly moved back to Naas once more but he returned to Dublin in 1918 to assume the editorship of *Nationality* because Arthur Griffith was under arrest. He undertook this task against his doctor's orders and in spite of his weak heart condition. His decision to stand in for the absent Griffith was to have fatal consequences. Various accounts are given of the circumstances surrounding his death but it is known that he was found unconscious on the morning of 14 November 1918 and removed to Jervis Street Hospital where he died. His brother Michael described how, on the third night after the signing of the Armistice, a crowd of drunken soldiers broke into the offices of Sinn Fein and wrecked the place and how Seumas O'Kelly, having vainly tried to defend himself with his walking stick, suffered the cerebral haemorrhage from which he died. The funeral procession, organised by Sinn Fein, was enormous and was watched by huge crowds in the streets of Dublin, as it wound its way to Glasnevin where O'Kelly was buried in the family grave. There were a number of posthumous publications, including the second of his novels, *Wet Clay* (1922).

THE LADY OF DEERPARK (1917)

In this curious specimen of 'Big House' fiction, Seumas O'Kelly takes an initial hint from Maria Edgeworth's *Castle Rackrent* in his choice of a servant as narrator. Paul Jennings is, however, a very different sort of servant from Edgeworth's Thady Quirke. Paul is a young man who, when his father dies suddenly, is abruptly called home from school to take his father's place as land-agent to the Heffernan property of Deerpark. The Jennings family has always served the Heffernans in this capacity and Paul is well pleased to escape the tedium of school and embark on his new existence as a responsible adult. The current landlord, William Heffernan, shoots himself to escape the hordes of debtors who surround his hopelessly encumbered estate and the place comes into the possession of his sister, Miss Mary Heffernan. The year of the novel's action is 1894, curiously enough the year which saw the publication of that notable literary swan-song of the Ascendancy, *The Real Charlotte*. Miss Heffernan, to begin with, has to live like a prisoner in the house she has unexpectedly inherited, huddling in one wing of the place and leaving the rest to moulder in the manner made familiar in numerous examples of the genre, both old and new. The Heffernan's story has been 'from start to finish a story of spending, of gambling, of running through the property'. Miss Heffernan believes that she is caring for the property on behalf of her nephew, George, William's sole surviving son who has emigrated to Australia. She regards her trust as a sacred duty and holds regular business consultations with young Paul Jennings, despite the wretched state of the property. She is deeply distressed by demands of various kinds conveyed to her in troublesome letters and often, on receipt of these, she calls for her housekeeper, Mrs Briscoe, to bring her smelling salts. Paul notes sardonically that 'the salts in the bottle were as dead as the estate' but, nevertheless, they seem to revive Miss Heffernan. This early part of the novel is well rendered and the reader soon acquires both a curiosity about Paul as narrator and also some knowledge of the curious relationship which grows up between him and his employer. He respects her efforts to keep up a bold front in difficult circumstances and willingly plays his part in the charade as a courteous upper servant who never fails to greet his mistress with a civil bow. Then, suddenly, Miss Heffernan's straitened circumstances are dramatically altered when news comes that the nephew, George Heffernan, has died in Australia, leaving a considerable fortune to his aunt, with a request that she devote it to the restoration of Deerpark. Unusually, we actually witness the resuscitation of a ramshackle and decayed Big House and, more importantly, the rejuvenation of its châtelaine. Miss Heffernan buys new clothes for herself as well as new furnishings for the house and the watchful Paul becomes 'keenly alive to the fact that a vital and very womanly personality was close at hand'. He gradually senses that her interest in him amounts to something more than the civility of a wealthy landowner to a conscientious agent. Mary Heffernan's long-suppressed emotions come to the surface as she begins to enjoy her new-found good fortune. While she and Paul are driving in the countryside one day, they encounter a beggar-woman with a tiny, new-born infant and Paul cannot fail to notice how deeply moved his employer is by the sight of the child in its mother's arms. The Deerpark servants are quick to see how the wind is blowing and Mrs Briscoe, in particular, voices her firm approval of Paul as a prospective master of Deerpark. Mrs Briscoe is a splendidly comic character who might have stepped out of one of O'Kelly's vivid short-stories – she recalls the vigorous tinker women of 'The Can with the Diamond Notch'. She is accompanied everywhere as she moves through the house by a splendid Persian cat, a kind of amiable familiar who becomes quite a character in his own right. Mrs Briscoe's comic dialogue has a finely Dickensian touch of bizarre inconsequence, as when she asserts her impregnable respectability to Paul:

> 'I hope I am a respectable widow woman ... and that Briscoe has not found out anything about me since that he did not know before the horse kicked him in the stomach and inflammation did the rest.'

All seems set fair for a marriage between the lady of Deerpark and her young land-agent. Unfortunately, however, Paul has already fallen deeply in love with young Betty Carolan, daughter of a local corn-factor and, though he feels a genuine fondness and respect for Miss Heffernan, he has no intention of marrying her. In a tense and subtly written scene in the library, Mary Heffernan comes as close as propriety will allow to a declaration of her love for Paul but his failure to respond in kind puts an end to her hopes of finding real love and she withdraws into herself, becoming hard and embittered. Part I of the novel concludes with the arrival in Deerpark of the future villain of the piece, one Kish Massy, a vulgar but vital horse-dealer, a kind of cross between Flurry Knox and Jason Quirke, who now sets about paying vigorous court to Mary Heffernan. Part II, which bears the title 'Kish Massy', develops this theme and concludes with the marriage of Kish and Mary Heffernan. Before she succumbs to Kish, Paul Jennings is granted a closer understanding of her loneliness and her yearning for a loving relationship with a man of her own choosing. He finds that her boudoir is cluttered with carefully dressed dolls – the room is, he feels, 'a strange medley, a nightmare of maternity' and he cannot fail to recall the encounter with the beggar-woman and her tiny baby. Mary Heffernan expresses through the passionate notes of her harp the emotions which she cannot voice to Paul but, in the end, she will marry the gross and pushing horse-coper, Kish Massy. O'Kelly imparts to the depiction of this character something of the comic surrealism which informs his most famous work, the novella-length short story, *The Weaver's Grave*. Kish is large and heavy, with an ape-like fondness for climbing which has survived from his boyhood when he constantly shinned up trees. In a memorable vignette at the end of Part II of the novel, Paul Jennings watches Kish Massy pay a call at Deerpark and sees him, on arrival at the front door, shin up one of the frontal columns of the house, in a comical impulse of sexual triumph at the winning of Mary Heffernan. O'Kelly succeeds in conveying the subtle unpleasantness of this mis-match of the refined and sensitive Mary Heffernan to the masterful and animalistic Kish Massy and our attitude to Paul Jennings, who is the privileged onlooker who sees every nuance of this painful situation, is inevitably coloured by Paul's failure to intervene.

Sadly, however, in Part III, which is entitled 'After the Marriage', O'Kelly fails completely to control or develop his story in a convincing manner and flounders into a morass of improbabilities and melodrama. It may well be that the novel's central weakness lies in the failure to develop the character of the narrator more fully. Paul Jennings' love for Betty Carolan is both uninteresting and unconvincing, since Betty herself appears only briefly and is clearly a mere device employed by O'Kelly to prevent the marriage of Paul to his employer. The depiction of Paul Jennings is seriously defective, in that we are early convinced of his intelligence and of his sympathetic awareness of Miss Heffernan's vulnerability but have to accept later that he can allow the ruinous intervention of Kish Massy to proceed unchecked. The observant, responsive narrator of the early stages of the story turns into a colourless recorder of Mary Heffernan's disastrous marriage and subsequent miseries and, as a result, a novel which had promised and sometimes achieved subtle insights into frustrated passion, lapses into gross caricature and muddled improbability. The reader simply cannot accept that the sympathetic Paul Jennings of Part I can turn into the cold fish who clinically reports the rest of the story.

Nevertheless, O'Kelly, conscious of the expectations aroused by this sort of novel, strives throughout to supply appropriately convincing background detail, and offers lively vignettes of the various levels of the society in which his protagonists move. The kind of telling precision which he brings to bear so memorably on the several personages in *The Weaver's Grave* surfaces here in Paul Jennings' lengthy account of the Deerpark tenants as they crowd in to pay their rent:

> A violent old man who remembered the famine, with a mouth like a vacant potato-pit, attacked me with blazing eyes, shouting and cursing, disputing records of rents which had been disposed of twenty years ago, striking the table with quivering fists, driving home arguments which had been nursed by the fireside a dozen years, astonishing me by a quotation from Virgil, learned from a hedge schoolmaster; others entered without a word, did their business without a single comment, their thin lips drawn across their teeth tight as the skin of a drum, men from some famished hillside; a widow with a rich colour in her cheeks wept for fifteen minutes for a husband who had died of consumption sixteen years ago . . .

O'Kelly also works hard to justify the improbable union of Mary Heffernan and Kish Massy by emphasising the disorderly nature of the society in this part of the west of Ireland. At a concert in the village, the various classes huddle together in the audience, gossiping and backbiting:

If Kish Massy was looking for snubs he had found the right company for them. The shouted words of greeting, the hearty good humour, the nods and smiles, the hand-shakes, the little salutes which were flying about, all concealed snubs and slights and insolent cuts . . . The social life of the locality was anaemic, morally run down. The aristocracy was bastard. The professional class was inconsequent and trying to shake off the shop-keeping element. The shop-keepers were endeavouring to rise above their ancestral peasantry. The clergymen hung like afterthoughts on the flanks of all classes. A little group of peasants near the door stood gloomily austere and apart.

It is a scene reminiscent of the social chaos which George Moore depicted with such malicious delight through his rumbustious account of the Spinsters' Ball in *A Drama in Muslin*. Appropriately, O'Kelly's village concert produces as its hilarious and vulgar climax a skirt dance performed by an ageing member of the local hunt, Mrs Hugh Quirke. This splendid comic figure would have been quite at home in one of the more riotous of the 'RM' stories of Somerville and Ross:

> Somebody in the farce said, 'And now comes forth the fairy dancer!' Without another word of warning Mrs Hugh sprang from the wings, prancing about the stage, throwing her legs in mid-air, shocking and horrifying, stimulating and delighting, a hard-looking thin woman, her eyes half closed, her breath coming short from her nostrils, her figure one of aggressive angles, her arms muscular, her elbows raw, her hands shaking the folds of her skirt about, displaying ankles that had no merit, shanks that were too wiry, limbs that were mercifully smothered in swathes of white frills under the semi-chorus-girl skirt.
> 'My God, it's Mrs Hugh!' said Colonel Burke, waking up.

O'Kelly's sense of black comedy comes to the fore at the end of the novel also, in the account of Kish Massy's ludicrous death. Poor old Kish, bled dry by his second wife and abandoned by her, drinks himself silly and, in a final parody of his penchant for climbing to great heights, clambers in his nightshirt to the very top of a crane in the local quarry. There he dangles helplessly, held up only by his nightshirt, accidentally hooked into the arm of the crane, his gross and naked body exposed to view. This ludicrous finale could have provided a marvellously comic climax to a different sort of novel but, coming as it does after the tragic death in childbirth of Mary Heffernan, it can only jar. Seumas O'Kelly tried the novel form once more and failed again, with *Wet Clay*, a story about a young American who returns to his ancestral home and tries to make a go of it as a farmer in an Ireland which treats him and his ideas with profound mistrust. Again, O'Kelly falls back on unlikely marriages and violently melodramatic climaxes. He seems to have been ultimately unable to exercise the kind of tonal control over a large mass of material which the longer form demands and to have found his true métier in the kind of long short stories which O'Faolain would later describe as 'tales', works such as 'The Can with the Diamond Notch' and, above all, his single real masterpiece, *The Weaver's Grave.*

SELECTED BIBLIOGRAPHY

RELATED WORKS

The Golden Barque and the Weaver's Grave, Dublin, 1919.
Wet Clay, Dublin & London, 1922.

BIOGRAPHY

George Brandon Saul, *Seumas O'Kelly*, Lewisburg, 1971.

CRITICAL STUDIES

George Brandon Saul, *op.cit.*

CRITICAL ARTICLES

A. E. Malone, 'Seumas O'Kelly', *Dublin Magazine* (July-Sept 1930), 39-46.
Seumas O'Sullivan, *Essays and Recollections*, Dublin & Cork, 1944, 118-122.
Aidan O'Hanlon, 'Seumas O'Kelly, 1880-1918', *Capuchin Annual*, 1949, 70-79.
George Brandon Saul, 'The Verse, Novels and Drama of Seumas O'Kelly', *Eire-Ireland* (Spring 1967), 48-57.
Anne Clune, 'Seumas O'Kelly', *The Irish Short Story* (ed. Rafroidi & Brown), Gerrards Cross, 1979, 141-157.
Alexander G. Gonzales, 'Seumas O'Kelly and James Joyce', *Eire-Ireland*, XXI, 2 (Summer 1986), 85-94.

VII

Daniel Corkery (1878-1964)

THE THRESHOLD OF QUIET

Daniel Corkery was born in Cork on 14 February 1878, the son of a carpenter. He received his early education at the Presentation Brothers' Elementary School in Douglas Street, Cork and later taught there as a monitor. Early in life he joined the Gaelic League and became an enthusiastic supporter of the Irish Language revival movement. He trained as a teacher at St Patrick's College in Dublin and returned to Cork where he worked as a Primary School teacher until about 1920. St Francis' and St Patrick's National Schools were among his places of employment at this time. He took a considerable interest in painting and attended evening classes at the Crawford Municipal School of Art in Cork. He also helped to organise the Cork Dramatic Society and wrote his first plays for this company. Among his pupils at St Patrick's National School were Seamus Murphy, who was subsequently to become a well-known sculptor and author of the highly successful book, *Stone Mad*, and also Michael O'Donovan, who eventually achieved a far wider literary fame than Corkery's own under his celebrated pseudonym of 'Frank O'Connor'. Corkery resigned from St Patrick's in 1921 when he was refused the headmastership. He began work on his only novel, *The Threshold of Quiet*, as early as 1912 but did not publish it until five years later, by which time his first collection of short stories, *A Munster Twilight* (1916), had enjoyed considerable critical acclaim. The novel was also favourably reviewed by many critics but was faulted by some for its sustained quietism, which seemed to the antagonistic reviewers to deprive the work of adequate incident and drama. In 1919, Corkery's play, *The Labour Leader*, a work inspired by Jim Larkin, had a success at the Abbey Theatre and *The Yellow Bittern* was well received at the same theatre in the following year. In that year also, 1920, he published another collection of stories, *The Hounds of Banba*. A book of lyrics, *I Bhreasail*, appeared in 1921. Between 1923 and 1928 Corkery worked as clerical assistant to the Inspector of Irish for County Cork. In 1925 he published one of the works most closely associated with his memory, a book which was to arouse ardent enthusiasm and fierce condemnation in almost equal proportions. This was *The Hidden Ireland* (1925), sub-titled 'A

Study of Gaelic Munster in the Eighteenth Century', which Sean O'Faolain, originally one of Corkery's proteges and eventually one of his severest critics, describes as 'a history, in effect, of 18th Century Ireland from the point of view of the penalised underdog.' Corkery himself, in his Introduction to the book, is suitably modest about his own lack of the historical scholarship needed for the work, but he was determined to attempt a polemical study which would restore respect for what he saw as the neglected Gaelic literary tradition of eighteenth-century Ireland. Corkery's missionary intentions produced both a flock of converts and a handful of vigorous non-believers. In recent times, the case against this hugely influential study has been most efficiently stated by L.M. Cullen in an essay published in *Studia Hibernica* 9 (1969). In 1929, Corkery published another highly successful set of short stories, *The Stormy Hills,* and in the same year was awarded the MA of the National University of Ireland for research on the works of J. M. Synge. This research work achieved book form two years later as *Synge and Anglo-Irish Literature,* a characteristically idiosyncratic work which applies the rigid standards of Corkery's cultural nationalism to the ebullient works of Synge with some curious results. In 1931, the year of publication of the Synge study, Corkery was appointed to the Chair of English at University College, Cork in succession to W.F.P. Stockley. His unsuccessful rival for the post was his young friend, Sean O'Faolain, who gives an entertaining account of his candidacy in the penultimate chapter of his autobiography, *Vive Moi* (1965). Corkery continued as Professor of English in Cork until 1947 and was awarded an Honorary D. Litt. by the National University of Ireland in the year following his retirement. He had published yet another collection of short stories, *Earth out of Earth,* in 1939 and his play, *Fohnam the Sculptor,* got an Abbey production in the same year, but increasingly, after his retirement from academic life, he began to devote himself to work on behalf of the Irish language. His short study, *The Fortunes of the Irish Language,* was published in 1954. Critics have not been slow to point out the contradiction between his propaganda for the Irish language as the natural medium of expression for the Irish writer and his own highly successful work as a writer in English. Daniel Corkery died at the house of his niece, Maureen, at Passage West just outside Cork on the last day of 1964.

THE THRESHOLD OF QUIET (1917)

In the Prologue to this, his only novel, Daniel Corkery, in defining the work's physical terrain, also identifies its moral range and quietly but firmly asserts a sturdily independent parochialism which is to pervade the book and give it its distinctive flavour:

> Leaving us the summer visitor says in his good-humoured way that Cork is quite a busy place, considering how small it is. And he really thinks so.

The amiable condescension of the departing tourist is firmly placed as an inadequate appreciation of the city's full significance. He sees only 'the flat of the city', where the more immediately obvious manifestations of urban life are 'flung higgeldy-piggeldy together into a narrow, double-streamed, many-bridged river valley.' He misses 'the true size and worth of things.' To appreciate these he would have to climb the hills which surround the city and enclose it, leaving the noise and bustle of the centre and taking refuge in the quietness and serenity which are to be found in the avenues and gardens on the slopes above:

> Go but three steps up any of these old-time, wide-sweeping, treeless, cloud-shadowed hills and you find yourself even at mid-day in a silence that grows on you. You have scarce left the city, yet you raise your eyes, you look around and notice little gable ends that finish in little crosses of stone, or arched gateways of sandstone or limestone or both, or far-stretching garden walls that are marked with tablets of brass on which are cut holy emblems and sacred letters . . .

To know the full story of the place you must attend to both 'the busy-body chatter of the valley' and the 'stillness of the hills.' Corkery then proceeds to equate this comprehensive geographical perspective with the novel's under-lying philosophical and psychological compulsions, and with its prevailing mood and tone:

> Self-knowledge is not easily won; and for me truly to know Cork is almost as difficult. Those faces I have been looking at in its streets to-day, how much do they know of that 'quiet desperation' in which, according to the American philosopher, most of the citizens of the world pass their lives? And if they do know something of this quiet desperation, whether is it the stillness of the hills or the busy-body chatter of the valley that gives it its local texture and colour, its tenderness, its snap, its gentleness, its petu-lance, its prayer?

Critics unsympathetic to the novel would probably contend that Corkery, in rejecting the superficial judgements of the mere visitor, himself errs too far in the other direction and offers us in this purposefully muted book an excess of the stillness of the hills and too little of the chatter of the valley. Nevertheless, he adheres throughout to the strategy laid down from the beginning. This is Cork's book, tightly, almost claustrophobically enclosed within the city until the penultimate chapter. The main characters will move from their residences on the outskirts and walk down into and across the city, whether it be Martin Cloyne emerging from his secluded nook by the Lough or Lily Bresnan high up on Fair Hill. Tragedy will come up out of the city to Lily when Stevie Galvin climbs the hills to tell her of the suicide of her brother, Frank, and it will be in 'the flat of the city' that Stevie and Martin will witness the violent scene involving the seaman and the prostitute, which intrudes on Martin's recollections of his idyllic day with Lily and spoils his dreams. Down in the flat of the city, also, Stevie Galvin will endure his lonely torments in his junk-filled eyrie on Morrison's Island, anguishing for his lost brother and their ruined friendship. In writing of the city of Belfast some two decades later, Michael McLaverty, the Northern Irish writer perhaps most akin to Corkery, adopts a similar strategy in his novel, *Call My Brother Back* (1939), in which he regularly allows his characters to escape from the sectarian strife of the town and take refuge on the hills above, from which the irrelevant absurdities of Belfast may be distanced and placed.

From the very beginning, therefore, the book states the terms on which it intends to appeal to us, the sort of intellectual demands which will be made. Vulgar superficiality is to be rejected. The excitements of the market-place must be deliberately fended off and truth sought in contemplation and reverie. The quietist mood is compounded by a profoundly pessimistic view of the Ireland of the day, a view which is essentially as grim as that taken by Joyce in *Dubliners*. Yeats's 'terrible beauty' might never have been heard of. There is no hint of such violent national stimuli in the Ireland of Corkery's only novel, though it was published in the year following the Insurrection of 1916 which had so excited Yeats. Corkery's Ireland is a place where young men gather to bemoan the sterility of their existences in comparison with the vivid life of the exile. The talk in Martin Cloyne's fire-lit room in the house by the Lough is all of the recently departed uncle who has returned to America as the book opens. 'Time out of mind,' we are told, 'perhaps as far back as the disaster of Kinsale, Ireland has been talking in this hopeless strain; the vigour of the nation seems to be abroad, only the timid at home.' Frank Bresnan, 'their brightest companion, their wit, their fellow of infinite jest', has already, though they do not yet know this, succumbed to despair and sought refuge in suicide from his Willy Loman-like existence as a commercial traveller through the dreary little county towns of Cork. Ned Connell, who will eventually leave and go to America himself, seems like 'the only live thing in a dead city' on the occasion in Chapter x when he inadvertently comes upon the distraught Stevie Galvin apostrophising the foreign ship and desperately seeking news of his estranged brother. When, in Chapter xxviii, Stevie comes to tell Martin of Lily's decision to enter the convent at Kilvirra, the talk is all of emigration, that 'disease-germ in the body-politic'. Out of their class of twenty-five at school, Stevie tells Martin, only two remain in Ireland. Cork has become for Stevie 'a city of dead houses . . . Yorick skulls every one of them . . . the lighted windows are a mockery'. All that is left in Cork is the life of its streets, which is dismissed as 'frivolous . . . musical comedy stuff'. Throughout, Corkery is at pains to counter the established literary view of the Irishman as a rattle, a good fellow full of drunken good cheer. There are several references to the characteristics which distinguish the true Celt. He is said to be oblique in his conversational responses and given to covering up his fundamental seriousness with banter. Old Mary, Lily's servant, is representative of the breed:

> She was a countrywoman, now old and small, but hardy, with pursed lips and sunken, grey eyes. Self-absorbed and silent, a true Celt, she despised sentimentality; yet, in spite of this native vigour of mind, there was in her grey eyes the trouble of a sense of mystery.

Linked with the characters' Celtic identity is their particular brand of religion, the Jansenistic Catholicism which is adduced often as the basis for their attitudes to life but, interestingly enough, never advanced as any kind of solution to their lonely struggles with self or with despair. Thus, we are told of Martin Cloyne:

> He was one of those rare people who do their thinking consciously, almost with a certain enjoyment. Perhaps his religion had helped towards this habit of introspection; perhaps it was in his nature, and certainly his very uneventful life had not discouraged it, if it was.

Lily Bresnan's personal dilemma is also explained in terms of her religious beliefs, when she is struggling to decide whether she should enter a convent or remain in the world to care for her father and brother:

> Whichever path she chose seemed the easier. On the one hand, to stay and attend on her father and Finnbarr was to choose the world. It seemed her duty to do so; no other course seemed reasonable; yet she leant greatly to the belief, common amongst Irish Catholics, that the right course in matters affecting the soul is that which does not seem to square exactly with what we call reason.

In spite, however, of this recurring tendency to explain the dispositions of various characters in terms of a particular kind of dogmatic conditioning, Corkery does not at any stage of the work allow his personages to seek refuge from their personal desperations in any simple, formulaic responses of a doctrinal nature. Patricia Hutchins is quite right when she points out that ' In Corkery's stories there is little or no sense of the supernatural, strangeness comes from men's minds or the effect of landscape upon them'.

Lily finally disappears into her convent refuge in Kilvirra but we hear no more of her thereafter and cannot know whether her flight from the world brings her peace or not. More to the point is the situation of Martin Cloyne, who is tormented by his awareness that his friendship with Frank Bresnan had come to an end long before Frank's dreadful death. Frank had not been at Martin's house, we are told, for six months, and Martin recalls that he had sometimes thought of calling on Frank but had failed to do so. They had, he is forced to admit, simply tired of each other, and he begins to fear that he may have abandoned his lonely and desperate former friend to his self-inflicted death. His failure to profess openly to Lily his love for her goes hand in hand with his guilt about her dead brother, rendering Martin impotent. He is allowed no simple solutions to his 'quiet desperation'. Indeed, as he struggles with his demons, he is made to realise with some bitterness and self-disgust that the seemingly stoical front which he habitually presents to the world is merely a façade for a dangerously corrosive brand of self-pity:

> All cruel people live in an atmosphere of self-pity: this he now saw; and he came to the conclusion that we should judge of our own state of mind by our actions, not by our thoughts; that, in fact, we should do with ourselves as we do with others, of whose intentions we take such little account. He would now shake himself free of dreams, he would play the man. He argued his mind into a state of rigidity, and this he mistook for self-control. And he experienced that luke-warm joy we all feel in having gathered a few crabbed philosophic fruits from wintry boughs.

Martin has lost both the man and the woman he loved. His dreams of any kind of future happiness are now shown to be illusory and he can interpose nothing between himself and pain other than a desperate determination to wait, to hang on grimly in a personal void, without consolation. Chapter XXIX is of vital importance here, for in it we see Martin struggle most desperately to come to terms with his anguish. Memories of the past and speculation about the future torment him equally and so he can only resolve to exist in some sort of perpetual present which admits of neither recollection nor speculation. The climax of the chapter is a powerfully imagined piece of dream fantasy in which Martin is cruelly shown what a Prufrock he really is. He dreams that he is about to attempt the hazardous feat of walking along the coping of a dangerous railway bridge, 'one of the tests of heroism among the boys of the district'. Suddenly, the dead Frank Bresnan appears to him in the guise of a heroic and beautiful boy, to warn him that he must not make the attempt. Heroic feats are not for him. And Lily stands by to witness his failure, his symbolic admission that he 'is not Prince Hamlet, nor was meant to be', that he is one of those fated to watch life pass him by, cursed with enough intelligence to suffer but always fated to miss the few real opportunities that come in his way. Corkery makes Martin Cloyne confront his dark night of the soul quite directly, allowing no doctrinal nostrums to ease his pain:

> ... 'Oh God,' he whispered, in a choking voice, and, again tossing his head angrily, would constrain his eyes to gaze wide-open at the darkness, forcing his thoughts at the same time to keep that narrow line which divides past and future. For here only was safety . . . Past, future, to either of which sleep would cruelly lead him, had suddenly become regions of pain . . . Inasmuch as it appeared, however, that the present could wound him only by virtue of some strange veto it exercised over past and future, he maintained his struggle against bringing either into being: and by this means he seemed able to disarm the present of its power; almost to be able to annihilate it, until nothing would remain except that vague sense of waiting.

Almost half a century later, in his two fine novels, *The Barracks* (1963) and *The Dark* (1965), John McGahern was to assign his heroes a similar painful struggle and a remarkably similar solution to their dilemmas. Both Elizabeth Reegan of *The Barracks* and young Mahoney of *The Dark* struggle grimly to evade the torment of time's flux by striving to exist in a continuing present which admits of no before or after. The general strategy of Corkery's novel is perhaps, closer to that of *The Barracks*, in that both Martin Cloyne and Elizabeth Reegan work out their solitary struggles largely by retrospection and there hangs over both these novels the sense of individual fates which have already been dictated by destiny, of lives which are running down. The more restive young hero of *The Dark* is made to struggle more turbulently against his destiny but, in the end, his resolution of his frustrations is remarkably similar to Martin Cloyne's. Daniel Corkery may be said to have established, in his only novel, a pattern of response to particular Irish situations which is to be rediscovered as fictionally appropriate by some of his most talented successors. In this respect, the book constitutes a significant contrast to Joyce's *A Portrait of the Artist as a Young Man*, the latter embodying the hazardous rejection of all traditional dictates of creed, nationality and language, while the Cork novel presents a pattern of agonising resignation. There are, inevitably, echoes of Joyce's work to be noticed in Corkery's novel, sometimes echoes of a remarkably precise kind. Finnbarr Bresnan, younger brother of the dead Frank, is made to embark on a regimen of pious practices remarkably similar to that undertaken by the repentant Stephen Dedalus and, interestingly enough, Corkery has Finnbarr undergo much the same sort of spiritual disillusionment as that suffered by Joyce's hero:

> He had laid down a rule of life some time before and to it he still rigidly adhered, finding it no more difficult than formerly. He had, however, grown accustomed to adorn it with tiny charities and little extra devotional practices – a weekly copper to a blind man who kept his station on Pope's Quay, attendance at Benediction in the Reparation Convent every Friday evening, and such like – and it was these, curiously enough, that became more and more difficult of fulfilment while he postponed the consideration of his fall. Such, he felt, were for more perfect souls than his. They grew irksome, until at last whenever he engaged in them a voice seemed to whisper 'hypocrite' in his ear.

Eventually, Finnbarr, Dedalus-like, abandons his intentions of becoming a priest and, again like Dedalus, leaves Ireland and takes refuge in flight upon the sea. No more than Martin Cloyne is he allowed sentimentalised, pseudo-religious solutions to his difficulties.

It has sometimes been suggested that Martin Cloyne is the figure in the novel who comes closest to being some sort of version of Corkery himself but, if this is the case, one must admire the decisively reductive view taken of this pensive protagonist. His prematurely middle-aged responses to experience seem to derive from some ruinous failure in the man to confront life directly on its own terms, a refusal to formulate intellectual conclusions on the basis of the evidence presented by life itself. He has, as it were, reversed the celebrated dictum of Robert Louis Stevenson by deciding that it is better to arrive than to travel hopefully. He calls to mind the dreadful Mr Duffy of Joyce's mordant story, 'A Painful Case' and, although Martin Cloyne merely drives the woman who loves him into a convent, whereas the rejected Mrs Sinico throws herself under a train, Corkery makes his central figure more cruelly aware of his sterility by compelling him to understand how he has deceived himself into mistaking frigidity for fortitude. As the passage from Chapter xxix quoted above indicates, Martin is forced to admit to himself the inadequacy of 'that luke-warm joy we all feel in having gathered a few crabbed philosophic fruits from wintry boughs.' Critics have sometimes expressed surprise at Corkery's never again attempting the novel form, but his decision may well be implicit in his profoundly pessimistic reading of the character of Martin Cloyne and his peculiar brand of sterile cerebration. When Samuel Beckett came to treat of a similarly incapacitated character in *Murphy* (1938), he coped with his fictional problem by making his book a black-comic assault on the form itself and by deploying an hilariously outrageous set of characters and circumstances to create a special kind of fictional spoof. Such exotic high-jinks are not in Corkery's nature as a writer. His humour, when it appears, is of the gentlest possible kind and derisive irony is not his response to the universe.

If one suggests that the novel is, in general, infinitely more successful in its treatment of men than of women, one must also concede that Corkery is astute enough to assign a very subordinate role to women and to thrust his male characters to the centre of the stage from the very beginning. The shade of the suicide, Frank Bresnan, haunts the little circle of friends who gather at Martin Cloyne's house by the Lough. Such little action as the book contains concerns Martin Cloyne in his relationship with Lily Bresnan and Stevie Galvin's tortured attempts at reconciliation with his only brother, Phil, who, it is eventually revealed, left Cork after a row with Stevie about Minnie Ryan. No woman, apart from Lily, is permitted any active part in the book and even Lily, when debating if she should enter the convent or not, is not allowed to include in her ruminations any thought of Martin Cloyne. One of the most compelling images in the novel is that of the dead Frank Bresnan during his wake. His corpse lies, newly-shrouded, in the bedroom, surrounded by chattering women:

> . . . he was left to the all-knowing, gossiping tongues of the women above; and, as if the talk itself were not torture enough, whenever it flagged for an instant some of those present, to improve the occasion, would be sure to hit upon some lugubrious reflection that would focus once again every eye in the room on the dead man's face. 'Look now, Mrs Moloney, do you mean to tell me he hasn't the look of his poor mother from here?' If the dead lip twitched, if the eyelids quivered beneath the dull and stupid scrutiny, would anyone who had known him alive wonder at it?

When Martin Cloyne looks through the press of chattering women and sees the white face on the bed, 'so piteous in its stillness', it seems to cry out to him, 'For God's sake, Martin, take me out of this'. Women, *en masse*, are gossiping busybodies. Individually, they are either saints like Lily or sinners like the raucous prostitute who makes a brief appearance in Chapter XVIII. The men are all unmarried, with the exception of Ned Connell, and it is made pretty clear that Martin Cloyne despises Ned and regards him as suitable only for export to America. Martin lives with his mother and sister, neither of whom impinges on our attention. Stevie Galvin lives alone in his toy-filled eyrie on

Morrison's Island, where he achieves an almost Dickensian grotesquerie with his pathetic and futile enthusiasms for odd hobbies and arcane branches of learning. Lily Bresnan, confronted like the heroine of Joyce's 'Eveline' by a choice between her duty to her family and some more self-indulgent alternative, is given no real option by her lackadaisacal suitor but to take the veil and become an enduring symbol of purity. Martin is left to comfort Stevie Galvin after the death of his brother in the wreck of the *Pinestar*, his only emotion at the end being 'a certain cold sense of loneliness' which Corkery is too honest to entitle peace. The book resounds with the tormented cries of lonely men. Lily hears Frank cry out in his sleep and, later; Ring brings Martin another account of Frank's desperation when he tells him how an acquaintance had heard Frank give two terrible cries, 'Help! Help!' while huddled asleep on a train. The desperately lonely Stevie Galvin seems to be begging an unfriendly universe for comfort when he is overheard by Ned Connell shouting at the unfriendly sailors for news from Rio de Janeiro.

In a book so lacking in action of an obvious kind, Corkery has to resort to a good deal of description and, in general, manages to fuse such material skilfully enough with the meandering nature of the narrative. He conveys a vivid picture of the city, of its busy dockland area, its surrounding hills where the streets are alive with children at play, its shops and offices peopled by clerks like Martin Cloyne. One is sometimes conscious of a limiting authorial omniscience which seems to preclude the exploration of character through dialogue and action. Thus, for example, when Martin Cloyne attends the wake at the Bresnan house, he is made to listen with a certain knowing weariness to the discussion between a figure who is vaguely and rather condescendingly identified as 'the inevitable Radical' and an equally stereotyped Irish Nationalist. One feels that, in such scenes, Corkery is rather restively attending to the obligatory depiction of a crowd scene without being at all interested in its details. The affair is generalised and the issues glossed over as though to suggest that the two men concerned, who are never identified by name, are simply rehearsing tired old attitudes which it would bore the author to explore. The result is that the reader is left dissatisfied with such uninterestingly imprecise portraits and wondering why Corkery has bothered to include such material at all. The principal figures in the story are sometimes assigned a Murphy-like preference for imprisoning themselves in armchairs, as though they are ill or convalescent, while their sexlessness is often conveyed in overtly religious images. Thus, at the opening of Chapter VII, we find Martin Cloyne so ensconced:

On the next Sunday, Martin Cloyne was again in the old arm-chair he loved so well, and sunk so deep in it as to suggest a state of convalescence. Unusually like himself he looked, his head, with his high, white brow, leaning a little towards the left shoulder, his eyes taking long rests, hardly moving at all, the lids drawn a little over them, and his lips as tender-looking as a nun's.

Stevie Galvin also appears chair-bound and like a religious after the shock of his brother's chilly and unfriendly letter, in Chapter XI:

> After some time he rose and approached the gramophone; once again he adjusted the funnel, unwound the wadding from the record, fixed it in the machine, turned the handle and set the music free. The roaring storm outside strengthened it and made it wild. Before the symphony had finished, Stevie was again back in his chair, arranging himself with a strange gravity. And again his hands were gripping the edges of his coat. Below its darkness hung his night-gown; it was not unlike a priest's vestment. His feet were bare.

In a significant authorial intrusion at the end of Chapter XIX, Corkery offers a revealing comment on Martin Cloyne which embodies his own awareness of the sort of book he is engaged in writing. At this point, Martin has left Stevie Galvin and is in some agitation of spirit after learning of Frank Bresnan's engagement to 'a good, simple, *stupid* girl' in Limerick and the likelihood of his death having being suicidal:

> . . . 'drowned himself,' 'drowned himself' was pulsing in his brain – as if he had not more than guessed as much long before! There are so many people in the world who feel it almost wrong to come up against plain statements of fact! Sensitive souls, they do not help the world to progress, but they almost make progress worth while. They test it: a world that would provide them with a suitable medium for working in, – what a world it would be!

It would not be entirely unfair to suggest that *The Threshold of Quiet* is a novel by a writer who has an instinctive distaste for 'coming up against plain statements of fact', a 'sensitive soul' whose characters shy away from the real world's vulgarities and pine for some unstained, ideal universe as their proper sphere. Corkery's most recent biographer, George Brandon Saul, is severe on the novel in his short study in the Bucknell 'Irish Writers' series, but hardly displays much understanding of the work. He is content to dismiss it with an inaccurate gibe about Corkery's religious sensitivity:

> Corkery's characters, obviously fearful of their own thought whenever they feel it may threaten to counter Roman Catholic doctrine, are simply tedious. The whole affair suggests the expanded reflection of a neurosis; in

long stretches it becomes almost as tiresome as the 'psychological' mean-
derings of George Moore.

In spite of the suggestive reference to neurosis, this is, in general, abuse rather
than criticism. As has been suggested earlier, Corkery's treatment of his main
characters most certainly does not allow them any easy doctrinal solutions
and Saul seems to emerge as someone who reads both Corkery and Moore
with equal insensitivity. Patricia Hutchins, a less pretentious critic, notes the
absence from Corkery's stories of any religiosity and, in a perceptively
sympathetic comment, suggests the nature of Corkery's achievement in his
novel and its importance for its period:

> In Corkery's stories there is little or no sense of the supernatural, strange-
> ness comes from men's minds or the effect of landscape upon them . . . The
> style was slow-moving at first, many of the impressions too colourful in a
> William Morris way, but the people and their problems were real and I
> soon became involved in them – Martin Cloyne who could not push
> himself against life enough, Stevie Galvin with his love of gadgets and
> hobbies hiding an empty space in him, the boy Finnbarr and his sister.
> Perhaps what made me continue, lazy as I felt, was 'that psychic sense of
> place,' to put it in the words used by Corkery of Synge. Here was a writer
> who could draw out of houses and streets and rooms some of the states of
> mind experienced there, and if the book as a whole is a description of 'lives
> of quiet desperation' it remains a valuable psychological assessment of its
> period.

Corkery's celebrated protegé, Sean O'Faolain, who was to be one of the
severest critics of some of his master's other works, was an early and
enthusiastic admirer of *The Threshold of Quiet*:

> The novel, delicate, brooding, sensitive, tragic, not without a grotesque
> note – as in the character of Stevie Galvin – fulfilled absolutely the prom-
> ise of the stories. It is, without question, a lovely novel, and for many even
> a perfect novel. Almost aggressively regionalist, it admits no view of life but
> the local, Irish view: a glimpse of other worlds serving only to support the
> sense of the inevitability of that view, and to sear the heart with a sense of
> the delimitation of life within a code, humbly accepted, loyally unques-
> tioned, despairingly followed to tragedy in the one case, to renunciation in
> the other.

These moderate and responsive readings suggest far better than Saul's
superficial dismissal the essential qualities of Daniel Corkery's passionately
celibate novel.

SELECTED BIBLIOGRAPHY

RELATED WORKS

A Munster Twilight, Dublin & Cork, 1916.
The Stormy Hills, Dublin & Cork, 1929.

BIOGRAPHY

George Brandon Saul, *Daniel Corkery*, Lewisburg, 1973.

CRITICAL STUDIES

George Brandon Saul, *op.cit.*

CRITICAL ARTICLES

Sean O'Faolain, 'Daniel Corkery', *The Dublin Magazine*, XI, 2 N.S. (April-June 1936), 49-61.
Patricia Hutchins, 'Daniel Corkery, Poet of Weather and Place', *Irish Writing*, 25 (Dec. 1953), 42-49.
Roibeárd Breathnach, 'Daniel Corkery – Creative Writer and Critic', University College, Cork, *Record*, 40 (1965), 31-37.
Séamus de Róiste, 'Daniel Corkery 1878-1964', Cork Arts Society Daniel Corkery Commemorative Exhibition, 1971.
Colbert Kearney, 'Dónall Ó Corcora Agus an Litríocht Angla-Éireannach', *Scríobh*, 4 (1979), 138-151.
Alexander G. Gonzales, 'A Re-evaluation of Daniel Corkery's Fiction', *Irish University Review*, 14, 2 (Autumn 1984), 191-201.

VIII

Eimar O'Duffy (1893-1935)

THE CUANDUINE TRILOGY

He was born in Dublin, the eldest son of a prosperous dental surgeon who was dentist-in-ordinary to the Vice-Regal household. His father, Kevin O'Duffy, was of Anglo-Irish stock and his fictional alter-ego is the Eugene Lascelles of O'Duffy's long novel, *The Wasted Island*, who muses in appropriately snobbish fashion about his small son's destiny:

> 'Public school and Varsity, of course. After that . . . the Army perhaps? No,' he decided, thinking of certain possibilities. 'We can do better than that. What about the Diplomatic Service? A Public School and Varsity man has the Empire at his feet.'

In real life, the public school proved to be Stonyhurst but the boy angered the father by preferring University College Dublin to Trinity. He took a Bachelor of Dental Surgery degree at UCD and finally broke with his father when the latter tried to persuade him to enter the British Army during the First World War. In fact, he took a quite contrary direction by joining the Irish Republican Brotherhood and becoming a captain in the Irish Volunteers. When the 1916 insurrection was imminent, O'Duffy was sent by Eoin MacNeill to Belfast to head off any possibility of insurrectionary action there. His eventual disillusionment with the Easter Rising is made clear in *The Wasted Island* (1919). It was inevitable that, holding such views, he should have found it difficult to settle down permanently in the new Irish Free State, though he did for a time work as a teacher and in the Department of External Affairs in Dublin. Then, in 1925, he moved his family to England. He had married in 1920 Kathleen Cruise O'Brien, aunt of the (later) well-known writer and politician, Conor Cruise O'Brien. There were two children of the marriage, Brian and Rosalind.

O'Duffy was playwright, versifier, novelist and would-be economist. Never very wealthy, he often had to produce fairly trivial literary work in haste, to make ends meet. His earliest writings of any importance were two plays for Edward Martyn's Irish Theatre, *The Phoenix on the Roof* and *The Walls of Athens*. Another early play was *Bricrui's Feast*. His first novel was *The Wasted Island*, a heavily autobiographical and excessively lengthy work which Robert Hogan charitably describes as being 'among other things, a painless and vividly dramatised course in Irish history'. In the early 1920s, O'Duffy published two light novels, *Printer's Errors* and *Miss Rudd and Some Lovers*, as well as the historical romance, *The Lion and the Fox*. *King Goshawk and the Birds*, the opening volume of the trilogy which was to be his major literary achievement, appeared in 1926. *The Spacious Adventures of the Man in the Street* followed in 1928 and the final volume, *Asses in Clover*, came out in 1933. In the early 1930s, he published a number of pot-boilers, detective thrillers of no great literary importance. He developed a keen interest in economic theory and published *Life and Money* in 1932 and a pamphlet, *Consumer Credit*, in 1934. For many years he had suffered severe pain caused by chronic ulceration of the stomach and he died of this condition in Surrey in 1935.

THE CUANDUINE TRILOGY (1926-1933)

The novels which make up the trilogy are *King Goshawk and the Birds* (1926), *The Spacious Adventures of the Man in the Street* (1928) and *Asses in Clover* (1933). The generic title, above, could be said to be something of a misnomer since Cuanduine, son of Cuchulain does not appear until Book II of the first volume, plays no part in the second, and, in the third, has to play second fiddle frequently to a host of other characters. The slightly unsatisfactory nature of the over-all title which is usually attached to this satirical trilogy is a comment of sorts on the diffuse nature of the work as a whole. Beginning as an attack on capitalist greed, it later broadens its scope to expose the various inadequacies of O'Duffy's Ireland and of modernity in general. The original plot, having to do with the seizure of all the birds of the world by the monstrous capitalist, King Goshawk, is abandoned during the entire length of the second novel and resumed rather late in the third in order to pull the loose fabric of the whole belatedly together. In a felicitous phrase, Benedict Kiely describes O'Duffy as 'an evangelical fantasist' and it is the serious imbalance between evangelism and fantasy which make the trilogy, by general agreement his major literary achievement, less than entirely successful, striking though it is here and there. O'Duffy belabours his particular targets too often and too predictably so that certain of his effects become tediously repetitive. His particular hatred is reserved for economists, the purveyors of 'the dismal science' which expresses itself in hideous jargon and never succeeds in solving any of the problems which it addresses. Thus, in

Book I of *Asses in Clover*, Mac an Rudai, the common-man figure who is a pauper in the midst of plenty, is made to encounter a series of economists who comment learnedly and pointlessly on his condition. They offer various futile diagnoses of his poverty and of its relationship to the aggressive capitalism in which his three brothers have managed to thrive. Cuanduine, nominally the central figure of the work, is pushed aside as Mac an Rudai is made during several chapters to encounter a string of financial morons, false priests and iniquitous judges. He is finally consigned to prison but O'Duffy rather undoes his own satirical effects by presenting Mac an Rudai not as an effective antagonist of the system which enslaves him but rather as the most conventional of believers in it, thus making him 'a not very inspiring person to fight for' as Cuanduine is forced to comment when he is permitted to re-enter the tale in Chapter XI.

Stylistically, O'Duffy interestingly bridges the period between the whimsical fantasy of James Stephens and the strenuously learned mockery of Flann O'Brien. The Philosopher named Murphy who resides in Dublin's Stoneybatter and sets going the action of *King Goshawk and the Birds* steps straight out of the pages of *The Crock of Gold*:

> Mundane things worried the Philosopher not at all. He never noticed whether he was comfortable or not, and he never cared what he ate. He did not even lament his lack of books, believing that there was more to be learnt from the talk of a child, the smile of a woman, or the folly of men than from all the books that were ever written.

His exchanges with Socrates and with Cuchulain himself, when he seeks them out in the ethereal regions to ask their assistance against King Goshawk, are a mixture of the profound and the comically bathetic in the true Stephens manner. Like Cuanduine, he has no part in the second of the novels and when he reappears in the third one he dies at the end of Book II because he is no longer needed after Cuanduine has slain King Goshawk. One recalls the decision made by the first Philosopher in *The Crock of Gold* who elected to die because he had not in the space of one week found any new truth. While he owes much to Stephens for the prevailing tone of certain aspects of his fantasy, O'Duffy can be seen to have exerted an evident influence on the author of *At Swim-Two-Birds*. His background and early career are interestingly similar in some respects to Brian O'Nolan's. Both were from well-to-do, middle-class families. Both attended University College Dublin and, like O'Nolan at a slightly later stage, O'Duffy too produced a body of light, satirical writing during his undergraduate days. These were collected in *A Lay of the Liffey, and Other Verses* (1918) and, although they are mere light-hearted drolleries, they show O'Duffy as someone with a keen interest in metrical pastiche and a lively delight in verbal pyrotechnics. Born almost two decades before O'Nolan, O'Duffy found himself involved in the political and military turbulence of the period during which Ireland strained towards independence while O'Nolan reached his early manhood during the early years of the newly formed Irish Free State, but they share a certain common disenchantment with the superficialities of Irish patriotism. O'Duffy was to elaborate his political cynicism at tedious length in the over-long *bildungsroman, The Wasted Island*, first published in 1919 and revised a decade later, but he achieves a more economical political derision in the early pages of *King Goshawk and the Birds* where he effectively satirises the Tweedle-Dum, Tweedle-Dee politics of the early days of the Free State in a manner worthy of Myles himself:

> As long as the Philosopher could remember, the Yallogreens and the Greenyallos had been thus abusing one another . . . The Philosopher sadly recalled to mind the great civil war that had been waged between them over the question of rejoining the British Empire, from which the Irish people had seceded some years earlier . . . The sequel of all this was burnt deep into the Philosopher's recollection; the mad declaration of war against the British Empire; the destruction of the Irish navy; the invasion of Ireland by the British; and the forcible re-establishment of the Republic.

Most importantly of all, O'Brien found in O'Duffy's novels a fine satirical capacity for producing hilariously effective contrasts by introducing into a shrunken modernity the giant figures of ancient Irish legend. Cuchulain, the champion of Ulster, the central figure of Yeats's Irish heroic pantheon, is made to walk the streets of a very dirty and decayed Dublin and, in an oft-quoted passage, finds himself playing tennis in the suburbs:

> You should have seen Cuchulain playing tennis with the gentry and ladies of the Bon Ton suburb. He learnt the whole art and skill of the game in ten minutes, and straightway beat the Champion of all Ireland six-love, six-love, six-love. Never had such strength and agility been seen before. He could cross the court in one leap; he never served a fault, and none but the Champion ever returned his service; he would take any stroke on the volley; and at the net his smash invariably burst the ball.

O'Duffy's Cuchulain and Cuanduine prepare the way for the Finn Mac Cool and Conan and Mad Sweeney of *At Swim-Two-Birds*. Yet, O'Duffy's anger is much nearer the surface and the tone of his work, as a consequence, lacks the happy anarchy of his successor's. Flann O'Brien's historically variegated characters inhabit a Dublin world of seedy undergraduates and pubcrawlers where the unnamed hero's uncle inclines to musical soirées involving Count John McCormack. O'Duffy's heroic Cuchulain takes an exploratory walk in Chapter VI of *King Goshawk* and the author can scarcely contain his loathing of the Dublin he describes:

> Come, O Muse, whoever you be, that stood by the elbow of the immortal Zola, take this pen of mine and pump it full of such foul and fetid ink as shall describe it worthily. To what shall I compare it? A festering corpse, maggot-crawling, under a carrion-kissing sun? . . .
>
> What ruin and decay were here: what filth and litter: what nauseating stenches. The houses were so crazy with age and so shaken with bombardments that there was scarce one that could stand without assistance: therefore they were held together by plates and rivets, or held apart by cross-beams, or braced up by scaffoldings, so that the street had the appearance of a dead forest . . . The streets were ankle-deep in dung and mire; craters yawned in their midst; piles of wrecked masonry obstructed them. Rivulets ran where the gutters had been. Foul sewer smells issued from holes and cracks.

Where O'Brien issues a manifesto on the absurdities of all literary pretences and subsequently embodies that credo in the absurd antics of his creatures, O'Duffy only succeeds in creating an impression of an author with too many bees in his bonnet for his novels' good. An overriding impression of mere crankiness unavoidably conveys itself in the presence of a parade of obsessively castigated *bêtes noires*. The pervasive vulgarity of modern life torments him unbearably. So, we get diatribes on everything from denatured food to vaccination, from trashy newspapers to pointless academic research, from birth-control to modern literature and the cinema – and, always and ever and anon, the gargantuan stupidities of bankers, politicians and economists. His trilogy is a farrago of digressions, some of them very funny, some less so, but all tending to draw us away from the plot of King Goshawk and his seizure of the world's birds. The most significant digression of all is, of course, the second volume in which O'Duffy abandons entirely the mode of the opening volume and writes instead a sort of Erewhonian satire on Earth itself, represented in the novel anagrammatically as the planet of Rathe. Cuanduine is abandoned in favour of the character whose body he has usurped, one Aloysius O'Kennedy, who himself usurps the body of a dead Rathean and embarks on a sub-Swiftian tour of the planet to which his spirit has travelled. Subsequently, the manners and practices of the Ratheans are recounted in order to contrast them directly wth the values which O'Kennedy/Ydenneko has brought with him from his own world. The Ratheans' attitudes to sex, crime, education, sport, marriage, divorce and many other issues are can-

vassed by a constantly amazed observer with the result that satirical light is
thrown on the absurdities of many of the standard practices of our own place
and time. Much of this is entertainingly and amusingly done. The lengthy
early sequence in which food is used as a convenient synonym for sex and the
Ratheans are depicted as monophagous, subsisting throughout their lives on
one fruit selected in youth, is cleverly developed. Brothels become secret
restaurants where hungry Ratheans, weary of monophagous existences,
huddle together in darkness to eat themselves sick on revoltingly greasy
messes. The process of satirical reversal is applied throughout, so that human
practices such as hunting of animals for sport are shown up for the vile
brutalities they are. Occasionally, the satire strikes a genuinely Swiftian note
of savagery. When the traveller penetrates to the Dark Country beyond
Rathe, he finds there a race of people who adjust their slaves to fit their small
houses in true Procrustean fashion by surgical reduction of their stature which
is achieved through removal of the shin bones in infancy. He meets also
a race of intelligent dogs who try to stand upright and ape the manners of the
humans. These passages are horribly convincing and gripping and the scene
where the traveller has a meal with the dog, Towser and his wife, Mrs Towser
and their two 'children', Dash and Flo, is quite splendidly nasty and yet comic,
almost as if Dickens's Wemmick had strayed into the fourth book of
Gulliver's Travels by mistake. Alf MacLochlainn has indicated how O'Duffy
began to employ his method of satirical reversal quite early, when he was
editor of the *National Student* in 1915. At that time, he wrote tongue-in-cheek
editorials of a political nature, simulating true-blue loyalty to Empire while
commending its opposite by implication. MacLochlainn refers also to O'Duffy's
'trick of happy anagram' but one wishes that this aspect of his technique had
not been overdone to a point where it tends to become shallow and
predictable. Antithetical situations of an effective nature, fully imagined and
carefully worked through in a convincing manner, are well enough but the
mere reversal or jumbling of letters in a name, so that Luther becomes Thelru
and Dickens appears as Sneckid, can easily deteriorate into a wearisome level
of schoolboyish sniggering, not very much above the level of *The Beano* or
The Dandy. *Asses in Clover* opens with a gathering of the world's great
financiers and the assembly includes Butterworth the Dairy King, Tanberg the
Tea King, Ah-Sin the Rice King and Gurgleheim the Liquor King. The worlds
of Swift and Butler appear, momentarily at least, to have given way to that
of the Famous Five and the Owl of the Remove.

Uneven and digressive, then, the trilogy clearly is. It varies from satirical
passages of great power to limp sections of authorial ranting, from genuine
comedy to schoolboy giggling. At its best, it impresses by its imaginative

range. This is a writer who can move from tennis-club trivia to science fiction, from grim realism to complex satire. *Saeva indignatio* there most certainly is, even if, at times, it is working at a rather journalistic level. Alf MacLochlainn, who appears commendably eager to counter the rather adverse judgements of Vivian Mercier, notes O'Duffy's range and the extent of his achievement in what was a tragically short creative life:

> In the twenty years of his adult life he had twenty published titles to his credit, an average of one a year, some of pamphlet form but ten of them substantial works. This industry alone is enough to make him notable as an Irish writer and further all his works are of considerable interest as documents of their time and a consideration of them brings us into touch with movements and works of great importance.
>
> He wrote plays, novels, verse, journalism, satire, detective stories and economics. In all he had an ease of style which is unobtrusive and showed a rare clarity and inventiveness of mind.

This is generous and just. O'Duffy's output, achieved in the face of constant and painful illness, is impressive enough to make us regret his death at a sadly early age when his gifts as a satirist seemed to be coming to maturity.

SELECTED BIBLIOGRAPHY

RELATED WORKS

Printer's Errors, Dublin & London, 1922.
Miss Rudd and Some Lovers, Dublin, 1923.

BIOGRAPHY

Robert Hogan, *Eimar O'Duffy*, Lewisburg, 1972.

CRITICAL STUDIES

Hogan, *op. cit.*

CRITICAL ARTICLES

Vivian Mercier, 'The Satires of Eimar O'Duffy', *The Bell*, XII, 4 (July 1946), 325-336.
Alf MacLochlainn, 'Eimar O'Duffy: a bibliographical biography', *The Irish Book*, 1, 1, 1959, 37-46.

IX

Brinsley MacNamara (1890-1963)

THE VARIOUS LIVES OF MARCUS IGOE

His real name was John Weldon and he was born in Ballinacor, Hiskinstown, Delvin, Co. Westmeath. His father, James Weldon, was the local schoolmaster at Ballinvalley School. As a young man of twenty, in 1910, the future writer joined the Abbey Theatre company as an actor and went to America in 1911, on the company's first tour there. He came back to Ireland in 1913 and lived in Delvin for five years, writing poems and stories for publication in various magazines. He came to wide public notice for the first time with his novel, *The Valley of the Squinting Windows* (1918). This unrelentingly savage attack on the endemic bitchery of Irish village life brought MacNamara an unenviable notoriety. In A.E. Malone's phrase, he was 'one of those who awoke one morning to find himself infamous'. The book so enraged the people of Delvin that they burned it publicly and vented their anger also on the author's father by boycotting his school, thus endangering his livelihood. James Weldon instituted a court action, claiming damages for alleged conspiracy to boycott, but the jury at the hearing disagreed and, despite a public appeal on James Weldon's behalf supported by such notables as W.B.Yeats, George Russell, Oliver St John Gogarty and James Stephens, the case was not re-tried. Brinsley MacNamara was to produce six further novels but the notoriety surrounding his first saw to it that it was to be that book with which his name would be most enduringly associated. He married in 1920 and his only child, a son named Oliver, was born the following year. MacNamara went to live in Dublin in 1922 and became Registrar of the National Gallery in 1925, in succession to James Stephens. He occupied this post until 1960, when he retired on pension.

His other novels included *The Clanking of Chains* (1920), *The Mirror in the Dusk* (1921), *The Various Lives of Marcus Igoe* (1929) and *Return to Ebontheever* (1930). In addition, he wrote numerous plays for the Abbey. His best-known comedy was *Look at the Heffernans* (1926) while his most successful tragedy was *Margaret Gillan* (1933). He also published numerous short stories and worked as drama critic for the *Irish Times*. He was a founder member of the Irish Academy of Letters in 1932. Because of the extraordinary *succès de scandale* of his first novel, he tended to be seen as a grimly realistic writer but, as Benedict Kiely and other critics have noted, this is something of an over-simplification. In a work like *The Various Lives of Marcus Igoe*, he can be seen to be striving to extend his technical range as a novelist in the direction of elaborately ironic fantasy. He wrote little after the publication in Belfast in 1951 of *The Whole Story of the X.Y.Z.*, a mildly comic novella on the theme of a Dublin clerk who inhabits a self-created fantasy world. Brinsley MacNamara died on 4 February 1963.

THE VARIOUS LIVES OF MARCUS IGOE (1929)

Brinsley MacNamara's fictional village, the object of his satire, is called Garradrimna, his equivalent of Patrick Kavanagh's Mucker or Drumnay. It is an unlovely and unlovable place, on which he made his first major assault in *The Valley of the Squinting Windows* (1918), the novel which was to bring down upon him the wrath of his native village of Delvin. As MacNamara depicts it there, Garradrimna is a small village peopled by mean-minded rustics who are incessantly engaged in maligning each other, rejoicing in the frequent misfortunes of their fellows and savagely envious of their occasional triumphs. Garradrimna has seven pubs, frequented by cadgers with insatiable thirsts. It possesses a post-office presided over by a post-mistress who makes it her regular business to steam open letters so that she may familiarise herself and her cronies with the supposedly private doings of the correspondents. The local school is dominated by an authoritarian clerical manager in the person of the local parish priest, who is ever on the watch to see to it that teachers and pupils conform absolutely to his own rigidly conservative standards of morality and behaviour. In this society, any aspiration towards the finer things of life is instantly sneered at as an absurd pretension. Everyone spies on everyone else and the very air of the place is suffused with envy and mean-minded calculation. The inhabitants of Garradrimna look out at their dreary little world through their 'squinting' windows and see the village and its people distorted into invariable ugliness.

This first novel was to earn its author the largely undeserved title of 'realist', and he was later to be hailed as the forerunner of an entire school of rural satirists. In fact, although in some respects the novel looks forward to such works as *The Green Fool* and *Tarry Flynn*, it is really a contrived and thinly characterised melodrama and the best thing about it may well be its memorably evocative title. In many respects, the story recalls the stagey effects of such nineteenth-century works as Gerald Griffin's *The Collegians*, and Rebecca Kerr, the pregnant school-teacher who is at the centre of the action, seems obviously indebted to the heroine of George Moore's *The Lake*, though MacNamara's novel possesses little of the plangently melodic quality of the earlier work. MacNamara seems, at this early stage of his career, to have been informed by a genuine desire to combat a kind of romantic sentimentality in literature, which he saw as stemming from a national sense of inferiority consequent on centuries of political oppression. That he knew at least some of the risks he was running is clear from some comments of his own:

> When a country has made a long flight for freedom, there is a feeling, pardonable enough, that it is in a sense traitorous to delve too deeply into the frailties of one's own people. The author should be patriotic and popular, write with his tongue in his cheek, and say of the Irishman anywhere that his vices are those of the stranger while his virtues are peculiarly his own. The writer should subscribe to the same inferiority complex and adopt the ostrich habit when events around him tend to belie the desired image. If a writer is a little earlier than his time, if he is fortu-nately or unfortunately influenced by nationalistic feelings of a different kind, if he believes that the best service he can do his country is to raise its self-respect by attempting to lift it out of the dark realm of sham and cant and humbug by holding up the mirror truthfully, he is set upon from all sides as if he has committed a shocking crime.

The impulse behind his first novel is, thus, sufficiently clear, but the book which caused such a furore in Delvin is, in fact, a poor one. If they had been capable of assessing it on artistic grounds, the furiously indignant book-burners of Delvin might have recognised that it is so unremittingly one-sided in its satire and so threadbare in its plotting and characterisation that, in the final analysis, it fails of its central satirical purpose. Its immediate successor, the political fable, *The Clanking of Chains* (1920), is also creaky and unconvincing. Its idealistic hero, Michael Dempsey, who begins by playing Robert Emmet on the local stage, proves far too fine a being for the corrupt society of the emergent Irish Free State and must, in the end, turn his back on his country and its incurable ills. The book is heavy with sentimental and didactic authorial intrusions and Michael Dempsey is an uninteresting, thinly realised hero who never succeeds in winning the reader's interest or sympathy to any worthwhile degree. The author has a thesis to urge, concerning the irredeemably craven nature of Irish society, and he implements his purpose by pontificating rather than by embodying his message in his washy and uninteresting central character. The novel dribbles towards its defeatist conclusion and the unlamented departure of its hopeless hero.

The novel which MacNamara produced a decade after the Delvin brouhaha, *The Various Lives of Marcus Igoe*, is in every way a more complex and technically sophisticated performance. The setting is once again Garradrimna, but the writer's attitude to place and subject has matured and his satire here is informed by a new geniality. Furthermore, as his ironic impulse becomes more various in its effects, he begins also to devise a much more adventurous literary technique. Though occasionally gauche in execution, this later work is ambitious in conception and, although by no means a complete success, constitutes a notable advance on the pedestrian early works with which his name is more often associated. He prefaces the novel with an epigraph taken from Montaigne: 'We are never present with, but always beyond ourselves.' This is to be the story or, rather, the stories, of a central character named Marcus Igoe, whose imagination constantly takes him 'beyond' himself and into the 'various lives' of the book's title. Igoe is a kind of Walter Mitty of Garradrimna, whose dreams and aspirations and longings are rehearsed for us against a background of village gossip and ill-nature. This time, however, the hero dominates the setting and an important aspect of the author's change of tactics has to do with a maturing of the satirical tone. Marcus is made to manifest a certain reluctant affection for his village, almost in spite of himself. 'I have', he tells us, 'loved my native village more than words can tell, or how else would I have hated it so much for what it would not be?' Marcus is the village cobbler, who looks out at his surroundings through the most squinting of all the windows in the place and fantasises lavishly, dreaming his way through a series of possible rather than actual lives. The main difficulty for the reader is that one easily becomes confused by the proliferation of tales relating to the many lives which Marcus either lives or imagines for himself. Even the enthusiastically uncritical A.E. Malone voiced some reservations about this aspect of the novel, admitting that 'the form of the novel is intricate and occasionally it becomes difficult to follow which is the dream and which the reality.' MacNamara is, in fact, striving to break away from the rather crude and simple form of his early works and is pushing his fiction in the direction of the anti-novel, a form required for the successful manipulation of the multi-faceted, layered plots which he devises for Marcus to experience. This becomes clear in Chapter XXXI when one of Marcus's 'lives' takes him to Dublin, where he meets a novelist who gives him a magazine which contains a story about a character very similar to Marcus himself, so that we are made keenly aware of the fictionality of the entire process and Marcus finds himself 'hovering perilously on the verge of literature . . . actually falling into it from moment to moment . . . as he sat there reading the story of himself'. Later in the novel, in Chapter XLVI, MacNamara sets going a literary debate between two village characters in a pub, an exchange which clearly anticipates the rather more celebrated discussion on the theory of fiction which is set up at the beginning of Flann O'Brien's *At Swim-Two-Birds*. Bartle Boyhan's account of the dangers attaching to unregulated fictions has the true O'Brien ring:

> 'Of course, the whole mistake occurs through having such an arbitrary power in the hands of playwrights and novelists and blackguards, instead of putting it on a properly organised system under Government control, the Government realising the paramount importance of the whole thing and setting up boards of Psychological inquiry in every district, so that everyone would be card-indexed with his proper name. Now, wouldn't that be suitable work for highly paid Civil servants instead of having it left to blackguards as in the past to perform unsystematically and indiscriminately. That'd be the way to do it, to give every fellow his correct place, according to his inclinations, in the social scheme. Look at the enormous convenience it would be to everyone, they knowing in consequence where exactly they were standing with everyone else, and the sense of protection it would be to the Government as well, they in turn knowing exactly where they stood with the whole population in general, in the case of Rebellions or declarations of a Republic.'

MacNamara's novel, however, never quite attains the happy anarchy of *At Swim-Two-Birds*, since it hovers rather unsteadily between passages of rustic realism and mockery of fiction's mimetic procedures. Flann O'Brien steers the reader through the crazy chaos of his numerous plots by brazenly interpolating frequent tongue-in-cheek recapitulations of the action of the novel (this, in itself, constituting an implementation of the work's pervasive mockery of the concept of fiction) and he also imparted some semblance of coherence to his literary pyrotechnics by providing one seemingly mundane level of plot, that involving the unnamed student hero and his bourgeois uncle. These more or less ordinary people appear and re-appear at intervals, providing a foothold in a version of everyday reality for readers bedazzled by a flying Sweeney, a Pooka MacPhellimey or a Finn MacCool. One of the problems with MacNamara's commendably adventurous account of Marcus Igoe is that he does not really distinguish sufficiently between the 'real' life of his hero and all his other fantasy lives. Late in the novel, when Marcus has retired from Garradrimna to live at Harbourstown, we are, indeed, offered a retrospective resumé of many of the phases which the novel has recounted, but these 'lost selves', as he calls them, are not clearly identified either as real or imaginary so that one is, more and more, led to assume that *all* are imaginary and a certain unavoidable confusion results:

Often it would strike him sadly, and he would think once more of going into Garradrimna to meet some one of his own lost selves. The Marcus Igoe of the dances in his young days and, later, the plums and pears; the Marcus Igoe of the time of the breach of promise action in the Four Courts in Dublin; the Marcus Igoe of the beard, and the summer morning romance upon the street of Garradrimna; the defeated Marcus Igoe of the cobbler's den; the Marcus Igoe who had been 'a Marquis'; the Marcus Igoe who had pondered in 'the Picture House', making life bend, as he thought, obediently to his will; the Marcus Igoe who had thought out a scheme for the perpetuation of his own memory; the Marcus Igoe who had failed to project himself into the part that had been written for him in the story of 'the Comedian'; the Marcus Igoe who had had the resignation to come out here.

As the many stories accumulate, the reader struggles to keep track of an increasingly puzzling chronology and the episodic nature of the work causes it, at times, to seem more like an amalgam of short stories than a well integrated novel. Indeed, it is interesting to note that one of the least satisfactory episodes of the novel, that dealing with Mrs Wyse and the marrying-off of her numerous daughters, surfaces again in the form of a short story entitled 'The Picture Gallery' in the collection of short stories which Mac Namara published in 1945, under the title *Some Curious People*. In that volume, also, he included another story, bearing the significant title 'The Different Mr Darlings', which revolves around the idea of multiple identity in a manner strongly reminiscent of the tangled story of Marcus Igoe. It would seem that the underlying idea of the novel had continued to interest him. The novel's defects can be said to stem from the work's ambitious scope. Muddled as it is, it nevertheless succeeds in conveying a powerful sense of a richly varied personality trapped in repressive circumstances and struggling to break free in order to realise its full potential. A rich social pageant unfolds, from the gentry level of the Honourable Reginald Moore and his hunting associates down through the strong farmers of the region to the village layabouts who inhabit the pubs and form a kind of Hardy-esque chorus to the action throughout. The whimsicality occasionally recalls the James Stephens of *The Crock of Gold* but, quite frequently, the new boldness of the author's technique looks forward to the more adventurous approach of anti-novelists such as Flann O'Brien or John Banville. The Dublin episodes are of particular interest and, in their often quite effective satire of the Irish Literary Renaissance, remind one that this is a work almost exactly contemporary with Denis Johnston's satirical play, *The Old Lady Says 'No!'*. All in all, *The Various Lives of Marcus Igoe* represents an impressive advance on the tawdry first novel by which this author is most often remembered. It has a geniality which was utterly lacking in the earlier work. Its scope is ambitiously wide, fusing together rustic satire with the artistic strivings and imaginative yearnings of the hero and looking beyond the rustic setting to a pretentious urban scene which is also, casually, given its congé. Its effects range from the anecdotal discursiveness of the short folk tale to the derisively self-conscious stance of the anti-novel, linking the Irish fiction of the earlier part of the century with its more adventurously modern successors.

SELECTED BIBLIOGRAPHY

RELATED WORKS

The Valley of the Squinting Windows, London, 1918.
The Clanking of Chains, Dublin, 1920.
Return to Ebontheever, London, 1930.

BIOGRAPHY

Brinsley MacNamara, 'Growing Up in the Midlands', *The Capuchin Annual*, 1964, 149-170.
Séamus O Saothraí, *An Dánlann Náisiúnta*, Dublin, Stationery Office, 1966, 36-38.
Marion Keaney, *Westmeath Authors: A Bibliographical and Biographical Study*, Mullingar, Longford-Westmeath Joint Library Committee, 1969, 98.
Séamus O Saothraí, 'Brinsley MacNamara (1890-1963)', *Irish Booklore*, 2, 1 (Spring 1972), 75-81.
Michael McDonnell, 'Brinsley MacNamara (1890-1963): A Checklist', *Journal of Irish Literature*, 4 (May 1975), 79-88.

CRITICAL ARTICLES

Andrew E. Malone, 'Brinsley MacNamara: An Appreciation', *Dublin Magazine*, July, 1929, 46-56.
Ruth Fleischmann, 'Brinsley MacNamara's Penny Dreadful', *Eire-Ireland* (Summer 1983), 52-74.

X

Elizabeth Bowen (1899–1973)

THE LAST SEPTEMBER

Elizabeth Dorothea Cole Bowen was born in Dublin, the only child of Henry Cole Bowen and Florence Colley Bowen. Her parents both belonged to long-established Protestant, Ascendancy, Anglo-Irish families. Her mother's family had first appeared in Ireland under the name of Cowley during the reign of Elizabeth I, one Walter Cowley being solicitor-general for Ireland in 1537. One branch of the Colley family changed its name to Wesley, or Wellesley, to inherit property in Co. Meath, and numbered among its more famous descendants Arthur, first Duke of Wellington. The Bowens, originally Welsh in origin, came to Ireland during the Civil War when Henry Bowen, originally of the King's party, switched his allegiance to Cromwell, became a lieutenant colonel and was assigned as a reward for his services a large tract of land in Co. Cork, between the Ballyhoura Mountains and the river Blackwater. The family home, Bowen's Court, was erected by the third Henry Bowen. It took ten years to build and was completed in 1775. Elizabeth Bowen, the last member of the family to occupy the house, wrote an account of it, *Bowen's Court*, in 1942. This house mattered greatly to her. She returned regularly to it throughout her varied and active life, struggled to modernise it and was profoundly saddened when, through lack of money, she was finally forced to sell it in 1960. The local farmer who bought the property was interested only in the land and the 'Big House' was soon pulled down. Elizabeth Bowen's experience in connection with Bowen's Court calls to mind that of her talented literary forerunner, Violet Martin, who as 'Martin Ross' achieved fame with her cousin, Edith Somerville, under the joint pseudonym of 'Somerville and Ross' and produced in *The Real Charlotte* and other novels work for which Elizabeth Bowen had a high regard. Violet Martin also had struggled gallantly and unavailingly to restore the lost grandeurs of her ancestral home at Ross. Edith Somerville and Violet Martin had been born some forty years before Elizabeth Bowen and had seen their comfortable, colonial world crumble around them. They recorded its inevitable decline in their fiction. The violent events which set the seal on that decline and ushered in a new political era in Ireland were taking place throughout Elizabeth

Bowen's early years and her imagination was haunted by the image of Bowen's Court in flames, though the house, unlike many other gentry residences, was to survive 'the Troubles'. When she came to write the novel which would enshrine her most profound responses to the Anglo-Irish situation, she inevitably concluded the book with the burning of 'Danielstown', the fictional equivalent of Bowen's Court.

During her first seven years, the future novelist's life was divided between summers spent at Bowen's Court and winters in the house of her birth, 15 Herbert Place, Dublin. The first great upset of her life took place when her father, a hardworking barrister, suffered a nervous breakdown. Her mother was advised to move to England with Elizabeth, to get away from her ailing father's dangerously depressing company so, at the age of seven, she found herself living with her mother in Kent, surrounded by a group of Anglo-Irish relatives who had settled there. Gradually, Henry Bowen recovered from his mental illness and came to visit his wife and daughter at Hythe but, in 1912, Elizabeth's mother died of cancer and the child was deprived of the loving relationship on which she had so depended. The strain of her father's illness had left her with a bad stammer which was to afflict her in varying degrees throughout her entire life. Physically, she was of a robust constitution but, as an only child with an unstable father and deprived of her mother at an early age, she grew up with a kind of nervous mistrust of life's accidents which was to inform the bulk of her fiction. After her mother's death, Elizabeth was cared for by various aunts. She went to school at Harpenden Hall and, later, at Downe House near Orpington. She seems to have enjoyed her schooldays. She left Downe House in 1917 and returned to live with her father at Bowen's Court. Her father remarried in the following year, his second wife being Mary Gwynn, sister of the writer, Stephen Gwynn. Elizabeth was on good terms with her step-mother and, for a time, she lived the life of the average young Anglo-Irish debutante, visiting friends, attending dances and generally enjoying herself. As a child, she had shown some skill at drawing and, at the age of twenty, she went for two terms to the London County Council School of Art, but she soon decided that she had no real talent to develop and left the school. She was later to describe her writing as 'verbal painting' saying that she was 'trying to make words do the work of line and colour'. In 1923, she published her first collection of short stories, *Encounters*, and married Alan Charles Cameron, who worked as Assistant Secretary for Education for Northamptonshire. In 1925 they settled at Old Headington, where he worked in the city of Oxford school system and they gradually came into contact with a large and interesting circle of university people, including C. M. Bowra and David Cecil. Now, for the first time in her life, she seems to have felt some kind of security, permanence and stability in her living arrangements. She published a second collection of stories, *Ann Lee's*, in 1926 and her first novel, *The Hotel*, in 1927. Her first important novel, *The Last September*, came out in 1929 and, in the following year, her father died and she became the owner of Bowen's Court. From now on, her life was to alternate for a long time between England, where she worked and made her considerable reputation as a writer, and Ireland, to which she and her husband regularly returned in the summer, to open the big house, tend the gardens and entertain their many friends. In the decade before the outbreak of the Second World War, Elizabeth Bowen published four further novels, *Friends and Relations* (1931), *To the North* (1932), *The House in Paris* (1935) and *The Death of the Heart* (1938), as well as a collection of stories, *The Cat Jumps* (1934). She and her husband settled in London, at 2 Clarence Terrace, in 1935. He worked for the BBC, while she got to know many of the celebrated literary figures of the day, from established Bloomsbury-ites like Virginia Woolf to her own contemporaries such as Rosamond Lehmann, Stephen Spender, Evelyn Waugh and L.P. Hartley. She remained in London throughout the war, working for the Ministry of Information and as an air-raid warden. She published no further novels during this period but she did write a great many short stories. In 1942 came *Bowen's Court*, her account of her ancestral home, and she followed this with the autobiographical work, *Seven Winters*, in 1943. Her survey, *English Novelists*, appeared in 1946. In 1949 she published *The Heat of the Day*, her first novel for over a decade, and in that year also she was awarded an honorary D. Litt. by Trinity College, Dublin. Alan Cameron retired from the BBC and in 1952 they returned to live at Bowen's Court as they had long planned to do but he died in August of the same year. During the last twenty years of her life, Elizabeth Bowen travelled a great deal. She worked for the British Council, lecturing in various parts of Europe, and also began to lecture regularly in America, visiting most of the major universities there, to lecture on the novel and to assist students with their own writing. She published another novel with an Irish setting, *A World of Love*, in 1955. Oxford awarded her an honorary D. Litt. in 1957. Shortage of money forced her to sell her beloved Bowen's Court in 1960 and she subsequently returned to Old Headington, Oxford, for a time. She came full circle in 1965 by buying a small house at Hythe in Kent, where she had first lived with her mother all those years before. In that year also she was made a Companion of Literature. She published her last novel, *Eva Trout*, in 1969 and it won her the James Tait Black prize. She died, of cancer of the lungs, in London in 1973 and was buried in Farahy churchyard, near her husband and her father and close to the spot where her ancestral home had stood.

THE LAST SEPTEMBER (1929)

This, which of all my books is nearest my heart, had a deep, unclouded, spontaneous source. Though not poetic, it brims with what could be the stuff of poetry, the sensations of youth. It is a work of instinct rather than knowledge – to a degree, a 'recall' book, but there has been no such recall before. In 'real' life, my girlhood summers in County Cork, in the house called Danielstown in the story, had been, though touched by romantic pleasure, mainly times of impatience, frivolity, or lassitude. I asked myself *what* I should be, and when?

'The house called Danielstown in the story' was, of course, Elizabeth Bowen's childhood home, Bowen's Court, and her heroine in the novel, Lois Farquar, constantly asks herself the same questions concerning 'what she will be, and when'. Yet, later in the Preface from which the passage above has been taken, the novelist insists that the book is 'many, many removes from autobiography'. Her account of *The Last September* as a work with a 'deep, unclouded, spontaneous source' is all the more remarkable in the light of her earlier confession in the Preface that, at this early stage of her career, she was much intimidated by the sheer difficulty involved in the business of writing a novel:

> . . . I was most oppressed, in advance, by the difficulty of assembling a novel's cast – bringing the various characters to the same spot, keeping them there, accounting for their continued presence (in real life, people seemed to be constantly getting up and going away) and linking them close enough, and for long enough, to provide the interplay known as 'plot'.

She solved these problems by bringing her characters together under one roof and keeping them there until just before the house is burnt to the ground on the last page. 'Danielstown' is yet another of the fictional 'Big Houses' which have provided Anglo-Irish fiction with one of its dominant and most poignantly evocative symbols. In this novel, Elizabeth Bowen's preoccupation with her enduring theme of the centrality of love combines with her hereditary involvement with her own distinctive Irish origins to produce a work which is animated by vital tensions on the personal, psychological plane and underpinned by profound social and historical concerns. Lois Farquar, her nineteen-year-old heroine, is the figure around whom Bowen creates an atmosphere of tensely questing, youthful uncertainty. An orphan, Lois is the niece of Sir Richard Naylor and, when the story opens, she is in residence at Danielstown along with her undergraduate cousin, Laurence, nephew of Myra, Lady Naylor. Between Lois and Laurence there exists a playful, cousinly relationship. He condescends to her intellectually, with all the world-weariness of a bright young man on vacation from Oxford, and she permits him to condescend, opposing her vulnerable uncertainties to his assumed sophistication. Fundamentally, they both know that they are similar in being at the beginning of their adult experience and, much later, when Gerald Lesworth has been killed and brutal reality has for the first time impinged on Lois's world of shifting possibilities, she will tell Laurence that, if she could bear to have anyone intrude upon her solitude, it would be he. Laurence's time at university has taught him a little about the realities of Irish politics, just enough to make his expression of his views at the dinner-table 'inconvenient' and his awareness of the fragility of the entire situation will cause him to declare outrageously, at the height of a summer tennis-party, that he would like to be around when the house finally burns. Lois, wrapped up in her preoccupations with her own destiny, has less time to spare for abstract political thought and one recalls the author's remarks on this aspect of her character, in the Preface:

> Why was Lois, at her romantic age, not more harrowed, or stirred, by the national struggle round her? In part, would not this be self-defence? This was a creature still half-awake, the soul not yet open, nor yet the eyes. And world war had shadowed her school-days: *that* was enough – now she wanted order. Trying enough to have to grow up, more so to grow up at a trying time. Like it or not, however, she acquiesced to strife, abnormalities and danger. Violence was contained in her sense of life, along with dance music, the sweet-pea in the garden, the inexorable raininess of days. Tragedy she could only touch at the margin – not Gerald's death, but her failure to love.

Lois's first attempt at love involves Hugo Montmorency. Hugo had once been in love with her mother, Laura Naylor, before Laura flounced off in a temperamental rage and precipitately married 'the rudest man in Ulster', Walter Farquar. Hugo later married the fragile Francie who is ten years his senior, and embarked on a wandering, unsettled existence with her. Lois is eager to find in Hugo a surrogate father and hopes for a loving relationship with him when he arrives at Danielstown, but the reality proves hideously disappointing. Hugo shows little interest in her and seems to have aged prematurely, turning into a sort of nurse-companion to his ailing and ageing wife. He brushes Francie's hair, looks after her clothes and fusses and frets about trivialities, seeming to live in a past which consists mainly of regrets for missed opportunities and lost companions. Later, he will be roused to brief animation by his interest in Marda Norton, the elegantly sophisticated visitor who turns up in Section 2 of the novel, but when Marda fails to respond to him he subsides once more into the role of fussy guardian of his older wife. The past, therefore, as represented by Hugo, offers Lois nothing in the way of human warmth and companionship, and her present existence offers her only the acerbic comments of Laurence or the predictably girlish gushings of her friend, Livvy Thompson, who is far from being a kindred spirit. Thus, when we first meet her, Lois is vulnerable and uncertain. Appropriately, we find that she likes to loiter in the ante-room on Danielstown's first floor, a curious, in-between sort of place, with bedrooms opening off it and people constantly passing through:

> Personally, she liked the ante-room, though it wasn't the ideal place to read or talk. Four rooms opened off it, and at any moment a door might be opened, or blow open, sending a draught down one's neck. People passed through it continually, so that one kept having to look up and smile. Yet Lois always seemed to be talking there, standing with a knee on a chair because it was not worth while to sit down, and her life very much complicated by not knowing how much of what she said had been over-heard, or by whom, or how far it would go.

This ante-room is an image of Lois's predicament. There she pauses, 'standing with a knee on a chair', in transit between two places, uncertain as to how much of her conversation has been overheard in the adjoining bedrooms, the doors of which tend to open if a passer-by treads on a loose floor-board. Here, Lois converses with the purposefully sardonic Laurence. From here she gets glimpses of Hugo patiently brushing Francie's hair. Later on, alone in her bedroom, she will herself overhear Lady Naylor and Francie discussing her in the ante-room and will be driven to making noise so that the pair may become aware of her presence. Within the outer shell of the doomed house, Lois waits in an ante-room of life, seeking for love and certainty. 'I was the child of the house from which Danielstown derives', said Bowen and, indeed, Lois is presented with a background of childhood experience which closely resembles the author's. Both her parents are dead and her father's memory is shrouded in some special sadness which might reflect Henry Bowen's intermittent, depressive illnesses. As Lois surveys those around her, she feels excluded from achieved relationships:

> 'We *can* sit out on the steps tonight, can't we?' persisted Lois. And because no one answered or cared and a conversation went on without her she felt profoundly lonely, suspecting once more for herself a particular doom of exclusion. Something of the trees in their intimacy of shadow was shared by the husband and wife and their host in the tree-shadowed room. She thought of love with its gift of importance.

Love has given 'its gift of importance' even to poor ailing Francie and will later give it to the glamorous Marda Norton who has gallantly broken off one engagement and embarked upon another. Even silly Livvy Thompson, once she has caught herself a subaltern, becomes surrounded by a peculiar glow of achievement and is accepted into the circle of army wives and sweethearts in the local garrison. Only Lois is excluded from the special privilege of loving and remains so even when Gerald falls in love with her:

> She would have loved to love him; she felt some kind of wistfulness, some deprivation. If there could only be some change, some movement – in her, outside of her, somewhere between them – some incalculable shifting of perspectives that would bring him wholly into focus, mind and spirit, as he had been bodily in focus now – she could love him.

Marda Norton, who is kind to Lois and close enough in age to be able to recall the torments of youth, sums her up to Hugo:

> 'Lois,' she said, 'is nice. She is in such a hurry, so concentrated upon her hurry, so helpless. She is like someone being driven against time in a taxi to catch a train, jerking and jerking to help the taxi along and looking wildly out of the window at things going slowly past. She keeps hearing that final train go out without her.'

Lois is quite unable to respond to Gerald's passion for her, as we see when he kisses her:

> So that was being kissed: just an impact with inside blankness. She was lonely and saw there was no future. She shut her eyes and tried – as sometimes when she was seasick, locked in misery between Holyhead and Kingstown – to be enclosed in nonentity, in some ideal no-place perfect and clear as a bubble.

Yet, as the affair progresses, she gradually comes to feel that she must marry Gerald, that his love for her deserves reward. One of the most effective aspects of the book's climax is the degree to which we resent Lady Naylor's interference between Gerald and Lois. Almost we begin to feel that Gerald's forthright desire for her might yet tutor Lois into some sort of response, but Lady Naylor's calculated intervention effectively prevents this.

If Lois Farquar's isolation and uncertainty were merely the customary and inevitable waverings of any hyper-sensitive girl of her age, it is possible that we might quickly tire of her as a character, might indeed come to find her merely irritating, in a juvenile sort of way. The vitally important use which Bowen makes of Lois in relation to her general theme redeems a character who might otherwise have receded into ordinariness, for the dilemma of Lois Farquar is made representative of the isolation and doom of her whole tribe. She is the child of the house, and the house itself and all it stands for are also inadequate and doomed. The link between the two is stressed and Lois's failure to connect her destiny either to the past, as represented by Hugo, or to the future, embodied in Gerald, bespeaks the failure of the Anglo-Irish to relate themselves fruitfully to either side of their nominal hyphen. Returning to the house after the dance at the army camp, Lois gathers flowers in the Danielstown garden and reflects on the way in which she and the house resemble each other:

> 'It is extraordinary,' said Lois, 'I feel as if I had been away for a week.'
> 'Yet you find us going on much the same?' He looked at her through the stems ironically but without intelligence. And she could not try to explain the magnetism they all exercised by their being static. Or how, after every return – or awakening, even, from sleep or preoccupation – she and these home surroundings still further penetrated each other mutually in the discovery of a lack.

'The discovery of a lack' in both house and heroine is one of the novel's main purposes, though it would be quite inaccurate to suggest that this purpose is effected in a sombrely tragic manner throughout. Quite the reverse is, in fact, the case, as Elizabeth Bowen achieves her serious purposes through unfailingly skilful social comedy. Yet, the serious purpose is never altogether forgotten. Early in the novel's first part, when Lois walks by herself in the shrubbery, she is an unseen observer of a menacing, trench-coated figure. There passes, 'within reach of her hand . . . some resolute profile powerful as a thought':

> It must be because of Ireland he was in such a hurry . . . Here was something else that she could not share. She could not conceive of her country emotionally: it was a way of living, abstract of several countrysides, or an oblique, frayed island moored at the north but with an air of being detached and drawn out west from the British coast.

Thus, the 'something else' which she, as the offspring of Danielstown, cannot share is the emotional concept of Ireland embodied in this shadowy and menacing figure in the shrubbery, who passes on his way without noticing or regarding her. Significantly, she is unable to respond emotionally either to Ireland or to Gerald, her English lover. Her double stasis is the characteristic emotional paralysis of her clan, caught between conflicting loyalties, not totally committed to either. Victoria Glendinning records how Elizabeth

Bowen would say jestingly that the Anglo-Irish were really only at home in mid-crossing between Holyhead and Dun Laoghaire. Lois, excited by her experience in the shrubbery, runs back to the house, eager to tell of her adventure, but she is suddenly overcome by a conviction of the sheer impossibility of conveying her excitement to the occupants of Danielstown:

> . . . as Lois went up the steps breathlessly her adventure began to diminish. It held ground for a moment as she saw the rug dropped in the hall by Mrs. Montmorency sprawl like a body across the polish. Then confidence disappeared in a waver of shadow among the furniture. Conceivably she had surprised life at a significant angle in the shrubbery. But it was impossible to speak of this. At a touch from Aunt Myra adventure became literary, to Uncle Richard it suggested an inconvenience; a glance from Mr Montmorency or Laurence would make her encounter sterile.
>
> But what seemed most probable was that they would not listen . . .

The extent to which Danielstown stands aside from the realities of Irish life is precisely conveyed by the carefully phrased sentence 'Conceivably she had surprised life at a significant angle in the shrubbery', a sentence in which the force of the sentiment expressed is deliberately blunted by the initial adverb. The entire experience, which has impinged so vividly on Lois only moments earlier, is transferred into some region of mental speculation and made to seem almost hypothetical as Lois rapidly becomes convinced that she will never succeed in communicating her sense of the moment's significance to her fellow residents in the house. This strange separateness is identified everywhere in the novel and is applied also to the other gentry houses in the neighbourhood. One afternoon towards the end of her visit, Marda Norton takes tea with the Careys at Mount Isabel and, here again, the same note of despondent isolation is struck:

> The yellow sun slanting in under the blinds on full-bosomed silver, hands balancing Worcester, dogs poking wistfully up from under the cloth, seemed old, used, filtering from the surplus of some happy fulfilment; while, unapproachably elsewhere, something went by without them.

When the police barracks at Ballyrum is attacked and destroyed with considerable loss of life, Lois cries out to Gerald:

> 'Do you know that while that was going on, eight miles off, I was cutting a dress out, a voile that I didn't even need, and playing the gramophone? . . . How is it that in this country that ought to be full of such violent realness there seems nothing for me but clothes and what people say? I might as well be in some sort of cocoon.'

Even Marda Norton, on her brief visit, is made to ask Hugo Montmorency:

'How far do you think this war is going to go? Will there ever be anything we can all do except not notice ?'

The year, of course, is 1920, the year in which the world of Somerville and Ross's *The Real Charlotte* and George Moore's *A Drama in Muslin* finally approached its violent end. Bowen's considerable achievement in *The Last September* is to have found artistic means to generalise that world's significance in terms of individual concerns and to do so in a novel which never sinks into solemnity and in a prose remarkable for its effervescent elegance. Not surprisingly, the place and the people inevitably recall the cast and setting of Somerville and Ross's finest novel, for which Elizabeth Bowen had a considerable regard. Sir Richard and Lady Naylor have a good deal in common with Sir Benjamin and Lady Dysart of Bruff. In both cases, the baronet is firmly subordinated to his lady. Admittedly, Sir Richard is not so complete a dafty as Sir Benjamin, but he is generally made to play the part of an elderly and slightly absent-minded commentator, always on the periphery of the action. His forceful spouse is a very different matter. One of the triumphs of the novel, Lady Naylor is both a vigorous comic creation and also a vital and dangerous protagonist in the part she plays in wrecking the relationship between Gerald and Lois. As she surveys the guests at her tennis party, she recalls unmistakably the mistress of Bruff in conversation with Charlotte Mullen:

'There seem to be many more people here than I thought we'd asked,' Lady Naylor was saying to Mrs. Carey of Mount Isabel. 'Lois asks people she meets at the Clonmore club, and then forgets . . . Why is it the Hartigans will never talk to men?'

The Hartigans, of course, are the 1920 equivalents of the Miss Beatties of *Charlotte* and the Brennan sisters of *Muslin*, sad spinsters, muslin martyrs doomed to be bitten by midges at many a summer tennis party. Elizabeth Bowen achieves some of her novel's finest comic effects by using Lady Naylor skilfully to point up an aspect of Anglo-Irish social discrimination which is of considerable importance to the work's detailed picture of a society on the verge of dissolution. This is Lady Naylor's aristocratic disdain of certain aspects of English life. Like the gentry of Somerville and Ross's novels, Lady Naylor has a firm way with the mere English. In her cruel interview with Gerald Lesworth at Mrs Fogarty's house, she seems at times like a more malign version of Lady Bracknell:

'Such a day,' she sighed briskly. 'We have lunched with the Boatleys. What a delightful colonel he must be. *She*, you know, is Irish; a Vere Scott. We must seem ridiculous to you, over here, the way we are all related.'

'Topping, I think,' said Gerald.

'Oh, I don't know! Now you lucky people seem to have no relations at all; that must feel so independent.'

'I have dozens.'

'Indeed? All in Surrey?'

'Scattered about.'

'That sounds to me, of course,' remarked Lady Naylor, pulling her gloves off brightly, 'exceedingly restless.'

She is unfailingly entertaining about her English friend, Anna Partridge of Bedfordshire, whom she contrives to introduce into her conversation as an illustration of the conventionality and boredom of English life, and she herself is quite resolved that there must be no defeatist conversation about 'the situation' at her dinner-table:

> 'From all the talk, you might think almost anything was going to happen, but we never listen. I have made it a rule not to talk, either. In fact, if you want rumours, we must send you over to Castle Trent. And I'm afraid also the Careys are incorrigible . . . Oh yes, Hugo, it's all very well to talk of disintegration in England and on the Continent. But one does wonder sometimes whether there's really much there to disintegrate . . .'

Thus, both England and the Continent are given their congé in one splendid flourish and Lady Naylor withdraws herself and her guests once again into the comfortable cocoon of cultivated indifference appropriate to the châtelaine of Danielstown. Throughout the novel, Elizabeth Bowen makes high comedy constantly out of this, one of her most serious concerns in the work, thereby imprinting this aspect of the lives of her characters indelibly on our memories. Again and again, the book blossoms into such comic vignettes. Even at night, dark comedy is made to invade the dream-worlds of Danielstown's sleepers:

> Sir Richard and Lady Naylor were sound asleep. She was dreaming about the Aberdeens, while he rode round the country on a motor bicycle from which he couldn't detach himself. His friends cut him; he discovered he was a Black and Tan. But night rolled on over them thickly and uneventfully.

This is authorial derision of a lovingly precise kind, in which the Naylors form a kind of comic composite, with her dreaming of Vice-Regal grandeur while poor, inoffensive Sir Richard imagines himself transformed improbably into a murderous mercenary and shunned by his kind. In fact, of course, Sir Richard has been depicted throughout as wanting only a quiet life and the minimum of military interference. He is far from pleased when he hears that Gerald Lesworth has captured the runaway Peter Connors and, indeed, quietly recalls this incident and sees the inescapable logic of terror when the family are informed of Gerald's own death at the end. Sir Richard, like the rest of his family, bitterly resents the way in which the Black and Tans rush about the country lanes, forcing everyone else out of their way. He is memorably funny about his chance encounter with an armoured car:

> 'I was held up yesterday for I wouldn't like to say how long, driving over to Ballyhinch, by a thing like a coffee-pot backing in and out of a gate, with a little brute of a fellow bobbing in and out at me from under a lid at the top. I kept my temper, but I couldn't help telling him I didn't know what the country was coming to – and just when we'd got the horses accustomed to motors. "You'll do no good," I told him "in this unfortunate country by running about in a thing like a coffee-pot." '

Bowen also evokes memorably the desperately hectic gaiety of the British garrison at Clonmore. Mrs Vermont and the other army wives are exposed in all their pathetic and vulnerable vulgarity and the novel is rich in scenes where the widely varying shades of loyalty to the British crown are delicately exposed by a perceptive and sardonic observer. The subtleties of the muddled colonial situation are beautifully observed. There is a general feeling among the Anglo-Irish gentry that the British army 'is not what it was' and the army wives constantly give offence to the local ladies by their insensitive talk about 'defending' the Irish. The voluminous Mrs Fogarty, with her Union Jack cushions and her house constantly full of British soldiers (though she herself is a Catholic) is an unfailing delight. In her cheerful, lower-middle-class vulgarity she recalls corresponding figures in the fictional world of Somerville and Ross (the McRorys of the 'R.M.' stories come to mind, as do Dr and Mrs Mangan of the novel *Mount Music*) and one recalls that the Protestant Ascendancy gentry reserved a special animosity for this class of people as they began to encroach on the social preserves of their betters. Jocelyn Brooke has remarked this aspect of Bowen's work:

> She seldom writes about working-class people, and the social group which, for her, represents the intractable and dangerous element in society is not the proletariat (or the near-proletariat – compare the Basts in *Howard's End*) but the pretentious, Philistine middle-class – such families as the Heccombs in *The Death of the Heart* and the Kelways in *The Heat of the Day*.

The Last September finely illustrates the two aspects of Bowen's work which have been remarked by Brooke as being most characteristic of her. The first of these is what he calls 'a preoccupation with the relationship between the individual and his environment'. It is natural that this aspect of her work should be most startlingly evident in this novel in which the environment is that in which she herself grew up. Repeatedly, her painter's eye evokes for us the landscape of Danielstown. The book is full of long, slow twilights and deepening shadows. We get to know the gardens and the shrubberies which surround the big house. We smell the laurels behind the tennis courts. The house itself is not merely a setting but an actor in the story, a living participant in the action. As Lois Farquar stands on the steps waiting to receive the Montmorencys as the story begins, 'the large façade of the house stared coldly over its mounting lawns'. Later, when the visitors have gone indoors, 'the mansion piled itself up in silence over the Montmorency's voices'. All through the long, sunny days of this last summer and autumn we shall get to know Danielstown as well as if we had indeed resided there. Its lofty drawing-room where 'voices went up in stately attenuation' to the distant ceiling; its terrace where the guests sit after dinner; its various bedrooms; the ante-room so beloved of Lois; the great front-door opening onto the hospitable entrance hall – with all of these the group scenes and the individual encounters of the novel will familiarise us. Rooms and their furnishings are conveyed in loving detail, so that we almost smell the 'bleaching cretonnes and ten days' emptiness' of the Blue Room where the Montmorencys are to sleep. Lois's doomed lover, Gerald Lesworth, will tell her that he thinks it 'a topping house' but he is, nevertheless, intimidated by it:

> The house so loomed, and stared so darkly and oddly that he showed a disposition – respectful rather than timorous – to move away from the front of it. They walked to the tennis courts and round one court in a circle.

The other major preoccupation remarked by Jocelyn Brooke is Elizabeth Bowen's 'fascination with the surface of life':

> . . . not so much for its own sake, as for the dangerous sense which it gives of existing upon a thin crust beneath which lurks the bottomless abyss. The crust is, too often, liable to crack – and, says Miss Bowen, 'the more the surface seems to heave or threaten to crack, the more its actual pattern fascinates me.'

In relation to the Anglo-Irish world she knew so well this particular obsession has a poignantly special relevance. Her preoccupation with the hazardous surface of life is one she shares with the important older contemporary to whom she is, clearly, most indebted for the distinctive aspects of her style. She presents her doomed tribe by means of an oblique and shimmering prose which, in its occasional syntactical inversions and frequent explosions of zany comedy, repeatedly recalls the work of Virginia Woolf, that other great celebrator of the precariousness of life,whose vulnerable solitaries so often comfort themselves with 'matches struck in the dark'. There are moments in *The Last September* when the echoes are quite specific. One such is when we are vouchsafed a brief glimpse of Gerald Lesworth's room immediately after his death:

> In Gerald's room some new music for the jazz band, caught in a draught, flopped over and over. An orderly put it away, shocked. All night some windows let out, over the sandbags, a squeamish, defiant yellow.

This evocation of the memory of the dead youth through his very absence from his usual haunts vividly recalls similar moments in Virginia Woolf's novel, *Jacob's Room,* when the dead Jacob Flanders is brought to mind in just such a way. There are some echoes also of E.M. Forster. When Francie Montmorency notes with surprise that, in coming to Danielstown she feels in some strange way that she is coming home, we cannot fail to recall the symbolic force of the house, Howard's End, in Forster's novel.

If Somerville and Ross celebrated what Conor Cruise O'Brien called 'the Indian Summer of the Irish Ascendancy', we may say that Elizabeth Bowen commemorates its sad, penultimate, autumnal moments. She climaxes her book with a passage which symmetrically recalls the work's opening paragraph. Once again the iron gate half way up the avenue under the beeches of Danielstown twangs, but this time the cars are sliding out with their executioners, not inwards with happy guests as at the beginning. And, with terrible ironic force, we learn that 'the door stood open hospitably upon a furnace'. Years before, Henry Bowen had written to his daughter in Italy an account of the burning of three gentry houses in the neighbourhood of Bowen's Court:

> I read his letter beside Lake Como, and looking at the blue water, taught myself to imagine Bowen's Court in flames. Perhaps that moment disinfected the future: realities of war I have seen since have been frightful: none of them has taken me by surprise.

Her imagination was haunted, like that of her celebrated predecessor Sheridan LeFanu by the image of the destruction of the great house:

> Bowen's Court survived – nevertheless, so often did I see it burning that the terrible last event in *The Last September* is more real than anything I have lived through.

Everywhere in her fiction she is concerned with love and its hazards. In *The Last September* she blends this central theme with a powerful threnody for her tribe in which the sense of impending doom is laced through with a sustaining and characteristic gaiety.

SELECTED BIBLIOGRAPHY

RELATED WORKS

The Death of the Heart, London, 1938.
The Heat of the Day, London, 1949.
A World of Love, London, 1955.

BIOGRAPHY

Victoria Glendinning, *Elizabeth Bowen: Portrait of a Writer*, London, 1977.

CRITICAL STUDIES

Jocelyn Brooke, *Elizabeth Bowen*, London , 1952.
Harriet Blodgett, *Patterns of Reality: Elizabeth Bowen's Novels*, The Hague & Paris, 1975.
Edwin J. Kenney, *Elizabeth Bowen*, Lewisburg, 1975.
Hermione Lee, *Elizabeth Bowen: An Estimation*, London & Totowa, 1981.
Patricia Craig, *Elizabeth Bowen*, Penguin pbk., 1986.

CRITICAL ARTICLES

David Daiches, 'The Novels of Elizabeth Bowen', *English Journal*, XXXVIII June 1949), 305-313.
Benedict Kiely, 'Elizabeth Bowen', *Irish Monthly*, LXXVIII(1950), 175-181 (In *Modern Irish Fiction: A Critique*, 151-159).
Sean O'Faolain, 'Elizabeth Bowen, or Romance does not pay', *The Vanishing Hero*, London, 1956, 169-190.
Barbara Seward, 'Elizabeth Bowen's World of Impoverished Love', *College English*, XVIII (Oct. 1956), 30-37.
Harry Strickhausen, 'Elizabeth Bowen and Reality', *Sewanee Review*, LXXIII (Winter 1965), 158-165.
Margaret Scanlan, 'Rumors of War: Elizabeth Bowen's *Last September* and J. G. Farrell's *Troubles*', *Eire-Ireland*, XX, 2 (Summer 1985), 70-89.
Phyllis Lassner, 'The Past is a Burning Pattern: Elizabeth Bowen's *The Last September*', *Eire-Ireland* XXI, 1 (Spring 1986), 40-54.

XI

Kathleen Coyle (1886-1952)

A FLOCK OF BIRDS

In her last published work, the autobiographical *The Magical Realm* (1943), Kathleen Coyle provides a vividly impressionistic account of her infancy and early youth in her native Derry. She was born on 23 October 1886, a tiny baby weighing only four pounds. The child was lucky to survive when a jealous servant named Kerrigan attempted to poison her. Kerrigan, a macabre and shadowy figure like something out of a black comedy by Molly Keane, had once, it seems, been engaged to marry Kathleen's father, John Coyle. Only the chance arrival of the baby's grandmother in the nick of time saved her life. Later, an accident with a perambulator, caused by a careless nursemaid, left the little girl with a badly injured foot at the age of three. Clumsy medical treatment of a most painful kind was to leave her with a permanent limp.

Her mother's family was Catholic and claimed descent from the aristocratic Kinel-Owens. Her father, whose religion (according to the autobiography) was 'a strict secret', was a charming, improvident alcoholic who returned to the family home from time to time to terrorise the household with his wildness and violence. He died in an institution while still in his forties. His daughter's moving account of her painful relationship with this lovable, maddening man is one of the most powerful strands of the autobiography. Apart from a brief spell at a Derry convent school, Kathleen was educated mainly at home, first by her parents and later by a succession of tutors and foreign governesses. 'I was born', she tells us, 'under stars that made schools as fleet as comets.' Her real education came from her avid reading of her father's books. Then, when she was twelve, she was given a Christmas present of a cheap edition of *Wuthering Heights* and Emily Brontë's great novel set her mind aflame:

> The story not only absorbed me. It altered me. It took me away forever from the world I lived in. It awoke me emotionally. It took me into a realm to which I belonged more than I belonged to what happened about me. This was the atmosphere in which all meanings beat. It was where what was *felt* was understood. . . This was the evocation, the call. It was what I had awaited. It was my baptism, my immersion in Jordan.

A financial crisis brought about the sale of the family home at Glendermott in 1906 and the Coyles moved to Liverpool, where Kathleen got work in a library. In 1909, they moved again, this time to London, where she worked in a newspaper office. The novelist, Rebecca West, who met Kathleen Coyle a few years before the outbreak of the Great War, later recorded that she was 'impressed, and almost alarmed, by her endowment of poetic sensitivity'. Rebecca West was later to contribute a substantial preface to one of Kathleen Coyle's more important novels, *Liv* (1928). In 1911, against her mother's wishes, Kathleen made a break from the family and went to live in Dublin. There, she became actively involved in the socialist movement and, in 1915, married fellow socialist, Charles O'Meagher, the handsome son of a working-class family from Co. Meath. The marriage broke up after only four years, leaving Kathleen with two children, a daughter, Michele, and a son romantically named Kestrel. She went back to London with the children and, for a short period, lived with her mother and sister. Then, she decided to try to make a living by her pen. She put the children into a foster home for a time, took a room in London and began to write. Her first novel, *Piccadilly*, was published in 1923. In the same year, she moved with her children to the continent, where she lived in Ostend and Antwerp before settling in Paris in 1926. During the following decade, she published a string of novels, almost one a year, including *It Is Better to Tell* (1927), *There Is A Door* (1931) and *Morning Comes Early* (1934). In a note which she contributed to Kunitz and Haycraft's *Twentieth Century Authors* (1942), Kathleen Coyle recorded the dismissive view that 'of my novels, only one, *A Flock of Birds*, is of any value. The others are, and were meant to be, means of earning a livelihood'. This was undoubtedly severe, and certainly unfair to work of the quality of *Liv*. That she set herself high standards is clear. She was annoyed when a blurb for *A Flock of Birds* recorded that the novel had run second to E.M. Forster's *A Passage to India* in a literary competition! The subsequent massive reputation of Forster's novel was to turn the apparent slur into a considerable compliment. In spite of her prolific output, however, Kathleen Coyle was often very hard up. On the advice of some American friends, she moved to the United States in 1937, with her daughter, and lived in new Hampshire, joining an aritsts' group known as 'The McDowell colony'. During the Hitler war, she wrote numerous short stories for women's magazines. She died of cancer in Philadelphia in 1952. Her work has remained virtually unknown in Ireland. This neglect may be due to her avoidance of the more garish aspects of the Ireland of her day and her concentration on what Robert Greacen has identified as her main preoccupation as a novelist, the exploration of the feminine psyche. The best of her fiction, in novels such as *Liv* and *A Flock of Birds*, deserves revival.

A FLOCK OF BIRDS (1930)

Quite the most striking aspect of this novel is the extent to which it eschews the more sensational implications of its theme. Published in the decade after the Civil War, at a time when memories of recent violence were still vivid, it might well have dealt in the obviosities which are normally associated with the kind of political violence which constitutes the hinge of the novel's action. Christy Munster has been sentenced to death for political murder and, as the novel opens, his family are emerging from the court-room where sentence has been pronounced. His mother, Catherine Munster, and his sister, Kathleen, and brother, Valentine, all strongly disapprove of his political affiliations. His fiancée, Cicely, alone shares his beliefs. What exactly these are we are never precisely told. It emerges later that Christy was one of a party of six attackers, one of whom (and it becomes clear that this was *not* Christy) fired the fatal shot. The victim is never identified for us. Christy is the only one of the six who was captured and he must pay the final penalty. The fact that an appeal for clemency is made to the Home Secretary indicates that the action of the novel is set in the pre-Independence period and there is mention of Marshal Foch and his conduct of a Great War campaign, so we may reasonably conclude that the period of the novel's action is about 1918 or so. The novel explores the consequences for the family of the death sentence, as they wait for Christy to be hanged and strive, by various kinds of intercession, to save him from the gallows. Coyle filters out of the book all the conventional details of such stories, so that she can concentrate on studying the effects of the crisis on the various members of the family and, in particular, on Christy's elderly mother, Catherine Munster. Christy himself remains a somewhat shadowy figure, immured in his fetid prison cell, playing a part in the novel only on the few occasions when various members of the family are allowed to visit him.

In addition to demoting Christy to a fairly minor role, Coyle also imposes a distinctive anonymity on the novel's setting. The obvious Irish city for events of this kind would seem to be Dublin, where a political crime of this sort would most probably be tried, but the novel never actually names Dublin as the scene of the action. It is clear that we are in a large and busy city, with lots of motor cars, taxis and other kinds of traffic about. Occasional details suggest Dublin. When Kathleen organises a petition, one of the people to whom she appeals for his signature is identified as 'Russell', which suggests 'AE' (he is, we are informed, 'full of the trouble in the Northern shipyards'). One of Catherine Munster's well-to-do friends, Lady Lysaght, seeks her at 'the Sheridan where you always stay', which suggests Dublin's most august hotel, the Shelbourne. They have, in fact, taken refuge in a less well-known hotel, the Stacpoole. Later in the novel, Catherine and Kathleen seek seclusion in a city park which is near the hotel and the account of this place, with its gravelled walks, Indian ducks, and swans on an island, suggests Stephen's Green, best-known of all Dublin parks, the one which Stephen Dedalus famously claimed as his own. In the grim unrolling of the few days of the book's action, however, all that matters is that we should be aware of the prison in which Christy languishes, the hotel in which the family waits for the end and the general sense of some large city containing all this anguish. That the Munsters are a wealthy family is clear. There is a family home, within driving distance of the city. It is called Gorabbey and is a lavishly furnished house, with beautiful gardens and various old retainers in constant attendance. Catherine and her children return there from time to time during the few days described for us, to eat or sleep or talk together about the horror which impends. Soon, Catherine can no longer bear to stay in this beloved house, where Christy was born. It is far too full of memories and she flees to the institutional anonymity of the Stacpoole Hotel, to be near the prison and within reach of Christy's lawyers. Christy's older brother, Valentine, who hates all that Christy stands for, nevertheless busies himself on his doomed brother's behalf. Valentine is himself a lawyer but has handed over the conduct of Christy's defence to another barrister, lest his own relationship to Christy should damage his brother's chances. In the event, Redmond, the barrister who takes the case in place of Valentine, does his best for his client but fails to secure his acquittal.

From the beginning, we are almost claustrophobically involved with the mother, Catherine Munster, and with her desperate attempts to come to terms with the awful inevitability of her son's death. Unlike the others, she never really believes in the possibility of a reprieve, though she is willing, in the interests of family concord, to go along with their desperate efforts to achieve one. In fact, she becomes more directly involved when events take an unexpected turn and, through the intervention of one of the family's influential friends, the *Times*, a government organ, comes out in favour of a reprieve for the condemned man. Harold Clontarf, editor of the opposing newspaper, which favours the views of Christy and his kind, now proposes to denounce Christy as a government spy and Valentine and his mother call at Clontarf's offices, in an attempt to dissuade him. Clontarf refuses to give way and a furious Valentine upbraids him for thus endangering Christy further:

> Valentine's shoulders heaved and went down again. He had the air of dealing with a fractious child, a boy who would not submit to discipline. 'I wish you to disclose nothing. I only wish to convince you that if you publish that article it means certain death to him. If you insist upon the

assertion that the government press is pleading for him because he is a government spy do you not realise that you force the government to hang him to prove that he isn't?'

Harold Clontarf refuses to budge, insisting that he and his supporters are at war and that, if Christy must be sacrificed for the cause, he will not shrink from the necessary action. Catherine, left alone with him, is granted a moment of visionary insight into the future:

> She stood up again, finally, looking for the last time at the man who was an instrument in the fate of her son and she had a queer premonition that one day his own life would be taken. He would fall on a roadside, the bullets whizzing like pebbles. Grey, and without shields. Emperors and captains. When a spear fell it lay dead like the sear of lightning that had passed. Poor man, she thought towards him, poor man. He knew not what he did.

The death sentence imposes a new valuation on past events and inflicts on Catherine the agonising search for a perspective on the future which will enable her to bear it. Before Christy was captured and sentenced, she had been concerned about other matters which now dwindle to their proper insignificance. She had worried about Valentine's possible involvement with prostitutes. She had resented Christy's engagement to Cicely. Now, the hideous certainty of his imminent death is all that matters and the past is of no moment when set against the horrific fact of the near future. That he should die for beliefs she cannot share makes for a peculiar bitterness. She resembles O'Casey's Juno Boyle in her contempt for male heroics:

> It was not that women loved sacrifice or glorified in it, drawing strength from it. The strength came right enough, but the love and glory were absent. Women hated sacrifice as they hated childbirth but they had to face it. They stood up afterwards as the day stands up from the night, washed from the darkness and full of singing birds and the business of life. . . She did not love sacrifice. A waste in the name of heaven was no less waste. It was that that she resented, his waste. To him it was a heroic purpose. Heroism or martyrdom was the fashion. What fools they were these young men, these weavers of wreaths! Other brows bore the thorns.

Catherine, bitterly aware of the lot of women, must now learn to accommodate her natural jealousy of her son's fiancée, Cicely, and her poignant desire to comfort the doomed son whom she cannot hope to save. Christy's death will radically alter all their lives. His sister, Kathleen, a writer who has been living in Paris, has been having an affair with a Frenchman, an air pilot named Andre Grenier. Her lover comes to Ireland to be with her at this trying time but, despite his touching willingness to stand by her, Kathleen recognises that their relationship is at an end and dismisses him. She explains to her mother how the disaster of Christy's impending execution has altered everything for her:

> 'Oh, Mother, I don't know. I don't understand. I love him differently from Christy. I want him, in my life, as I never could want Christy, and yet this. . . . this about Christy has killed everything else. Nothing else matters . . . I have sent Dede back to his wife and for two years I've been begging him to leave her!'

Cicely, of course, will never marry Christy (she considers marrying him romantically in his prison cell, thereby recalling Grace Gifford's marriage to Joseph Mary Plunkett in his prison cell on the eve of his execution, but she is dissuaded by the outspoken Valentine who tells her that 'people would only say you had to, and afterwards that you were mistaken'). Valentine himself decides to marry the woman he has been visiting in Windyridge and tells his mother of his decision, asserting that he believes that nothing 'more genuine will ever come into my life'. So, Christy's siblings and his fiancée fashion their maimed futures in the awareness of his impending death. His mother, on the other hand, is an old woman. Most of her life is in the past, a compound of memories. Christy's death will make it impossible for her to go on living at Gorabbey, where he was born and reared, and she pays the place one final, painful visit and bequeaths it to Valentine. Her agonised progress from a stricken paralysis of the emotions to the reality of genuine grief is charted by Coyle with masterly tension. When she leaves the courtroom at the beginning, after hearing sentence of death passed on Christy, Catherine can only stare unseeingly at the inappropriately named 'Felicity's hat shop' opposite. She can, at first, feel nothing at all. Her mind tells her that she ought to be experiencing conventional grief but, at first, she cannot. Returning home to Gorabbey, she finds the kitchen table full of dishes piled with strawberries and, still insulated against easy and usual responses, she sets about making jam (but she will, she knows, never eat strawberries again). She watches her daughter, Kathleen, who resembles her mother in her fierce independence, shredding an evening dress into small pieces which she then stows away pointlessly in a drawer. The futility of conversation, even between close members of the family, is achingly clear. The occasion demands passionate responses but reality produces only futile trivia. When Catherine first visits Christy in prison, she is distressed by his tangled hair and wants to take a comb to it, and wash his face and tidy him as though he were still a little boy. She does not join the others in collecting appeal signatures, though she understands that they have to labour on Christy's behalf. In her wanderings through the city, she finds her way into a Catholic church. It is made clear that the Munsters are not Catholics but Catherine achieves a moment of significant vision as she gazes on a painting of Mary with the dead Christ:

> She was transfixed and stirred, devastated by understanding. It was so much older than she, this happening, this – leaving of the mother. They took him down from the cross and Mary hid many things in her heart. How many mothers had hidden things in their hearts! Men died and women stayed on after them to learn the full meaning, the bitter, unsatisfying taste of life . . . the life they had created! . . . Before the stricken figure of Mary she was humiliated as a woman of her age; and her grief lessened . . . whatever unity was meant by God she was desolated into its need.

The novel compresses into the few days preceding Christy's execution an almost unbearable intensity of feeling. In its painful evocation of the past, Coyle's taut, detailed prose often recalls Virginia Woolf's manner of particularisation in moments of heightened emotion. Here, for example, is Catherine recalling Mitchell, the man she had loved before she married her husband, Luke.

> All through her life Mitchell had been in the background. It was natural that he should send a telegram. His eldest boy had been eaten by sharks in the Pacific. And now he was with his daughter and grandchildren. They were playing tennis at Santander.

The short, clipped sentences, with their focussing on seemingly grotesque detail ('his eldest boy had been eaten by sharks in the Pacific') recall Clarissa Dalloway's tremulous probings of her menacing past. Elsewhere, as Catherine strains towards the doomed Christy in a desperate effort to achieve some sort of unity in suffering with him so that he will not face his dreadful end alone, the prose assumes a Lawrencian density:

> She had come in with the dawn blazing in the sky, with the beginning day. She had been sheltered in the dark moonless night and with the break of day she had come in to bed, to sleep, to oblivion. The night had been a sacrament to her, a communion with Christy. She could not recover it now. It was stored in her – for ever.

At the end, when the appeal to the Home Secretary has been turned down and they must all visit the doomed man for the last time, Catherine asks only that she be the very last to visit him. Her request is granted and she tells Christy that she means to return to her hotel room to keep a special vigil until he is executed:

'Listen, Christy! I want you to take this in. All this night I shall keep vigil for you ... on my knees.' She would shut herself into the hotel bedroom. 'I shall not stand up ... until ... until it is all over. I want you to dip into my soul, into my prayers and take courage from me. I will not fail you.' 'And I!' his voice was wrought for her and bound on her, 'I will not fail you. I will die like your son!'

Despite this touching final compact between mother and son, the novel ends on a bleak note of despair. Emerging from the prison, Catherine is met by Valentine who steers her clear of the crowds gathered outside. The people are being led in their prayers by Cicely, and Catherine characteristically shies away from such public shows of emotion:

'Take me,' she said steadily, 'to the little bedroom in the hotel.' She raised her face to the prison and from the prison to the sky above, the dark clouded chimera of the sky, the flying clouds of the night that had yet to come. 'What is that dark cloud in the sky?'

He offered comfort to her comfortless soul: 'It is going to rain.'

A smile widened her mouth: and she gave him back madness: 'It is only a flock of birds.'

In closing thus, with the book's title, and by declaring it 'madness', Coyle seems to set the seal on a conviction of the hopelessness of the suffering she has been plumbing so painfully throughout. The phrase, 'a flock of birds', is one which Catherine devised to comfort Christy as a child. When clouds darkened the sky, she would tell him that they were only 'a flock of birds' but there is no comfort in the well-worn family formula at the end. This is a remarkable novel which denies itself the facile slogans and political clichés to which the theme might have tempted it, to concentrate minutely on the pain of individual suffering. All the main characters are closely observed in their separate identities, as they respond to the appalling crisis which afflicts them. The family's instinctive antipathy to Christy's fiancée, Cicely, is not shirked – sentimentality is everywhere avoided in favour of a tough, gallant realism. The concentration on individuals rather than issues has seen to it that the novel has not dated as more politically explicit 'historical' novels have done. In *A Flock of Birds* and, particularly, in its memorable heroine, Catherine Munster, Kathleen Coyle speaks with startling freshness to the troubled condition of modern Ireland.

SELECTED BIBLIOGRAPHY

RELATED WORKS

Youth in the Saddle, London, 1927 (published in New York in same year, under title, *Shule Agra*).
Liv, London, 1928.

AUTOBIOGRAPHY

The Magical Realm, New York, 1943.

CRITICAL STUDIES

John P. McBride, *Kathleen Coyle 1886-1952: An Irish Writer Rediscovered.* (Unpublished dissertation, The Queen's University, Belfast, 1981).

CRITICAL ARTICLES

Robert Greacen, 'Kathleen Coyle: Explorer of the Feminine Psyche', *Ulster Tatler* (Nov. 1980), 46-47.
Robert Greacen, 'The Magical Realm: A Derry Childhood', *Ulster Tatler* (April 1981), 49-50.

XII

Kate O'Brien (1897-1974)

THE ANTE-ROOM

Kate O'Brien was born in Limerick, the fourth daughter of Thomas O'Brien and Catherine Thornhill. There were eight children in all and the family lived at Boru House, Mulgrave Street. Her mother died when Kate was six years old and the child was then sent as a boarder to the local convent school, Laurel Hill, where she had her entire schooling. In the light of her fiction's preoccupation with the emotional stresses of the religious life as lived by nuns and her concern with issues of beleaguered faith, it seems reasonable to suggest that the dozen or so years spent at Laurel Hill were significantly formative ones for the future writer. She went up to University College, Dublin in the troubled days after the Insurrection of 1916 and was later to speak with warm affection of her time at university during that grim and troubled period:

> I came up to a Dublin still smoking from Easter Week. The first European War was on, and all general conditions were sad and miserable. We were a hungry, untidy, dirty lot – we of 1917-1919. But did we enjoy ourselves? Did we read, did we think, did we loaf, did we argue? . . . Stephen's Green was very important in our student life. We used to follow W. B. Yeats all around it . . . We used to track Maud Gonne about, too, when she was out of jail. She was marvellous and tall, with her accompanying Irish wolf-hounds.

She graduated with honours in English and French in 1919 and worked for a time in the Foreign News section of the *Manchester Guardian* and later at a convent school in London. In 1921 she travelled to Washington as secretary to her brother-in-law, Stephen O'Mara, who was acting as chairman of the de Valera Bonds Drive. She later worked as governess in Spain for a family resident near Bilbao, a period of her life on which she was to draw for her novel, *Mary Lavelle* (1936). From Spain she went back to London where she married a young Dutchman, Gustav Renier, in 1924. The marriage proved unsuccessful.

Her first literary achievement was the play, *Distinguished Villa*, which was staged in London in 1926 and attracted favourable comment from Sean O'Casey, among others. In the following year, her play, *The Bridge*, was put on at the Arts Theatre Club in London. She retained her interest in the theatre throughout her career and several of her novels were later adapted for the stage. Her first novel, *Without My Cloak*, a chronicle of an Irish industrial family, appeared in 1931, and had a great success, winning her both the Hawthornden Prize and the James Tait Black Memorial Prize. Later novels include *The Ante-Room* (1934), *The Land of Spices* (1941), *The Last of Summer* (1943) and *The Flower of May* (1953). Her most considerable international success was achieved, understandably perhaps, with a novel on a non-Irish theme, *That Lady* (1946). She herself described this as being not so much an historical novel as 'an invention arising from the curious external story of Ana de Mendoza and Phillip II of Spain'. The novel was dramatised in 1949 and Katherine Cornell took the lead in the Broadway production. It was later made into a successful film with Olivia de Havilland in the role of Ana de Mendoza. Kate O'Brien's treatment of Philip II in the novel earned her official Spanish displeasure and she was refused entry to Spain for a time. This ban was lifted in 1957 through the intervention of the Irish ambassador in Madrid.

In addition to her novels and plays, she also wrote a travel book, *Farewell Spain* (1937), a biography, *Teresa of Avila* (1952) and various works of a personal and reminiscential nature such as *My Ireland* (1962) and *Presentation Parlour* (1963). She also wrote a number of short stories and was a prolific writer of articles for various journals as well as a perceptive reviewer of new fiction. She was, for example, one of the few professional reviewers to respond warmly to the idiosyncratic excellences of Samuel Beckett's *Murphy* at its first appearance in 1938. In 1950 she settled at Roundstone in Co. Galway but financial difficulties forced her to sell her house there in 1961. She then went to live in a small cottage in the village of Boughton in Kent, where she spent the rest of her life. She died in hospital at Canterbury in 1974. Her work had won considerable acclaim during her lifetime and she was recognised in Ireland and elsewhere as a novelist and playwright of stature. She was elected a member of the Irish Academy of Letters in 1947. After her death, her novels went out of print for a time, but, in recent years, Arlen House, The Women's Press did sterling work in reissuing many of the novels in attractive paperback editions.

THE ANTE-ROOM (1934)

There is a remarkable contrast between Kate O'Brien's first, prize-winning novel, *Without My Cloak* (1931) and the work with which she followed it in 1934, *The Ante-Room*, which appears to have been her own favourite among her books. While both have similar settings and explore the same social group, the earlier work is leisurely and diffuse where the latter is tautly concentrated. In *Without My Cloak* she was staking out her territory, tracing the dubious origins of her comfortable burghers and showing their rapid rise to commercial success and social confidence. This novel is a chronicle of the growth and development of a Catholic merchant family in the south-west of Ireland and of their successful progress from early struggles as small shop-keepers to full-blown Victorian prosperity in well-furnished villas tended by numerous servants. The Considines are, as it were, Irish Forsytes. Indeed, Kate O'Brien may well have had Galsworthy's famous saga in mind during the composition of her own seminal chronicle, since there are many points of similarity both in matters of detail and in the general strategy of the work. The principal Considine residence, Anthony Considine's new house, River Hill, clearly corresponds to the mansion which the ill-fated Bosinney designs for Soames Forsyte at Robin Hill. The beautiful and unhappy Caroline Consid-ine, who marries the Soames-like lawyer, Lanigan, is the Irene of the Irish novel who, in middle life, abandons her husband and her home and comes perilously close to flouting all the Catholic proprieties of the tribe. Like the Forsytes, the Considines and their closer relatives inhabit comfortable dwellings and delight in family gatherings. They come together for birthdays and weddings and funerals and gradually over the years create a wealthy, claustrophobic ambience from which Anthony's beloved son, Denis (the young Jolyon of this book, in a sense) will try to break away. Neither Caroline nor Denis will carry revolt to the point of no return. The centrifugal pull of the Considine circle always prevails in the end and Caroline returns to her family, while Denis reconciles himself to separation from the socially inferior girl with whom he has fallen in love and finds a bride more to his father's and the family's liking.

In concentrating her creative efforts on this social group, Kate O'Brien, in addition to identifying fictionally her chosen people, was also fulfilling a long-standing impulse of the Irish novel. For there is a sense in which the Irish novel of the nineteenth century hankered after the middle ground so familiar in the English novel, an area generally denied to Irish novelists by the fearsome turbulence of a sharply divided colonial society. Broadly speaking, early Irish fiction tends to be a matter of extremes, swinging as it does between the gentry of the Big House and the peasantry of the cabin. When Gerald Griffin, recently returned from London, embarked upon his panoramic melodrama, *The Collegians* (1829), he built into the book a middle-class Catholic family, the Dalys, who might be said to be the fictional ancestors of Kate O'Brien's Considines. It was a matter of some personal importance to Griffin that he should incorporate such a loving, thriving group of Catholics in his novel to show the English reader that such people were not only domestically serene but also politically loyal, since it was a declared part of Griffin's consciously didactic intention to show the English reader that Irish Catholics, when properly treated by their English overlords, could be as decent and law-abiding as their Protestant fellow-citizens. The fact that Griffin knew perfectly well that Irish Catholics were not decently treated by their English rulers imparted to this aspect of his fiction an element of strain and make-believe, and the jovial domesticity of the Daly family rings more than slightly false. Kate O'Brien, of course, was writing over a century later than Griffin, in a modern Ireland which had recently ejected its old rulers and undertaken the running of its own affairs, but it is highly interesting to notice how careful she is to stress the apolitical nature of her nineteenth-century Considines. Here, for example, is Teresa, who will later figure as the dying mother in *The Ante-Room*, as she appears early in the first novel:

> Being Irish, Teresa obviously couldn't be a Conservative, but being a woman she was spared the necessity of knowing for certain which party was which. In any case, political feeling never ran high in Considine blood. The destiny of mankind, or of any race of it, mattered only in so far as it furthered the interests of an established family. Teresa was inclined to regard politics as she regarded firearms – things that shouldn't be left about the house.

It is with such gentle, protective ironies that Kate O'Brien steers her prosperous characters away from the shoals of Irish politics and keeps her novel firmly settled on issues of property and family relationships. She is most certainly not interested in political violence or exile or famine or land-hunger, those familir staples of early Irish fiction. No Griffin or Kickham she, or Edgeworth either. Eavan Boland, in her introduction to a welcome paperback re-issue of *The Ante-Room* in 1980, identified the precise area of Kate O'Brien's interest:

> There was an Ireland between the mortgaged acres of Maria Edgeworth and the strong farms of Mary Lavin's short stories. It was an Ireland of increasing wealth and uneasy conscience, where the women wore stays,

and rouged their cheeks, had their clothes made by Dublin dressmakers and tried to forget the hauntings of their grandparents. This was Catholic Ireland; it was never nationalist Ireland.

The third and final section of *Without My Cloak* carries the story of the Considines through to the year 1877, at which point the rebellious Denis finds his suitable partner, Anna, and the book closes in a transport of amorous delight and general family satisfaction. *The Ante-Room*, in one sense, follows directly, in that its action is placed in the year 1880, the place is still Mellick (that fictional counterpart of Kate O'Brien's native city of Limerick) and we are again involved with a branch of the Considine family. Teresa Considine, whose ignorance of political matters was glanced at earlier, inexplicably marries 'a mere clerk in some hole and corner office' but, having done so, settles down as the tribe's matriarch and produces a large family of her own:

> After her marriage she became once more the strongest pillar among them of the family pride. Danny and she had so far contributed eight to Honest John's quota of grandchildren, the eight plainest perhaps, but indubitably eight grandchildren.

When, twenty fictional years later, some of these plain Mulqueen offspring are re-introduced in *The Ante-Room*, their plainness is forgotten. One of them, Marie Rose, is an acknowledged beauty and her younger sister, Agnes, hitherto overshadowed by her blonde sister, is beginning at twenty-five to discover her own dark and impressive good looks. Marie Rose has married and departed from the family home, 'Roseholm', and Agnes is now its châtelaine. Her mother, Teresa, is dying of an incurable cancer and requires constant nursing. Her father, the despised Danny Mulqueen, is heart-broken at the imminence of his wife's death and leans on Agnes in his sorrow. The other principal member of the family is Agnes's older brother, Reggie, who is thirty-five and has long suffered from syphilis, a disease which, in 1880, was still incurable. The mercury treatment which is all that is available to him, while holding his disease at bay, has made him a physical wreck:

> He had always been vain of his loose and swarthy good looks, and these were puffed and bloated now. He had always half-desired to play the piano well – but now his thickened hands were more tentative than ever as he fooled at his eternal Chopin.

One thing only stands between him and final despair and has done so since the first diagnosis of his disease. This is his mother's fiercely protective love. Teresa has devoted herself totally to her ruined son and, in gratitude, he now repays her devotion by trying desperately to amuse her and keep her happy during these, her final days. He reads to her, gossips with her, plays his snatches of Chopin and sings to her. What he simply cannot do is accept that she is dying. If Teresa leaves him he will have nobody to comfort him and he cannot face this grim solitude. He therefore clings to the fiction of her possible recovery, though it is known that her case is hopeless and this will be confirmed in the course of the novel by a celebrated London cancer specialist who is called in as a last resort by Teresa's physicians. In her turn, the dying woman clings to life only for the sake of her helpless son, tormented by the awful fear that when she dies he will be quite alone and unable to cope with the fearsome wreckage of his life. The tremulous, loving, doomed tie between diseased son and diseased mother is one of the most poignantly effective of the book's many relationships. This is to be a novel about the conflict between duty and passion and Kate O'Brien presents her main events through a story which is as rigorously disciplined as her first was diffuse. The action of *The Ante-Room* is confined to a mere three days and for that short period we are confined to the emotional claustrophobia of 'Roseholm', the title of which is presumably meant to recall to our minds Ibsen's passion-riddled 'Rosmersholm', where suicide also provides the final resolution of the conflict. All the characters will be tested by love in one form or another during the short, tense period of the novel, which has the neo-classical density of a well-crafted play, with its several relationships enacted and explored in an atmosphere of almost stifling religious intensity. All the characters are Catholics and most of them practise their demanding religion to the hilt with an almost Jansenistic fervour. A compelling aura of religiosity is thrown over the entire household when Teresa's brother, Canon Tom Considine, ordains a Triduum of prayer for the dying woman, urging the household to storm heaven with their entreaties for a solution to Teresa's agony. The action of the book takes place on three Holy Days, Hallowe'en, All Saint's Day and All Soul's Day and the climax of the book's religious ritual comes with the celebration of Mass by Canon Tom in his dying sister's bedroom.

The central conflict of the novel involves Agnes Mulqueen's guilty passion for her sister's estranged husband, Vincent de Courcy O'Regan. Marie-Rose seizes upon her mother's dangerous condition as an excuse to visit her old home when, in fact, she merely wishes to get away from her husband, but Vincent soon follows her to 'Roseholm'. Agnes, a devout Catholic, has been unable to attend Confession for some ten weeks because she feels that she has sinned by harbouring lustful thoughts of Vincent. She is now faced with the need to confess her sins as a preparation for taking Communion at the Mass in her mother's sick-room. Torn between her passion for Vincent and her profound love for her sister, she decides to make a good Confession and renounce Vincent forever. She puts the first part of this resolution into effect and achieves at least a temporary command over her feelings, substituting for her fevered longings a chilly serenity which follows on the priest's absolution of her sins:

> How simple! How formal and civilised was the method of the Church in its exactions. As she prayed and allowed the priest's words to flow into her mind, she was aware of coolness in herself, that her heart was only beating normally now, that the tiny twitchings had ceased under the flesh of her fingertips. She had done that which her belief exacted, and here, without fuss or probing, was the immediate reward – the cold comfort which assured her with gentle contempt that everything dies except the idea of God – even sin itself, being more mortal than the sinner.

Thus, for the moment at any rate, Agnes achieves a cold command over her feelings. She herself has unwittingly upset the calculating sexual composure of young Dr Curran who attends on her mother and, contrary to his best-laid plans, falls deeply in love with Agnes. Curran is presented in an unattractive light and directly linked with the ruined Reggie, since it is made clear that he too has indulged his sexual inclinations while abroad but that, unlike Reggie, he was professionally knowledgeable enough to avoid the worst consequences of his philanderings. Now that he is back home in Ireland it has been his intention to play safe, build a prosperous practice and eventually marry some suitably sensible wife who will help him to further his professional ambitions. His sudden wild passion for Agnes shatters all his tidy plans. His repellent emotional calculations are efficiently exposed:

> William Curran had always been clear in his views about women. Every inch a doctor, he deplored the mischief which the amorous instinct had done and continued to do to the human race. It would always have to be reckoned with, he knew, but he did not see that it was worth its own high and often hysterical claims. The sane thing was to despise, since you could never kill it . . . He had enjoyed himself abroad and kept his head. Here at home he was continent, because he believed in continency and found it practicable.

His sudden passion for Agnes shatters his complacency but Agnes, her mind filled with images of the handsome Vincent, simply cannot take Curran's ardours seriously. This is, in fact, a deeply sardonic novel in which 'the amorous instinct' plays havoc with all the people it touches. Vincent and Marie-Rose have ceased to love or desire each other. The dreadful Reggie has garnered love's most fearsome rewards and can never achieve a normal marriage. Curran's prim professionalism is thrown into disarray by an unplanned and unreciprocated love. Agnes is forced to choose between her guilty desire for Vincent, her loyalty to her faith and her long-standing love for her sister. A particularly bleak version of the love-game is offered us in the case of Nurse Cunningham, the dying woman's attendant. She has nourished the conventional matrimonial aspirations of her profession but now, as she approaches thirty, has to admit that she is unlikely to trap a doctor into marriage. Having had to work hard all her life, she luxuriates in the wealthy comfort of the Mulqueen home and will eventually make the grisly decision to marry the diseased Reggie, with her eyes wide open to the implications of her action. Her terrible decision brings relief and final comfort to Teresa who can now die in peace, happy in the knowledge that another woman has assumed the care of her beloved and helpless son. 'The amorous instinct' produces disaster and unhappiness for all its victims, but Nurse Cunningham's economic instincts, ironically, produce final happiness for her dying patient. Agnes feels a profound sense of shock and horror when she is told of the nurse's decision by Dr Curran:

> Agnes's face became in a wave of lightning speed suffused in red, and then drained white again before a breath could be taken.
> 'Marry – Reggie?'
> 'Yes'.
> 'But – '.
> 'She knows about him. A formal marriage – which will give him companionship and very competent protection and care. It's an excellent idea.'
> Agnes stood up.
> 'I think it's horrible – ' she whispered.

Later, she wonders ironically what her uncle, Canon Tom Considine, 'made of this answer to his intercession'. The God who inflicts the amorous instinct on his luckless creatures and imposes on them a moral code which forbids them to indulge their natural passions, grants happiness to a dying woman by bringing about a non-marriage between a normally amorous young woman and a hopelessly diseased syphilitic. The novel ends with the suicide of Agnes's lover, Vincent, a melodramatic contrivance perhaps but, in the circumstances of this novel, an unavoidable one. The book's peculiar strength resides in the author's determination to test the demands of romantic love with complete consistency against the rigours of a stringent ethical code which allows its practitioners no convenient loopholes, no possibility of self-deceit or comfortable evasion. Its most obvious weakness lies in its frequent failure to provide its troubled and thoughtful characters with genuinely convincing dialogue. Kate O'Brien seems conscious of this hazard and, at one point, attempts to defuse the charged atmosphere between Agnes and Dr Curran by having her jokingly accuse him of sounding 'as if you had read Miss Braddon'. This is a rare escape into mild humour and the novel is not elsewhere in the least humorous. Kate O'Brien is no prude and was quite prepared in her other novels to deal with sexual issues in a variety of ways. She ran into trouble with the Censorship Board because she made the plot of her excellent novel, *The Land of Spices*, hinge on a brief incident of male homosexuality. In *Mary Lavelle* she permits her Irish heroine to have a brief *affaire* with her Spanish lover before returning to Ireland. Nor is she incapable of writing lively dialogue, as *Without My Cloak* demonstrates again and again. It would seem to be the case that in this one novel, *The Ante-Room*, she decided to set herself the challenge of writing about what she called (in *Mary Lavelle*) 'the mighty lie of romantic passion' in a setting of rigid Catholic orthodoxy and even if the resultant novel is sometimes dangerously close to melodramatic mawkishness it has too a curious, consistent power which derives from its relentless determination to play fair by its own ground rules. Vivian Mercier records that Kate O'Brien told him

> 'I am a moralist, in that I see no story unless there is a moral conflict, and the old-fashioned sense of the soul and its troubling effect in human affairs.'

The same critic rightly describes *The Ante-Room* as 'a masterpiece of compression and symmetry'. When one looks for other, similar Irish novels to range alongside it one finds it far from easy to match its peculiar *gravitas*. Kate O'Brien's contemporary, Sean O'Faolain, has regularly tackled similar issues in his longer stories but he has done so by means of a distinctively ironic comedy which has grown more genial all the time. His 'Lovers of the Lake' does not shirk the serious issues it raises but it hardly traps its protagonists in the same moral cul-de-sac provided for the various lovers in *The Ante-Room*. Nor does O'Faolain's work ever adopt as pessimistic a view of romantic love. There are no diseased mock-marriages in his stories. Rather do we find that the painful tensions of a story like 'Lovers of the Lake' are resolved into the gentle ironies of the later 'In the Bosom of the Country' where illicit passion is given its congé by tranquil domesticity rather than suicide. Among later writers who have occupied themselves with the amours of the Irish middle-classs in realistic novels one might single out John Broderick for attention but it is obvious that he plays the romantic game by entirely different rules. In his fiction, Catholic moral conventions are treated merely as a social façade behind which his characters bed each other with brutish abandon. As Vivian Mercier points out, commentators have sometimes gone outside Ireland to find Kate O'Brien's fictional fellows and she has sometimes been compared to Mauriac as an analyst of the conflict between passion and duty. One might also, perhaps, link her wih the Graham Greene of such novels as *The Heart of the Matter* and *The End of the Affair*, except that Greene occupies himself with the consequences of the failure of his characters to live up to the demands of their ethical code while Kate O'Brien, in *The Ante-Room* at any rate, compels her characters to an agonising conformity. Her consistently serious approach to sexual matters, her refusal to fudge the issues she raises through either fantasy or farce, her characters' rigorous questioning of their moral dilemmas, all these aspects of her fiction make her an exceptional figure among Irish novelists at any time. In the censorious Ireland of fifty years ago she was a remarkable pioneer and the high quality of her best fiction still offers a challenge today.

SELECTED BIBLIOGRAPHY

RELATED WORKS

Without My Cloak, London, 1931.
The Land of Spices, London, 1941.
The Last of Summer, London, 1943.

BIOGRAPHY

No biography has yet been published. There are helpful notes in Robert Hogan's *Dictionary of Irish Literature* and Henry Boylan's *A Dictionary of Irish Biography*.

CRITICAL STUDIES

Lorna Reynolds, *Kate O'Brien: A Literary Portrait*, Gerrards Cross & Totowa, 1987.

CRITICAL ARTICLES

Vivian Mercier, 'Kate O'Brien', *Irish Writing*, 1 (1946), 86-100.
John Jordan, 'Some Works of the Month: Kate O'Brien – A Note on her Themes', *The Bell*, xix (Jan. 1954), 55-59. 'Kate O'Brien: First Lady of Irish Letters', *Hibernia*, 11 May 1973, 11.
Eavan Boland, 'That Lady: A Profile of Kate O'Brien 1897-1974', *The Critic*, xxxiv, 2 (Winter 1975), 16-25.
John Liddy (ed.), *The Stony Thursday Book,* Limerick, 1981.
Joan Ryan, 'Women in the Novels of Kate O'Brien: The Mellick Novels', *Studies in Anglo-Irish Literature* (ed. Kosok), Bonn, 1982, 322-332.
Adele M. Dalsimer, 'A Not So Simple Saga: Kate O'Brien's *Without My Cloak*', *Eire-Ireland*, xxi 3 (Fall 1986), 55-71.

XIII

Sean O'Faolain (b. 1900)

BIRD ALONE

He was born John Whelan, third son of Denis Whelan and Bridget Murphy. His father was a member of the Royal Irish Constabulary, a faithful servant of the Crown, who looked to his children to grow up in a similar mould. A fictionalised version of the father is to be found in the Johnny Hussey of *A Nest of Simple Folk*, and the emergent antagonisms between the future writer and his policeman father are reflected in Denis Hussey's battle with Johnny towards the end of that novel. Commenting on his relationship with his father, in his autobiography *Vive Moi* (1965), O'Faolain tells us that 'he always evoked my respect, and sometimes my admiration but, although he loved me with a father's love, he rarely warmed me to love him'. The mother was 'very tall, slim as a reed and quite beautiful' and came from Co. Limerick. *Vive Moi* presents her as a devoted mother, intensely ambitious for her children and given to a rather gloomy piety. The family home in Half-Moon Street was just behind the Cork Opera House and the mother took in the 'arteestes' as weekly lodgers, so that the house was often filled with exotic creatures, members of touring companies, whose clothes, scents, accents and general romantic aura gave the young JohnWhelan an early whiff of other, more cosmopolitan worlds. Taking his lead at first from his father, he revelled in stirring tales of Empire, read G.A. Henty and R.M. Ballantyne and went as often as free tickets allowed to see Esmé Percy or Zena and Phyllis Dare at the Opera House. Then, at the age of fifteen, he happened to see (also at the Opera House) the Abbey Theatre players in Lennox Robinson's play, *The Patriot*, and for the first time awakened to the possibility that Irish lives and Irish experiences might form the stuff of literature in place of the gaudy romances to which he had hitherto given unswerving emotional allegiance. Soon he was to come into contact with the Cork writer, Daniel Corkery, whose house on the north side of the city became something of a refuge for the young man hungry for intellectual stimulation. In 1918, he entered University College, Cork, where he read English Language and Literature and began to take an interest in Irish politics. He joined the Irish Volunteers, became intensely nationalistic, began to learn the Irish language and take his holidays in the Gaeltacht, and took the decisive public step of changing his name from plain JohnWhelan to the Irish version of 'Sean O'Faolain'. He graduated from UCC in 1921 with an Honours BA in English. In the Civil War, he took the Republican side and was for a time Director of Propaganda for the IRA. He had his first experience as an editor with the journal *An Long*, to which he contributed also as a reviewer. He returned to the university in Cork and was awarded an MA in 1924 for a thesis on the Irish poet, Dáibhidh Ua Bruadair. He then taught for a time at the Christian Brothers' school in Ennis, Co. Clare, but returned to the university yet again, this time to take an MA in English and a Higher Diploma in Education in 1926. In the same year, he became Harkness Commonwealth Fellow at Harvard University, where he received an AM degree in 1929. He married his Cork sweetheart, Eileen Gould, in Boston in 1928. He taught subsequently at Boston College and at Strawberry Hill in Middlesex and brought out his first collection of stories, *Midsummer Night's Madness*, in 1932. It was promptly banned in Ireland. In spite of this, he returned to live permanently in Ireland and began to set about making a living by his pen. The Thirties saw him flourishing as short story writer, novelist, dramatist and biographer, with *A Nest of Simple Folk* (1933); *Constance Markievicz* (1934); *Bird Alone* (1936); *She Had to Do Something* (1937); *A Purse of Coppers* (1937); *King of the Beggars* (1938); *DeValera* (1939). In 1940, he published his third novel, *Come Back to Erin*, and embarked on his most famous public role as editor of the literary magazine, *The Bell*, a position he occupied until 1946, when Peadar O'Donnell succeeded him as editor. During the entire period of the Hitler war, *The Bell* opened its pages to a host of distinguished contributors from home and abroad and battled energetically against the censorship and the general intellectual obscurantism of the time. Although he abandoned the novel form (suppressing a novel entitled *Alien With a Passport*, which had been accepted by Jonathan Cape), he continued to work busily as biographer, short story writer, essayist and critic. He wrote travel books, lectured at various universities in the United States, and was honoured with a D.Litt. from Trinity College, Dublin, in 1959. Over the years he had become Ireland's most celebrated man of letters, the elder statesman of the Irish literary world. His short stories were published in three handsome volumes by Constable (1980, 1981 and 1982) and, most surprising of all, he made an unexpected return to the novel form, after a lapse of almost four decades, when he published his fourth novel, *And Again?*, in 1979.

BIRD ALONE (1936)

O'Faolain made his debut as a novelist, as did Kate O'Brien, with a lengthy saga or chronicle novel. *A Nest of Simple Folk* (1933) was published a year after his first collection of short stories, *Midsummer Night's Madness*, and has much in common with it stylistically. When he reviewed his own performance some quarter of a century later, at the time of the publication in 1957 of a selection of his 'Finest Stories', he noted with characteristic urbanity his early inclination towards a lush romanticism both of vocabulary and outlook. He charged himself, in retrospect, with being 'drowned in himself' and wryly admitted his early fondness for a vocabulary

> . . . full of romantic words, such as *dawn, dew, onwards, youth, world, adamant* or *dusk*; of metaphors and abstractions, of personalizations and sensations which belong to the author rather than to the characters.

He voiced his admiration for writers who could express themselves succinctly and instanced Hemingway as a case in point ('Hemingway is the real man') but acknowledged his own early tendency to expand and develop his ideas to an unnecessary extent:

> . . . the writer who luxuriates goes on with his first image or idea. His emotions and his thoughts dilate, the style dilates with them, and in the end he is trying to write a kind of verbal music to convey feelings that the mere sense of the words cannot give. He is chasing the inexpressible. He is interested mainly in his own devouring daemon.

There is a good deal of 'verbal music' in the first novel, as there is in the early short stories. It manifests itself particularly in the many extended descriptions of place with which *A Nest of Simple Folk* is studded, from its beginnings in rural Co. Limerick to its climax in the city of Cork. Again and again, the varying moods of the characters are related to their surroundings in leisurely descriptive passages evocative of the particular joy or sorrow which is then upon them. The writing is often pensive and slow and one cannot escape the suspicion, particularly in the closing section ('The City') that what we are being offered is O'Faolain's own fond memories of his native place. He delights in evoking for us the streets and quays of Cork, the ships in its busy harbour, the tall houses, the surrounding hills, the family picnics to nearby beauty spots, the whole bustling self-absorbed life of a provincial town which likes to fancy itself a city. The obvious contrast which inevitably suggests itself is with Corkery's *The Threshold of Quiet*, a work which O'Faolain greatly admired. In comparison with *A Nest of Simple Folk*, Corkery's novel gives an impression of austerity and restraint in matters of description and, importantly, in the use of dialogue. Where the older writer seems to eschew quite deliberately both picturesqueness of place and of language, O'Faolain luxuriates in both. He is prodigal in his use of local idiom (which Corkery entirely avoids), sprinkling this first novel and later ones also with Cork slang. His early novelistic style is often more reminiscent of Dickens or Hardy (or, even, of Carleton) than of any more modern writers. He is weaving a vast fabric of Irish nineteenth-century life in loving detail and tracing his characters' gradual journey from rural to urban surroundings. Unlike Kate O'Brien who, in *Without My Cloak*, concentrates exclusively on the commercial and domestic doings of her fictional family and assiduously expunges from her narrative all traces of matters political, O'Faolain makes his lengthy first novel into an overtly political and historical work. It begins in the mid-nineteenth century and traces the life of Leo Foxe-Donnell, offspring of a match between a peasant farmer and a daughter of the gentry, who is brought up by a pair of aged aunts in their crumbling Big House and turned into a semi-educated half-sir without much in the way of property or ability. His destiny is decided by a chance visit to a meeting addressed by the Fenian leader, James Stephens, at which Leo is converted to Fenianism, anti-clericalism and an active involvement in revolutionary politics which soon earns him a lengthy gaol sentence. He continues a rebel throughout his life and, at the end, rushes off at the age of seventy-six to participate in the Easter Rising of 1916 in Dublin. The other main character is his grandson, Denis Hussey, who finally espouses his grandfather's republicanism in defiance of his policeman father's middle-class British respectability. This first novel establishes the patterns which are to recur in those which followed it. The setting for both *Bird Alone* and *Come Back to Erin* is once again Cork and both engage with the tensions set up by the opposition of a revolutionary republican outlook to respectable middle-class social conformity.

In *Bird Alone*, we once again encounter the charismatic grandfather figure, again an old Fenian who imposes his influence on his grandson, while the boy rejects his dreary, penny-pinching father who is made to seem the embodiment of joyless respectability. The autobiographical undertones are clear and have often been remarked. The second and third novels, like many of the early short stories, trace the development of a gradual disenchantment with republican idealism, as modern Ireland moves out of its period of military struggle against the British into the anti-climax of independence and the limp realities of the new Free State. The ultimate indignity for the inveterate republican of the third novel, Frank Hannafey, is to be offered, at the story's end, a post as a Warble-Fly Inspector in one of the government departments of the new state, a bathetic irony of an almost excessively comic kind. *Bird Alone*, however, is set not in the post-independence era but in the period of the fall of Parnell. This is the protracted reminiscence of one, Corney Crone who, at the beginning, is an old man looking back at the events of his boyhood and early manhood. His retrospections intertwine the turbulent political events of the period with the tragic story of his doomed love for his sweetheart, Elsie Sherlock. Corney is the 'bird alone' of the title, his life having turned him into a sad solitary who has abandoned all his inherited pieties and been rejected by his society. 'It was not that I could not believe in men, but that I could not believe in what men believed', he tells us at the end. While this novel, at one of its levels, recalls *A Nest of Simple Folk*, with the ardent Fenian of the first book finding a clear successor in the rumbustious grandfather of *Bird Alone*, it is equally clear that, in this second novel, O'Faolain was straining to draw his fiction away from historical preoccupations so that he might concentrate his attention on problems arising from intimate personal relationships. The backward pull of history is here being resisted and the work is striving to explore new places and the vital dilemmas of individuals. Accordingly, the tortured and tortuous love affair between Corney and Eileen achieves its doomed consummation not in their native city of Cork but in London, an excitingly cosmopolitan setting in which they make new friends and feel the stimulus of new sights and experiences. Throughout the book, there is an evident tension between Corney's deep affection for his own small city, with all its faults of gossipy mean-spiritedness, and a growing contempt for the repressive and puritanical nature of provincial society. When Corney has to leave Cork, he is torn by conflicting emotions about this beautiful but claustrophobic little place where he has grown up, fallen in love and come to grief:

> No longer now a city-under-the-sea, she was the Lilliput she had always been, where the carts trundled to the doorsteps on Saturdays and the cattle dropped their dung on the streets, and the churches were crowded to the doors on Sundays and Holidays. And it mattered nothing to me that she had nothing one would wish to look at – neither wide streets, nor great houses, nor buildings to catch the breath, nor memories of greatness; that she had no history; nor that she was merely a country town filled with half-rich and pauper-poor, and small merchants and petty tradesmen who like my own people fatted the priests, and kept the monks and nuns and starveling beggars alive and made those half-rich happy in their half-wealth.

Corney's ambivalence is, in fact, O'Faolain's also. He defined it amusingly, in the course of a Foreword to the selection of his 'Finest Stories', when he indulged in entertainingly ironic self-analysis and came to the conclusion that

> . . . when it comes to writing about people who, like the Irish of our day, combine beautiful, palpitating tea-rose souls with hard, coolly calculating heads, there does not seem to be any way at all of writing about them except satirically or angrily . . . the reader may recognise a few mildly tentative efforts in this direction in the last few stories in this book. They started out to be satirical; they mostly failed dismally to be satirical; largely, I presume – I observe it to my dismay and I confess it to my shame -- because I still have much too soft a corner for the old land. For all I know I may still be a besotted romantic. Some day I may manage to dislike my countrymen sufficiently to satirise them; but I gravely doubt it – curse them.

This openly confessed ambivalence of attitude on the writer's part proves to be a considerable strength in his comedy, imparting a delightful geniality to such short stories as 'Unholy Living and Half Dying' and 'In the Bosom of the Country' but it unfits him for the simpler severities of the tragic mode and robs his novel writing of the cutting edge of a Joyce. It is, indeed, Joyce, in particular the Joyce of *A Portrait of the Artist as a Young Man*, who most obviously looms behind *Bird Alone* as an influence and as a dangerous model. O'Faolain's Cork manifests the same cosily claustrophobic Catholicism as Joyce's Dublin. Life here, too, marches to the music of church bells and is surrounded by rituals, at once protective and dominant, of a guardian Church which offers either salvation on its own terms or damnation on any others. The desperate spiritual agony which Elsie Sherlock endures at the end finds its Joycean emotional counterpart in Stephen Dedalus's nightmare visions of hell after the Retreat sermon in *Portrait*. Stephen, at once attracted and repelled by conformity, anticipates Corney Crone, who begins as a believer but finally asserts: 'Not one single thing would I change: except that once, for a week, I was untrue to my sins.' Joycean echoes are everywhere in the novel. Corney's mother is, like Molly Bloom, a fine singer who

> . . . was always singing at charity concerts, and while her family were tearing wild at home, she would be in the wings with three priests around her, laughing and joking, or even joking with the other business-men who helped my miserable-faced father at these affairs.

Shades, also, of Mrs Kearney in the *Dubliners*' story, 'A Mother'. Clearest example of all in the way of Joycean influence is found in Chapter v of *Bird Alone*, where O'Faolain, in the novel's most ambitious set-piece, daringly offers a pastiche of the celebrated Christmas dinner scene from *A Portrait*.

This is built around the central figure of Corney's aunt, Virginia, his mother's sister who visits the family from London. She is a handsome and gracious woman who, at first, makes a favourable impression on Corney and all his relatives but is later revealed, shockingly, as a London prostitute. At the dinner party, however, she has not yet been exposed and, to begin with, she is able to queen it appropriately at her sister's table, pouring wine hospitably for the visiting men and charming the company generally. As in the famous Joycean scene, it is the dead Parnell who causes the diners to quarrel furiously. Foran, a solicitor, produces a series of maliciously ambiguous remarks about Parnell and his mistress, Kitty O'Shea, inviting Virginia to join in the hints and implications of impropriety which he tosses into the general conversation at table. Parnell is vigorously defended by Corney's grandfather and his friend, Arthur John Coppinger, while the visiting clergyman, Canon Whitley, tries in vain to smother this dangerous talk of politics and possible immorality. The scene, entertaining enough in its own right, never quite attains the crisp force of its great predecessor. It goes on too long and the combatants are not as clearly identified as they might be, so that one tends to lose track of the individuals involved. Also, O'Faolain breaks up the scene, allowing Corney's mother to separate the angry disputants in mid-quarrel by prevailing on the children to play cards in one room while the adults adjourn to the sitting-room. This deprives Corney, the narrator, of the opportunity to know what goes on in the next room, until there is a ring on the door-bell and Canon Whitley's driver arrives to take the Canon to the station. The driver appears to know about Virginia's London life and the scene rapidly deteriorates into vulgar personal abuse between the two of them, with Corney's mother in despair at the ruin of her party. O'Faolain further dissipates his effects by inserting a confusing scene at the end of the chapter, concerning the purchasing of some houses by the grandfather and a friend of his, a separate issue which blurs the argument over Parnell and weakens the impact of the revelations about the aunt.

There is a corresponding lack of clarity on the matter of Corney's abandoning of his religious faith. This is made to hinge on a supposed disenchantment consequent on the ruin of Parnell but this is hardly convincing since it is the grandfather, not Corney, who is an embittered Fenian. As narrator, Corney has sometimes had the task of presenting the old man's fierce republicanism in a richly comic light, as in the extended comic scene in Chapter III, where the grandfather refuses to comply with Catholic requirements for the burial of his Fenian friend, Arty Tinsley. As a result, when Corney is made to identify with the grandfather's bitter rejection of the Church, the effect is less than entirely convincing:

It was the end of our piety. All the bitterness of the miserable years after Parnell soured us both – made us full of hatred and contempt. Less and less often we went into the city for the faction fights and the tar-barrels and the speeches.

Corney's dual role in the novel, as narrator and chief participant, is not easy to control and this weakens somewhat the final moral conflict between Elsie's terror at her sin and Corney's adamant refusal to accept that their sexual union has been sinful. O'Faolain hardly succeeds in fusing convincingly the book's broad historical concerns and its more intimate personal dilemmas. Elsie's family, the Sherlocks, are introduced into the narrative in a somewhat arbitrary fashion and, later on, when the exigencies of the plot require the extension of the action to the seaside town of Youghal where the tragic denouement is to be enacted, O'Faolain has recourse to coincidental encounters of a boldly Hardy-esque kind. Corney strolls along the beach at Youghal and chances upon an English artist, Stella:

It was then I met Stella – how, is of small matter now: all I will say is that when we met I was in a very disturbed state of mind, and there is no reason why I should tell more. My first impression of her was that she was a very kind woman and we were soon talking.

Stella, thus casually encountered, represents the larger world outside Ireland. She chaffs Corney about his excessive seriousness, his idealism and his 'Search for the Absolute', telling him that he reminds her of Dante's people in Hell who 'lived wilfully in sadness'. His mind, she insists, is ' a core on core of prisons' and she cheerfully admonishes him to come with her to enjoy a ride on the roundabout at the local funfair, or the 'merries' as Cork-man Corney dubs it. Stella soon disappears from the story but her friend, Marion, remains to act as confidante for Elsie in her pregnancy and to provide a setting for the final tragic scene at the cottage in Youghal which she has shared with Stella. The powerful climax, with the frantic Elsie attempting suicide in the wintry sea in preference to confessing her predicament to her prudish family, is reminiscent of much that is memorable in nineteenth-century fiction. Lucetta, from *The Mayor of Casterbridge*, comes to mind, as does the shipwreck scene in *David Copperfield* or the knife-edge excitement of 'The Cliff without a Name' in *A Pair of Blue Eyes*.

A bitter and powerful irony is achieved by the contrast in the novel between Elsie's death without a priest and the grandfather's eventual reconciliation with the Church which he has so long rejected and maligned. This is one of the most effective of the novel's tactics. Its implications, not laboured by O'Faolain, are surely considerable. The old rebel, Philip Crone, at the behest of his pious daughter-in-law, goes through a comical process of final repentance in which he manages to have the best of both worlds, here and hereafter. The tone of this section of the novel is reminiscent of the amused geniality remarked above and evident in such short stories as 'Unholy Living and Half Dying', stories in which lackadaisical Catholics make easy bargains with a tolerant God on the basis of a philosophy with the motto 'make me virtuous but not yet'. At Corney's final meeting with his dying grandfather, the old man gleefully claims to have 'codded' the priest into giving him his final absolution while he still clings to his Fenian principles:

> I went up to my grander, and I said, cheerfully:
> 'Well, grander, the old skillet is clean at last?' He was very weak, but he beckoned with the finger and I leaned to him.
> 'Clean as a whistle. There was only one thing I found hard. He asked me to forgive the clergy for not wanting Arty Tinsley, God rest him, to be buried in Christian ground. We had a terrible tussle over that but I said I forgave them.'
> 'That's right, grander,' I said, and patted his head.
> The finger beckoned.
> 'But, sure, you know, I don't forgive 'em. Nor never will. Only you have to cod them blokes of priests, you know, now and again.'
> His eyes closed and he smiled like a man who has, in his last years as in his early life, had the best of both worlds and knows it. At his request I handed him his beads and he fell asleep praying on them.

On the other hand, the wretched Elsie, who is Corney's victim (as Corney, in his turn, has been his grandfather's victim) is granted no such easy passage to the hereafter. In the final analysis, the novel implies a powerful condemnation of the Fenian grandfather's damaging influence on the young. We recall that, in Chapter v, Corney reminisced about the school chosen for him by his grandfather and saw through the old Fenian's motivation when it was too late:

> There was that school my grandfather sent me to. I thought I chose it for myself, for my father wanted me to go to the little gentlemen's school up the hill and I wanted this one because Christy Tinsley was there . . . For years I was grateful to my grander who took my side; but now I know the truth. If it was a place where the innocence of me was forced and pampered, he wanted it pampered only because he could feed on it. You don't believe that? Then why else did he send me there – an old lecher who had long since lost the Faith?

O'Faolain was to record his disenchantment with intransigent republican-ism (with 'the way in which the Rebel spends and wastes himself') in many of his writings but the point can scarcely ever have been made as forcefully as it is in this novel.

Elsie's final undoing is made possible only by the repressive mores of the society which has produced her and Corny's scathing contempt for the 'Lilliputian' nature of his native Cork is, in some sense, an echo of O'Faolain's broad conviction that the emergent society of the Irish Free State was too thinly composed to act as a satisfactory subject for a novelist. His own fate as a novelist was shaped by his un-Joycean decision to remain within that thinly composed society and write from within it. The decision was a conscious one. O'Faolain rejected the Joycean formula of 'silence, exile and cunning', contending that Joyce had paid too high a price for his outright rejection of his Irish heritage. Joyce, according to O'Faolain, 'rejected his own fated field of life wherein he might have read the signatures of mortal things and made them tolerable, intelligible, meaningful'. That judgement on Joyce, voiced in *The Vanishing Hero* (1956) over thirty years after the publication of *Ulysses*, says much about O'Faolain's reading of that greatest of all Irish novels and much also about his own chosen entanglement in the nets of his native place. Sharing Joyce's revulsion from the constraints imposed by Ireland on the artist, O'Faolain, nevertheless, like several of the figures in his third novel, 'came back to Erin' and, like them, found it a small, mean-minded place, forgetful of its heroic past and of its recent revolutionary ardour. If one feels a certain regret that he chose to remain and adopt the role of critical gadfly to his infuriating place and people instead of shaking the dust of Ireland from his feet and attempting some sort of conclusive statement as a permanent outsider, his views on Joyce may suggest that his own novelistic technique, purposefully anti-modernist as it was, might not have given him access to the stylistically kaleidoscopic universe of Bloom and Stephen, that universe in which Joyce simultaneously aggrandizes and flays the Lilliputian Irish world. The Luciferean decision that it is better to reign in hell than serve in heaven does not suit all tastes or all talents.

SELECTED BIBLIOGRAPHY

RELATED WORKS

A Nest of Simple Folk, London, 1933.
Come Back to Erin, New York, 1940.

AUTOBIOGRAPHY

Vive Moi, London, 1965.

CRITICAL STUDIES

Maurice Harmon, *Sean O'Faolain: A Critical Introduction,* Indiana, 1966 (revised & updated edition, Dublin, 1984).

CRITICAL ARTICLES

Donat O'Donnell, 'The Parnellism of Sean O'Faolain', *Maria Cross*, London, 1954, 95–114.

Grattan Freyer, 'Change Naturally: The Fiction of O'Flaherty, O'Faolain, McGahern', *Eire-Ireland*, XVIII, 1 (Spring 1983), 138–145.

XIV

Samuel Beckett (1906 – 1989)

MURPHY

'Friday, the thirteenth' is traditionally regarded in Ireland as a day of ill-omen, a day on which, for example, no sensible farmer would take his beasts to market or begin to plough a field. In the light of this, one feels, Samuel Beckett must have derived a certain amount of sardonic amusement from his own natal day, for not only was it Friday, 13 April but it was also Good Friday of 1906. If the Dublin of the day had possessed, as Beckett's first novel does, 'a swami who cast excellent nativities for sixpence', one wonders what 'little bull of incommunication' he might have produced for the new arrival. Prospects might well have seemed bright enough, if one ignored the planets and attended only to social considerations. Samuel was the second son of William and Mary Roe Beckett and the family home was 'Cooldrinagh' in the well-to-do Dublin suburb of Foxrock. William Beckett was a quantity surveyor who had married a nurse and the Becketts were Protestants of Huguenot stock. Samuel went to kindergarten and preparatory school in Dublin and was a boarder at Portora Royal School in Enniskillen from 1920 to 1923. He began to learn French while at prep school and demonstrated his considerable intellectual and academic ability from an early age, excelling particularly in French, Classics and English and combining his scholarly abilities with a talent for athletic activity. He enjoyed boxing and distance swimming but his favourite sports were rugby and cricket. Between 1923 and 1927 he read for a degree in Modern Languages (French and Italian) at Trinity College, Dublin, got the best First of his year and was awarded the Large Gold Medal in Modern Literature in 1927. He was briefly a teacher at Campbell College in Belfast, a city which he dubbed 'a terrible place full of bigotry' and then, late in 1928, he went to teach at the École Normale Supérieure in Paris. He met James Joyce and, in 1929, contributed an essay to the anthology, *Our Exagmination Round His Factification for Incamination of Work in Progress*. His poem, 'Whoroscope', won the £10 prize in a poetry competititon organised by Nancy Cunard and he also completed a critical study of Proust.

In the summer of 1930, Beckett returned to Dublin to take up a post as a Lecturer in French at Trinity but he resigned this post after a few terms and went back to France at Easter, 1932. He lived for brief periods in Kassel, Paris, London and Dublin and worked on but did not complete a first novel, *Dream of Fair to Middling Women*. Some of the material from this went into his first collection of short stories, *More Pricks than Kicks*, which was published in 1933 and sold very poorly. Beckett spent two rather dreary years in London between 1933 and 1935, the period from which much of the bleak landscape of *Murphy* derives. It was at this time that Beckett worked as an orderly at a hospital for the mentally ill where one of his friends was a doctor. His consuming sympathy for the sick was reinforced by the pain he felt at the deaths of various members of his own family, including his father who died of a heart attack in 1933. During late 1935 and much of 1936, Beckett travelled widely in Germany. In 1937, he settled in Paris, taking up his residence in a seventh-floor flat at 6, rue des Favorites, which he retained until 1961. *Murphy* was published in London in 1938 and when war broke out the following year Beckett, who was then visiting his mother in Dublin, returned to Paris and, by 1940, was a member of a Resistance group engaged in gathering information on German troop movements. The group was betrayed to the Gestapo in 1942 and Beckett fled to Roussillon, a village in the Vaucluse, where he remained for two years, during which time he wrote his second novel, *Watt*, which remained unpublished until 1953. He returned to his old flat in Paris after the war. There followed half a dozen years of seclusion during which many of the works he submitted to publishers were rejected. In 1951, however, *Molloy* was published in Paris and *Malone Meurt* appeared later in the same year. The third volume of the famous trilogy, *L'Innomable*, came out in 1953 but, earlier that same year, had appeared the work which was to win Beckett world-wide fame, his celebrated play, *En Attendant Godot*. This most discussed of all modern plays had its world premiere at the Théâtre de Babylone in Paris early in 1953. The work transformed Beckett from a lonely, idiosyncratic writer long inured to failure into a hugely successful literary giant who had now to exert all his talent for privacy to escape the pestering attentions of press interviewers.

Public honours were showered upon him: an honorary degree from his old university in 1959; the Prix Formentor in 1961; the Nobel Prize for Literature in 1969. As he grew older his writings became ever more dessicated and, more and more, Beckett concerned himself with the minutiae of play production, often working with favourite players such as Billie Whitelaw and the late Jack MacGowran and Patrick Magee. Beckett's *Collected Poems in English and French* appeared as recently as 1977. The fortunate few who were privileged to get close to this austere and private man testify to his great natural courtesy and unfailing generosity.

MURPHY (1938)

Beckett's reputation is now so considerable that one has to make an effort to credit his earlier obscurity. Reviewing his career before the outbreak of the Hitler war, one might have been excused for classifying him as an able academic with a dilettante's interest in the production of the occasional poem or short story. His essay, 'Dante . . . Bruno, Vico . . . Joyce', appeared in 1929, his study of Proust in 1931, and both could have been seen as the productions of a talented academic critic equipping himself for a chair at one of the universities. He put aside his first attempt at a novel and subsequently fed some of the discarded material into his first collection of short stories, *More Pricks Than Kicks* (1934). The poems, *Echo's Bones and Other Precipitates*, came out in 1935 and for the next few years he published little apart from an occasional poem or short story. *Murphy*, appearing in the year before Europe plunged into chaos, evoked little critical interest or enthusiasm. Iris Murdoch, herself of Anglo-Irish origin, read it with obvious pleasure and profit. Her first novel, *Under the Net* (1954), was to show the influence of Beckett's comedy. Its hero, Jake Donaghue, a peripatetic like Murphy, is gifted with the curious 'surgical' charisma which makes Beckett's hero such a focus of interest to all his friends and, like Murphy, Jake goes to work in a hospital at the climax of the novel. *Under the Net*, however, while sharing *Murphy's* tendency to philosophise rather obviously, avoids the corrosive mordancy which distinguishes the earlier novel and is, in general, a much more cheerful work. Kate O'Brien, herself an Irish writer of a very different kind from Beckett, was another honourable exception to the general pattern of neglect. Her review of *Murphy* in the *Spectator* of 25 March 1938 was both warmly enthusiastic and remarkably accurate in its astute responses to the book's peculiar nature. The entire review is worth reading for its intelligent communication of the novel's distinctive flavour and for the sensible advice it offers on how it should be approached. Kate O'Brien went to the heart of the matter by dubbing *Murphy* 'a sweeping bold record of an adventure in the soul' and went on:

> It is erudite, allusive, brilliant, impudent and rude. Rabelais, Sterne and Joyce – the last above all – stir in its echoes, but Mr Beckett, though moved again and again to a bright clear lyricism . . . is not like Joyce evocative of tragedy or hell. He is a magnificently learned sceptic, a joker overloaded with the scholarship of great jokes.

She further sensibly suggested that a first reading of *Murphy* should make no attempt to tease out the many references with which the work is packed but should rather 'sweep along, acknowledging points lost by lack of reference in oneself, but seeing even in darkness the skirts of his tantalising innuendo, and taking the whole contentedly, as a great draught of brilliant, idiosyncratic commentary, a most witty, wild and individualistic refreshment.' More profound analysis could, Kate O'Brien urged, be undertaken during later readings.

While Kate O'Brien, herself a talented exponent of social realism in the novel, might well have been expected to baulk at *Murphy* yet did not, one might have looked to Dylan Thomas, another Celtic word-smith, to have responded with delight to Beckett's verbal high-jinks. Paradoxically, however, Dylan Thomas was much less favourably disposed. He found *Murphy* to be 'difficult, serious and wrong'. His review is the self-conscious effort of a very young man and is itself badly cluttered with poor puns and clumsy attempts at humour. His reasons for finding the book 'wrong' are ironically close to Beckett's deliberate design:

> I call the book wrong for many reasons. It is not rightly what it should be, that is what Mr Beckett intended it to be: a story about the conflict between the inside and the outsides of certain curious people. It fails in its purpose because the minds and bodies of these characters are almost utterly without relation to each other.

Clearly, the Welsh poet had perceived the Cartesian dislocations of Beckett's figures but he made no attempt to pursue the matter further, simply protesting that these strange, fragmented people refused to comport themselves in the proper manner of the realistic novel for which Thomas was apparently searching. There are genuine perceptions in Thomas's piece on the novel but they are swamped by his unsuccessful attempts at wit. There were, however, no jokes, heavy-handed or otherwise, in the brief review accorded to the book by J.H. (Joseph Hone?) in *The Dublin Magazine* the following year. Quite simply, J.H. accused the book of being neither Irish nor a novel. The philosophical basis of the book might possibly interest, he said, 'the few who like to search out recondite ideas':

> Murphy, the chief character, hardly exists as a human being, so it would be difficult to label him with any nationality. The most feasible explanation is that Mr Beckett was trying to follow in the wake of, say, *Gulliver* or *Penguin Island*. And being modern he is casual and broken-winged compared with the soaring and classical coherence of the older works. The whole thing is a bizarre fantasy with a nasty twist about it that its self-evident cleverness and scholarship cannot redeem.

This reviewer also anticipated many subsequent commentators by finding Celia 'the one really human character in the book'. It is worth noting that, generally unsympathetic to the novel as he was, 'J.H.' nevertheless clearly responded to the mordant bleakness underlying Beckett's vision of Murphy's universe and sensed in the book a darkness which the surface brilliance ultimately failed to conceal.

Most readers of *Murphy* are bound to experience in some degree the sort of irritation which assailed the youthful Dylan Thomas when he wrote his early review. It would be a most unusual person who would fail to experience the troubling sense of dislocation to which Thomas adverts. Familiar links in the chain of causes and effects seem to be missing, characters seem to dash about pointlessly on frantic journeys which produce no positive results, almost as though Beckett had rewritten Stevenson's celebrated aphorism as 'it is better to travel hopelessly than to arrive'. Murphy himself, who appears to be the focus of impassioned though futile interest for all the other characters, remains unaware of the others' interest in him, with the sole exception of his brief involvement with Celia. Coming to terms with the novel requires coming to terms with Murphy himself, the only character in the book who 'is not a puppet' and, indeed, there might be something to be said for beginning one's reading of the novel with the sardonic authorial explanation of 'Murphy's mind' with which we are lengthily supplied in Chapter 6. Beckett himself, of course, would probably reply to this impertinent suggestion that had he wished the reader to behave in this outrageous manner he would have made this his opening chapter! Perhaps one might settle for the suggestion that the purposeful reader might begin his *second* reading of the novel with Chapter 6. This is the point where Beckett signals to us his clear realisation that his principal character, of his very nature, must prove an uneasy inhabitant of the traditional novel form. One's responses to Beckett's unremittingly sardonic authorial tone in Chapter 6 will determine whether one is prepared to heed his astringent guidance there or, alternatively, commit oneself to the view that Beckett's wry acknowledgement of the chapter's regrettable necessity is, in itself, a clear admission of his failure to contain his principal character within a viable fictional structure which could dispense with such 'bulletins'. The opening paragraph of the chapter in question is one of the most nervously contrived and one of the most vital in the entire novel. It is at once engagingly apologetic and firmly assertive:

It is most unfortunate, but the point of this story has been reached where a justification of the expression 'Murphy's mind' has to be attempted. Happily we need not concern ourselves with this apparatus as it really was – that would be an extravagance and an impertinence – but solely with what it felt and pictured itself to be. Murphy's mind is after all the gravamen of these informations. A short section to itself at this stage will relieve us from the necessity of apologizing for it further.

Two points at least are worth remarking about this authorial intrusion. Beckett begins with a courteous gesture towards traditional expectations by admitting that it is 'unfortunate' that he must come between us and the progress of the fiction at this point. He is telling what he refers to simply as a 'story' but he is creatively concerned lest Murphy's concept of his mind should interfere with our understanding of the story. The essential point here is that Beckett is at pains to make clear that he will not perpetrate the 'impertinence' of undertaking to explain to us what Murphy's mind really was. After all, the story itself will presumably reveal that to us. What requires to be painfully explained to us just now is what Murphy himself *thought* his mind to be. In other words, it is clearly implied that Murphy's theory of his own mind will not be matched by his practice in the story. Murphy's theory of his mind, we are being warned, will not work out in this story. In the event, of course, it does not. Murphy is self-deceived from the very first lines of the novel, in which he is shown, Hamlet-like, sitting carefully out of the sun 'as though he were free'. He is not free, of course. His attempts to implement his theory of mind inevitably founder in ludicrous disaster. Strapped naked into his rocking-chair at the very beginning, he can only topple over helplessly and is saved from early extinction only by the arrival of Celia. His assumptions about little Mr Endon, later in the story, prove to be equally mistaken and only serve to produce chaos in the Magdalen Mental Mercyseat. His delighted flight to his garret at the end culminates in his fortuitous destruction. The novel is constantly at pains to demonstrate the inaccuracy of Murphy's theory of mind, or at any rate its inappropriateness to the world in which he is required to function. What holds him in that world is his desire for Celia and her 'music'. In Chapter 3, Murphy himself announces to Celia the inevitability of his own destruction:

> 'What have I now? he said. 'I distinguish. You, my body and my mind.' He paused for this monstrous proposition to be granted. Celia did not hesitate, she might never have occasion to grant him anything again. 'In the mercantile gehenna,' he said, 'to which your words invite me, one of these will go, or two, or all. If you, then you only; if my body, then you also; if my mind, then all.'

Murphy will be but briefly detained in the 'mercantile gehenna' to which Celia invites him. His carnal desires have been accurately placed as early as Chapter 1, where we are told that 'the part of him that he hated craved for Celia, the part that he loved shrivelled up at the thought of her'. A special pathos attaches to Murphy as he endeavours to escape the flux of circumstance, just as a similar poignancy emanates from Celia as she is abandoned in it, entirely alone. Each of them, hopelessly separated as they are, possesses a dignity denied to all others in the story. Their brief encounter, presented through brilliantly comic exchanges which serve marvellously to heighten their separate kinds of pain, is the centre of the story. The minor characters all riccochet madly around in the 'commercial gehenna' of the pointless universe which Murphy's mind is so anxious to eschew. Celia will disappear utterly from Beckett's fiction as he progresses rapidly via *Watt* to the inevitable solipsism of the moribund narrators of the trilogy. It is one of Beckett's most signal triumphs that he can take one of the most absurd clichés of romantic fiction, the whore with a heart of gold, and turn her into a painfully moving evocation of human loneliness.

Murphy himself derives from the Dantean hero of Beckett's earlier work, the short stories of *More Pricks Than Kicks*. Belacqua, a character in Dante's *Purgatorio*, was required to spend in purgatorial expiation of his sins an amount of time equivalent to that which he had squandered upon earth. He is, thus, the embodiment of indolence and, in the sense that he seems to imply ultimate salvation achieved only after the maximum possible delay, he constitutes a highly appropriate figure for the embodiment of Beckett's moral cliff-hanging. Murphy is made to dub one of the stages in his dream of total freedom 'the Belacqua bliss'. Appropriately, this stage is conceived of by Murphy as that of the 'half light', midway between the two other stages of light and dark:

> In the second were the forms without parallel. Here the pleasure was contemplation. This system had no other mode in which to be out of joint and therefore did not need to be put right in this. Here was the Belacqua bliss and others scarcely less precise.

Eugene Webb suggests that there is a progressive moderation of the narrator's tone towards the protagonists in Beckett's novels. He argues that, while Belacqua is given fairly rough handling by the narrator in *More Pricks than Kicks* where he is dubbed 'an impossible person' and shown to be selfish and mendacious, Murphy, on the other hand, is treated more ambivalently. While it is true that he is the only one in the novel who does not 'whinge', he could scarcely be said to fare much better than Belacqua in the end. The authorial process which Webb is identifying is, in fact, the gradual elimination from the fiction of the intrusive narrator altogether. In *Belacqua and the Lobster*, the opening story of *More Pricks Than Kicks*, the narrator enters at the climax of the story to deflate Belacqua's self-deception concerning the hideous cruelty of the lobster's death. When Belacqua consoles himself and excuses his greed with the thought 'Well, it's a quick death, God help us all', the narrator instantly contradicts this escapism with the flat concluding statement 'It is not'. This authorial presence, as we have seen, is most evident in *Murphy* in the crucial Chapter 6 but, as Beckett's fiction develops, he progresses towards an elimination of this commentator. The narrator in *Watt* is not made to be Watt's judge and, in the trilogy, the narrator is eliminated and the protagonists speak to us directly with the interpretative gloss submerged deep in the novels' intricate patterns of complex black humour.

Modern Irish fiction has displayed some fondness for Oblomov-like heroes of the Murphy type, though they may not all come to us trailing the threads of Cartesian or Geulincxean explication quite as obviously as Beckett's hero is made to do. The nameless hero of Flann O'Brien's *At Swim-Two-Birds* spends much of his time sleazily abed and even spawns surrogate figures of the same kind so that Trellis, one of his principal imaginings, also spends much of his time between the sheets. Young Mahoney, hero of John McGahern's *The Dark*, though not an addict of the bed, seems in the end to arrive at a Murphy-like stasis in which he abandons the Herculean strivings of his youth in favour of a dark philosophy of accommodation to quotidian reality on the basis of some sort of stoical indifference to worldly success. McGahern's deadly seriousness, however, does not permit him the sardonic ironies in which Beckett's figures bandage their unavoidable wounds. Where the Beckettian hero purposefully exiles himself from the world of accident, the McGahern protagonist is prepared to involve himself in it, convinced of the pointlessness of all worldly strivings but resigned to going along for the moment with the necessity to survive at some level in the 'commercial gehenna'.

Murphy is, in fact, a Cartesian or Geulincxean hero, but the world in which Beckett places him is not one in which such a figure can find a resting-place, unless it be a lasting resting-place among the spits and sawdust of a bar-room floor. The world of *Murphy* is no kinder to Cartesians than it is to the rest of us. It is a sort of reach-me-down version of the world of Jacobean drama, full of self-seeking, vicious characters in restless pursuit of each other, a world of hungry lusts and perverted grotesques, a mad world indeed, my masters. The whirligig of unsatisfied human lust is comically presented to us early on in the hilarious exchanges between Murphy and Neary, from whom Murphy has failed to learn any skill which might help him to control his 'Petroushka' heart:

> Of such was Neary's love for Miss Dwyer, who loved a Flight-Lieutenant Elliman, who loved a Miss Farren of Ringaskiddy, who loved a Father Fitt of Ballinaclashet, who in all sincerity was bound to acknowledge a certain

vocation for a Mrs. West of Passage, who loved Neary.

Murphy's need of Celia's 'music' will briefly involve him with this endless and wearying cycle of desire but what all the others in the book admire most about him is his 'surgical' quality, his ability to detach himself from the tumult of event which is their natural environment. Only Celia lacks the others' egocentricity and, instead of persuading Murphy to her own way of thinking, she herself becomes a sort of apprentice Murphy, experimenting with his rocking-chair and resigned to losing her strange swain. All the others are self-seeking and nasty in various ways. Miss Carridge, she of the dreadful body-odour, is a hypocrite whose charity 'stopped at nothing short of alms'. Murphy's pursuers, who group themselves around Neary, exude a special brand of selfish nastiness. Neary himself, the appropriately named Needle Wylie, Miss Counihan, Cooper, the revolting Ticklepenny, all these are in their various ways hell-bent on pursuing their limited personal ends. They are all treated to the narrator's special brand of scathingly learned obliquity and one of the novel's major triumphs consists in its comically caustic revelation of the futility of egoism, even if it never descends to the vulgarity of optimism by any suggestion of genuine mutuality. The closest it comes to that is Celia's moving reflection on her lost lover, 'I was a piece out of him that he could not go on without'. Typically, the pathos even of that lonely claim is undercut by our awareness of the real circumstances of Murphy's demise. In general, even the most enthusiastic of Beckett critics tend to find his first novel, in comparison with the later trilogy, a cluttered affair, over-burdened with learned humour, ponderous puns and verbal extravagances of all kinds. Genuine pleasure in the effects achieved seems often to be mingled with an attendant conviction of authorial excess. Such responses are entirely valid, since *Murphy* is, clearly, too much of a good thing altogether. It outrageously gluts our quantum of wantum. Yet, in the spaces between the work's anti-novel dimension and the relentlessly ebullient jesting, Beckett achieves moments of poignancy which remain in the memory. All the same, it is clear that he would soon decide to escape from the Hibernian logorrhoea of *More Pricks than Kicks* and *Murphy*. In doing so, he would renounce all connection with his gabby Anglo-Irish forebears from William Carleton to Samuel Lover, from Somerville and Ross to John Millington Synge. In an article on 'Recent Irish Poetry' in *The Bookman* for August 1934, he had declared his reservations about the 'antiquarians' of the Irish Literary Revival and was to find the fellowship of writers like Denis Devlin, Brian Coffey and Thomas McGreevy more congenial than that of Stephens or Clarke. Wylie calls Murphy 'the ruins of the ruins of a broth of a boy' and Beckett had no intention of continuing to act as a sort of literary jaunting-car jarvey for such relics of oul' dacency.

His impulse takes him away from the Irish past and its customary literary modes to a European modernism and the stern linguistic disciplines of an adopted second language in which he would find it easier 'to write without a style'. The style which must be discarded was the florid, top-heavy jocosity of *Murphy*. Like Stephen Dedalus, Beckett was sensitively aware of the hazards of the English of Ireland but, where Joyce solved his problems by embracing a multiplicity of languages, Beckett took refuge in an alternative tongue. 'The more Joyce knew the more he could', he said, distinguishing between his idol's expansive genius and his own reductive tendencies. Soon, the sardonic authorial commentary of *Murphy* would give way to the solipsistic reflections of a Molloy or a Malone, the streets of Dublin and London fade out into the understated landscapes of the trilogy. *Murphy* is at once Beckett's derisive salute and decisive farewell to an overworked and outworn tradition of Anglo-Irish literature.

Like Joyce, Beckett has been the subject of quite exhaustive critical attention and, in recent years, much of this has been applied to the fiction, in contrast to an earlier critical emphasis on the plays. The bibliography of Beckett studies grows space and *Murphy* has not been neglected. Sighle Kennedy devoted an entire book to tracing in minute detail the work's astrological and astronomical systems; Samuel Mintz has produced a detailed examination of its Cartesian allusions; David Hesla offers a minute exploration of the novel's range of philosophical references. In the presence of the inevitable spate of learned explication, much of it of interest, it is something of a comfort to find a critic who himself performs in an impressively learned manner, ultimately reaching much the same sort of sensible conclusion as that voiced by Kate O'Brien in her early review of the novel. Hugh Culik, who entertainingly probes the medical detail of the book, advises:

> We are asked to approach the novel in terms of its technique, rather than to translate it into philosophy, theology, field theory, or any other extraliterary mode. He forces us to accept the integrity of literature as literature, and not as something else. Beckett's novel represents a complex and self-conscious form of direct expression that suggests the direction his mature fiction later takes.

SELECTED BIBLIOGRAPHY

RELATED WORKS

Watt, Paris, 1953 (written 1941-42).
Molloy, Paris, 1951. English translation, Paris, 1955.

Malone Meurt, Paris, 1951. English translation, *Malone Dies*, New York, 1956.

L'Innomable, Paris, 1953. English translation, *The Unnamable*, New York, 1958. (The trilogy, *Molloy, Malone Dies* and *The Unnamable* was published in a single volume in London in 1959.)

BIOGRAPHY

Deirdre Bair, *Samuel Beckett: A Biography*, London, 1978.

CRITICAL STUDIES

Richard Coe, *Beckett,* Edinburgh & London, 1978.
John Fletcher, *The Novels of Samuel Beckett,* London, 1964.
Hugh Kenner, *Samuel Beckett: A Critical Study,* London, 1965.
Francis Doherty, *Samuel Beckett,* London, 1971.
David H. Hesla, *The Shape of Chaos*, Minneapolis, 1971.
Sighle Kennedy, *Murphy's Bed*, Lewisburg, 1971.
A. Alvarez, *Beckett*, London, 1974.
John Pilling, *Samuel Beckett*, London, 1976.
Eric P. Levy, *Beckett and the Voice of Species*, Dublin, 1980.

CRITICAL ARTICLES

Ross Chambers, 'Beckett and the Padded Cell', *Meanjin Quarterly,* 21 (1962), 451-468.
Morse Mitchell, 'The Contemplative Life According to Samuel Beckett', *Hudson Review*, 15 (Winter 1962-63), 512-524.
Richard Coe, 'God and Samuel Beckett', *Meanjin Quarterly*, 24 (1965), 65-86.
Sighle Kennedy, 'The Devil and Holy Water – Samuel Beckett's *Murphy* and Flann O'Brien's *At Swim-Two-Birds'*, *Modern Irish Literature* (ed. R. J. Porter & J. D. Brophy), Boston, 1972, 251-260.
J.C.C. Mays, 'Mythologized Presences: *Murphy* in its Time', *Myth and Reality in Irish Literature* (ed. J. Ronsley), Waterloo, 1977, 197-218.
Hugh Culik, 'Mindful of the Body: Medical Allusions in Beckett's *Murphy'*, *Eire-Ireland*, XIV, 1 (Spring 1979), 84-101.
Hugh Kenner, *A Reader's Guide to Samuel Beckett*, London, 1980, 57-71.

XV

Flann O'Brien (1911-1966)

AT SWIM–TWO-BIRDS

As Anne Clissmann indicates in her sympathetic and valuably comprehensive study of the writer, he was a man who worked under numerous pseudonyms and constantly frustrated the activities of naïve interviewers and literal-minded biographers. It may, therefore, be useful to sort out some at least of the potentially confusing proliferation of identities. The family name was Ó'Nualláin and its English equivalent either O'Nolan or, more simply, Nolan. The writer's correct name in its Irish form is, accordingly, Brian Ó'Nualláin and, in English, this could be represented as either Brian O'Nolan or Brian Nolan. When he wrote *At Swim-Two-Birds*, he did so as 'Flann O'Brien', a pseudonym which he had first adopted while conducting a controversial exchange of letters with Frank O'Connor and Sean O'Faolain in the *Irish Times* early in the year of the novel's publication. It seems that he himself came to dislike this particular pseudonym and wanted to publish his first novel under the name of 'John Hackett'. Mercifully, Longmans refused to allow this. For his journalistic work in the *Irish Times* he assumed the alias of 'Myles na gCopaleen', a close approximation to the correct Irish form of that name – this was later simplified to 'Myles na Gopaleen'. He borrowed this name from a character in Gerald Griffin's novel, *The Collegians* (1829). It means 'Myles of the Ponies' and its original bearer is a sort of Arcadian mountaineer and horseman who is given affectionately comic treatment in Griffin's novel. It is conceivable that O'Nolan may have been attracted to the character because, when he first appears in the novel, he is depicted as a honey-tongued cajoler who succeeds in humouring a group of gentry into granting him a favour. The original Myles is a fast and skilful talker who puts his particular brand of blarney to excellent practical use – the link with his twentieth-century alter-ego seems clear enough. Anne Clissmann and others list a spate of other names which the writer assumed at various stages of his career, some of them adopted during his undergraduate days at UCD, but for ordinary purposes it suffices to know that his real name was Brian Nolan, his novelistic alias Flann O'Brien and his journalistic persona Myles na Gopaleen.

He was born at Strabane in Co. Tyrone in 1911, the third son of an officer of Customs and Excise, Michael Victor O'Nolan. The father's work involved frequent transfers and soon after Brian's birth the family moved for a short time to Glasgow. They moved again shortly afterwards and at the time of the Easter Rising of 1916 were living in the Dublin suburb of Inchicore. When the father was established in his post, he was assigned to the district of Tullamore and the family lived in the town of Tullamore until 1923, when promotion resulted in yet another move back to Dublin. Brian's older brother, Ciarán, records in his memoir of their youth, *Óige an Dearthár* (1973), the odd fact that none of the boys attended any school until the family settled in Dublin in 1923, by which time Brian was already twelve years old. From Ciarán's account of the matter, however, they do not seem to have felt at any educational disadvantage as a result. The father and mother were both lively-minded and highly intelligent people. The house was full of books of all kinds and the father, a long-time devotee of the Irish language movement, had seen to it that his children were fully bilingual. The boys at first attended the Christian Brothers' school at Synge Street and remained there until the family went to live in the more fashionable suburb of Blackrock in 1927. At that point, the boys transferred to the rather more easy-going Blackrock College. The father was appointed a Revenue Commissioner in 1925 and remained in this very senior and well-paid post, stationed in Dublin Castle, until his death from a coronary attack at the age of sixty-two in 1937. Brian left school in 1929 and enrolled at University College, Dublin, where he graduated as a BA with second-class honours in German, English and Irish in 1932. In the following year he won a travelling scholarship which enabled him to study at the University of Cologne during the first six months of 1934. He was awarded the MA degree in 1935 for a thesis on modern Irish poetry. He had begun to write for a student magazine, *Comhthrom Féinne*, while he was at the university.

On leaving university, he entered the Civil Service in 1935 and began work in the Department of Local Government. He remained in this Department until he retired from his post in 1953. He began work on his celebrated first novel in 1935 and completed it in 1937. It was published by Longmans in 1939. *The Third Policeman*, completed in 1940, failed to find a publisher, to O'Nolan's great disappointment, but his novel in the Irish language, *An Béal Bocht*, appeared in 1941 and met with general acclaim from those competent to read it, a highly appreciative but necessarily limited audience. At the invitation of R. M. Smyllie, the Falstaffian editor of the *Irish Times*, O'Nolan began to contribute a regular column to that newspaper. *Cruiskeen Lawn* (originally the title of a rollicking Irish drinking song, meaning, literally, 'Little Full Jug') began in bilingual form and then appeared in the Irish language mainly until the end of 1941. In 1942 it alternated between

English and Irish, day by day. Later the column was mainly in English. It was to endure for more than twenty years and enjoyed huge popularity among the newspaper's readers. A play, *Faustus Kelly*, enjoyed a modest success in 1943. Brian O'Nolan married a fellow civil servant in 1948. After his premature retirement on pension from the Civil Service in 1953, he seems to have been hard pressed for money at times and tried unsuccessfully for various university and other appointments. In 1960, however, a reissue of *At Swim-Two-Birds* by McGibbon & Kee brought him into notice once again. The book sold well and the author was sufficiently encouraged to embark on novel writing once more. *The Hard Life* appeared in 1961. During his later years, O'Nolan was dogged by constant ill-health but he drew on the unpublished novel, *The Third Policeman*, for material for his last work of fiction, *The Dalkey Archive*, which came out in 1964. It seems, surprisingly, to have been his own favourite among his works. He did a great deal of writing for television in his later years, working for the newly established studios of Telefís Éireann. He died of cancer on 1 April 1966 and was buried in his parents' grave at Deans Grange, outside Dublin.

AT SWIM-TWO-BIRDS (1939)

For a first novel completed while its author was still in his twenties *At Swim-Two-Birds* represents an amazing achievement, an astonishing virtuoso performance which, sadly, he was never again to equal during a curiously sporadic career. The book appeared in 1939, a year in which Europe was turning its thoughts to somewhat grimmer matters. Anne Clissmann records that on its first appearance the novel knocked Margaret Mitchell's celebrated *Gone With the Wind* off the top of the Dublin best-seller lists for one heady week in April but, since she goes on to remark that O'Brien's novel sold fewer than two hundred and fifty copies in all, its brief stay at the top of the best-seller lists seems pretty meaningless. In fact, the novel was treated coolly by some uncomprehending reviewers and was largely disregarded, rapidly becoming a mere coterie taste and remaining so until its re-issue in 1960. It was commended by the American writer, William Saroyan, and also by Graham Greene. O'Brien's friend, Niall Sheridan, presented a copy to James Joyce who seems to have enjoyed it greatly in spite of his ruined eye-sight. On the other hand, Ethel Mannin, to whom O'Brien sent a copy, pronounced it 'altogether too latter-day James Joycean' and clearly disliked the work. Commercially the book was a failure and a worse blow was soon to follow.

O'Brien completed his second novel, *The Third Policeman*, early in 1940 and offered it to Longmans who turned it down on the grounds that it was too fantastic. William Saroyan tried to find an American publisher for the novel, without success. O'Brien was deeply hurt by this second failure and put away the rejected manuscript, telling his friends that it had been lost. He was to use parts of it for his last novel, *The Dalkey Archive*, towards the end of his life but *The Third Policeman* itself did not appear in print until the year after O'Brien's death.

The failure of his first novel to win wide acceptance combined with the rejection of his second novel to trivialise and distort O'Brien's reputation from the beginning. Had his second novel come before the public when it was completed in 1940 its disturbingly sombre quality, unmistakeable in spite of large elements of hilarious incidental comedy, might have produced a more thoughtful re-assessment of the first novel. Instead, *The Third Policeman* remained unpublished throughout its author's lifetime and his next published work after *At Swim-Two-Birds* was to be the Irish-language novel, *An Béal Bocht*, which proved a great success but, necessarily, with a limited audience. Once again, though for different reasons this time, a powerful work of sombre comedy became a coterie taste and no comprehensive view of the author's remarkable talents emerged even after he had completed three notable works of fiction. His subsequent career as a full-time civil-servant and part-time writer makes unhappy reading in the accounts given of it by Anne Clissmann and his various friends and associates. His heavy involvement in journalistic work for the *Irish Times* served to justify the emerging public view of him as a sort of Dublin version of 'Beachcomber', the English comic journalist, J. B. Morton. The rapid popularity of the 'Cruiskeen Lawn' column meant that Myles na Gopaleen quickly took over from Flann O'Brien and one of the most impressive novelistic talents of the century was to be dissipated in an endless series of amusing but essentially trivial pieces for a daily paper. The strain of producing a stream of 'Cruiskeen Lawn' columns must surely have exerted a ruinously corrosive effect on O'Brien's great gifts as a writer of fiction. Irish literary history is choc-a-bloc with tales of the might-have-been but, in this case, the coruscating brilliance of the first novel surely entitles one to express profound regret for the eventual deterioration into quotidian journalistic ephemera. Some sense of what was lost is conveyed by the remarkably unstinting praise lavished on *At Swim-Two-Birds* by the English poet and novelist, John Wain, in his well-known *Encounter* piece, 'To Write for My Own Race' (1967). Reading this warmly generous paean of praise now, one is sardonically moved to recalling the old yarn about the man who, having just been informed of the Crucifixion, rushed into the streets and tried to start a persecution of the Jews! Wain's genuine but belated panegyric which appeared in the year after its subject's death, his sense of sharing with Philip Larkin and Kingsley Amis the excitement of a great literary 'discovery' nearly thirty years after the novel's original publication, reveals the English literary establishment of the Sixties paying homage to an unacknowledged master. Reading Wain's piece now, one is again pointlessly infuriated by O'Brien's early failure, by the refusal to publish the second novel and the subsequent trivialisation of a remarkable talent. It all helps, perhaps, to explain why the middle-aged O'Brien who appears in Anthony Cronin's literary memoir, *Dead As Doornails* (1976), seems such an unattractively embittered figure.

The writer himself seems to have developed a distaste for his exciting first novel quite early. Shortly after its publication he began to disparage it in a rather self-conscious fashion. 'It is a belly-laugh or high-class literary pretentious slush, depending on how you look at it', he told Ethel Mannin when sending her a copy of the novel in July, 1939. In 1960, in a letter to Brian Inglis, he called it 'juvenile nonsense'. At all times, the critics' recurring tendency to link the work to Joyce seems to have infuriated O'Brien. 'If I hear that word "Joyce" again, I will surely froth at the gob!' he wrote to Timothy O'Keefe in 1961, and he took a characteristically comic revenge on the Great Cham of Irish letters in *The Dalkey Archive* where he resurrects Joyce and installs him as a bartender or 'curate' in a pub near Dublin. 'I've had it in for that bugger for a long time', he told O'Keefe in 1962, when he was working on his last novel. In fact, of course, it was not a little disingenuous of O'Brien to object to critical commentary which linked his first novel to Joycean sources. The connections are quite obvious and have often been closely documented, notably by such critics as Bernard Benstock and Del Ivan Janik. The nameless student narrator of *At Swim-Two-Birds* clearly derives in some way or another from the Stephen Dedalus of *A Portrait of the Artist as a Young Man*. A student at the same university, he also spends much of his time in bed and treats his studies in a similarly cavalier manner, thereby infuriating the uncle with whom he resides, a figure who bears a resemblance to Simon Dedalus. Just as Stephen's father was, in his son's derisive description of him, 'something in a distillery', this narrator's uncle is 'holder of Guinness clerkship the third class'. Like Simon Dedalus, the uncle tends to voice doubts about the academic doings of the younger man, whose closest companions bear an obvious resemblance to Stephen's. Kelly recalls Davin and Lynch, while Brinsley is a sort of composite of Lynch and Cranly. When the narrator makes one of his rare visits to University College he is almost indistinguishable from Stephen Dedalus on similar forays in the *Portrait*:

It was my custom to go into the main hall of the College and stand with my back to one of the steam-heating devices, my faded overcoat open and my cold hostile eyes flitting about the faces that passed before me. The younger students were much in evidence, formless and ugly in adolescence; others were older, bore themselves with assurance and wore clothing of good quality.

This combines recollections of Stephen's visits to the university with his later, detached scrutiny of the naked bodies of his fellows as they swim at the Bull Wall. Like Stephen also, the narrator is made to discover lice on his person, and at the very end of the novel, in the *Conclusion of the book, ultimate*, O'Brien, via the mythical Professor Unternehmer, ascribes the dire misadventures of the fictional Trellis to 'an inverted sow neurosis wherein the farrow eat their dam', mockingly subverting one of the most celebrated of Joycean *dicta*. It may be that O'Brien read his Joyce a little too straight, if his pervasive mockery of Dedalus through the thoughts, actions and conversation of his own protagonist are indeed intended as a general debunking of that most famous of Irish fictional youths. Joyce himself had already undertaken the deflation of Stephen, whose adolescent vauntings are subtly undercut throughout the novel. Joyce pointed out to his American friend, Frank Budgen, how many readers of the *Portrait* failed to notice that the full title of the work was *A Portrait of the Artist as a Young Man*, emphasising, Budgen tell us, the last four words of that title. Thus, Joyce himself fired the first salvoes at his young prig-hero, something which O'Brien, in view of his calculated derision, would seem to have missed or at any rate chosen to ignore.

Quite apart from similarities between Stephen and O'Brien's narrator, *At Swim* is heavily indebted to Joyce in the comic gigantism of the Finn episodes which inevitably recall the controlling technique of the *Cyclops* episode of *Ulysses*, while O'Brien's huge, simple-minded Celtic hero owes much to Joyce's Citizen. In general, O'Brien's riotously funny mélange of different historical periods and many different kinds of literary style cannot but recall the variegated fictional world of Leopold Bloom. The quality in *Ulysses* which T.S. Eliot commended, its capacity for manipulating a continuous parallel between contemporaneity and antiquity, is clearly a formative influence on O'Brien's novel.

All that has so far been remarked by way of literary indebtedness, however, could, in the light of O'Brien's central strategy, be seen as incidental. However pervasive the Joycean influence on his successor's technique, *At Swim-Two-Birds* essentially constitutes a spirited rejection of the Joycean aesthetic in regard to the whole art of novel-writing as propounded by Stephen Dedalus in his celebrated definition of the literary work of art in Chapter v of the *Portrait*:

The artist, like the God of the creation, remains within or behind or beyond or above his handiwork, invisible, refined out of existence, indifferent, paring his fingernails.

Early in O'Brien's novel, his narrator outlines to Brinsley a brazen counter-theory designed to highlight the flagrant unreliability of the entire fictional process:

The novel, in the hands of an unscrupulous writer, could be despotic. In reply to an inquiry, it was explained that a satisfactory novel should be a self-evident sham to which the reader could regulate at will the degree of his credulity.

The narrator develops his ideas at length, providing in fact a theoretical basis for the very novel which O'Brien is engaged in writing and, when he has finished his explanation, his listener, Brinsley, fulfils his Cranly-like role by crudely pronouncing the elaborate thesis 'all my bum'. Similarly, Stephen's auditor had responded mockingly also, if a little less coarsely, when he had imagined the God of creation refining his own finger-nails out of existence as he detached himself from his handiwork in a divine determination to fulfil the Joycean aesthetic. O'Brien's novel, with its multiple beginnings and conclusions, its laminated plots and incessant authorial intrusions, embodies an hilariously entertaining mockery of any organic view of the novel as a world apart, self-justifying and entire unto itself between its first page and its last. The O'Brien formula deliberately flouts the view of the novel proposed by Henry James in *The Art of Fiction*, that 'a novel is a living thing, all one and continuous, like every other organism, and in proportion as it lives will be found . . . that in each of the parts there is something of each of the other parts.' Elsewhere in the same work, James had faulted Anthony Trollope for the very practice which O'Brien deliberately makes the principal strategy of his own novel:

Certain accomplished novelists have a habit of giving themselves away which must often bring tears to the eyes of people who take their fiction seriously. I was lately struck, in reading over the pages of Anthony Trollope, with his want of discretion in this particular. In a digression, a parenthesis or an aside, he concedes to the reader that he and his trusting friend are only 'making believe'. He admits that the events he narrates have not really happened, and that he can give his narrative any turn the reader may like best. Such a betrayal of a sacred office seems to me, I confess, a terrible crime . . . It implies that the novelist is less occupied in looking for the truth than the historian, and in doing so it deprives him at a stroke of all his standing-room.

O'Brien commits the Jamesian 'terrible crime' with enormous glee again and again and, ironically, thus acquires for his book a special kind of demented liberty in regard to plot and setting. As late as 1963, in a letter to Mark Hamilton, O'Brien was to describe *The Dalkey Archive* as 'an essay in extreme derision of literary attitudes and people' and the use of this phrase thus late in his life suggests the constancy of his determination as a mocker of high literary seriousness.

The book's various plots derive from and are controlled by the figure of the student-narrator, himself a fiction. He is engaged in writing a novel about one Dermot Trellis, also a writer. Trellis is the proprietor of the Red Swan Hotel and has spent the last twenty years mainly in bed, rising only to supervise the laundering of his linen by the slavey, Teresa. Trellis is, thus, a sort of congenial older version of the student-narrator himself, with a similar inclination to retire contemplatively between the sheets, in order to avoid the hurly-burly of outside events. Trellis's own literary purpose is to write an intensely moral book which will expose the dangers of vice of all kind but the central credo of *At Swim* is realised in the failure of Trellis's purpose which is brought about by the purposeful independence of the characters he creates. His chosen villain, Furriskey, who is intended as a ravisher of innocent maidens, falls in love with one of his supposed victims and embarks on a virtuous union with her. Since Trellis's creatures are free of his control only when Trellis is asleep, they have to live a double life, functioning as his puppets while he is awake and achieving freedom to go their own way only when he slumbers again. The limited nature of Trellis's control over his own creations further implements the novelistic programme outlined earlier. His characters manage to achieve at least a measure of that 'democracy' which has been advanced as the desirable state of all fictional characters and, having achieved it, they then turn on their creator, using Orlick, the bastard son fathered by Trellis on one of his own characters, as their instrument. O'Brien presumably adopted the name of Trellis's chief tormentor from Dickens's *Great Expectations*, in which the villainous Orlick murders Mrs Joe Gargery and almost murders the hero, Pip. The Dickensian Orlick, like his Irish namesake, is a savage tormentor, who delights in gloating over his victim. In the climactic scene in the Dickens novel, when Orlick has captured Pip and bound him fast he first vengefully informs him that he will kill him and then proceeds to rave savagely at the helpless Pip:

> 'Now, wolf,' said he, 'afore I kill you, like any other beast – which is what I mean to do and what I have tied you up for – I'll have a good look at you and a good goad at you. Oh, you enemy!'

O'Brien must have relished the lurid melodrama of this and his own Orlick does, indeed, have a good 'goad' at poor old Trellis, devising for him brutal torments which bring him, like Pip, to the very verge of destruction.

The main structural strategies of *At Swim* are clear enough. We are frequently returned to the student-narrator's mundane domestic surroundings and are regularly supplied with his helpful synopses of the action and this provides a fundamental kind of reassurance in the general fictional mêlée. Furthermore, within that mêlée itself, the various levels of plot constantly provide us with supportive parallels and correspondences. Thus, Trellis's torments are an evident echo of Sweeney's, and Trellis himself, as has been indicated earlier, is a version of the student-narrator. We are even given advance warning of Trellis's trial quite early in the book in the form of a 'Shorthand Note of a cross-examination of Mr Trellis at a later date . . . ' One of the more reassuring ploys is the student-narrator's comforting insistence on his own sense of confusion, which comically leads into the first of the 'synopses' of the action 'FOR THE BENEFIT OF NEW READERS' on the grounds that the narrator has himself mislaid 'four pages of unascertained content'. This consoling sense of general and unavoidable muddle is reinforced by Brinsley's subsequent insistence that he cannot tell the difference between Furriskey, Lamont and Shanahan, a trio who, according to Brinsley, 'might make one man between them'. Undoubtedly, the cheerful admission from within the fabric of the fictions themselves of the near-chaos of the entire enterprise is one of the cleverest of O'Brien's many contrivances. The book's cat's-cradle of cross-references and multiple openings and conclusions is signalled to us from the very first page and we are prepared for the demands the work will make on us by the early introduction of the important figure of Finn MacCool, whose highly diverting account of the doings of his companions of the Fianna are deliberately placed cheek by jowl with the drab quotidian activities of the student-narrator as he borrows small sums of money from his uncle and corresponds with dubious racing tipsters. From the beginning, the worlds of the ordinary and the extraordinary, of the contemporary and the antiquarian, of the factual and the mythological, are laminated and intermingled in the work's heady fabric.

O'Brien's friend and contemporary at UCD, Niall Sheridan (the 'Brinsley' of the novel), earned the undying gratitude of all subsequent readers by pruning the novel severely when O'Brien gave it to him for comment on its first completion. Anne Clissmann records that Sheridan cut the book by one third. Sheridan himself makes the more modest claim that he deleted a fifth. He applied his red pencil in particular to the Finn MacCool sections. Even then, only the most besotted of Flann-eurs would wish to claim that the novel in its present form is altogether devoid of tedium. Sheridan might well have taken his scissors to the lengthy exchanges between the Pooka MacPhellimey and the Good Fairy, an area of the novel in which O'Brien himself may be self-consciously voicing his own awareness of the excessive verbosity of it all when he has the Good Fairy assert that 'there is nothing so bad as the compression of fine talk that should last for six hours into one small hour'. The irony may be on the heavy side but it is amply justified.

It is in the very nature of parody that it pre-empts or obstructs criticism, since parody is itself a form of criticism, constituting as it does a commentary on whatever is being parodied. *At Swim-Two-Birds*, whatever else it may be, is certainly a manic medley of literary styles and periods. Self-consciousness is its very *raison d'etre*. Yet, in the end, we must still try to define a total impression made on us by the book and, for one reader at least, the mere awareness that this novel is a deliberate flurry of literary artifice ultimately solves very little. It may be the grim bleakness of the ending, or it may be the repellent brutalities inflicted on Trellis (as on Sweeney) but, as with other works by Flann O'Brien, the final impression left on us by *At Swim* is not just of literary high jinks. The book has about it a kind of spiritual gloom which may imply some serious imbalance in its parodic details. Perhaps the Sweeney episodes go on too long. Perhaps the cruelties practised on Trellis are over-stated, or it may be that Bernard Benstock has a point when he identifies in O'Brien 'a serious lack of commitment in any direction'. The fun is fast and furious and the author himself is heavily involved as self-proclaimed puppeteer. It is precisely because he is so involved that we feel entitled to look to him for guidance in the wild whirl of jest and contrivance. We get no such guidance and no final note of a decisive kind is struck. The book is wildly funny, often savagely cruel and, in the end, Stygian in its gloom, but it provides from within itself no containing judgement on all these ingredients. The novel's unsettling mixture of hilarity and gloom has been noted by many commentators. In a *Spectator* review of the reissue, in 1960, John Coleman identified as peculiarly Irish a certain 'distaste for life' exhibited by such Irish writers as Swift, Joyce and Beckett, and commented further:

> Mr O'Brien just misses this by holding resolutely to his norm of fantasy; the Augustan periphrasis and earthy deflations, the mock-scholastic debate of *At Swim-Two-Birds* result in something peculiarly wild and sweet. Only the prolonged pains inflicted on Trellis at the end begin to move the comedy on to uglier ground.

Timothy Hilton, reviewing the Penguin Modern Classics edition in 1967, noted the detailed savagery of the cruelties inflicted on the mad King Sweeney in the source work, the medieval Irish poem, *Buile Suibhne*, which he describes as 'a document unparalleled for the vicious oddity of its hero's mishaps' and, discussing O'Brien's use of this material, he comments:

> O'Brien's sense of humour is a sharp instrument; it penetrates the myth, its inexplicable and implacable violence and desolation, leaves it intact and makes it comic . . . In that myth . . . O'Brien hit on precisely the subject of his best, early work, a strange union of laughter with beauty and pain.

O'Brien's chosen weapon is irony and it is, as Benstock remarks, an irony without a centre of gravity. Benstock concedes that 'it would be unjust to overlook Brian O'Nolan's constant desire to set the smug world on it ear' but accuses him of exhibiting 'a perpetual tendency to cold feet'. This weakness Benstock ascribes to O'Nolan's failure to achieve a Joycean distance from his target through the well-tried strategy of exile. Certainly, O'Brien would seem to have been submerged by the parochial literary world of Dublin. He early became a big fish in a small pond and subsequent circumstances trapped him for good. Thereafter, perhaps, his drinking and his journalism contributed to his gradual decline. Of all his books, perhaps, only *The Third Policeman* (to which Benstock scarcely does justice) achieves a genuinely organic completeness. The cyclical pattern of hellish retribution envisaged there seems to provide O'Brien with a controlling context for his wild flights of comic fantasy. This dark story of murder and retribution, a sort of *Playboy of the Western World* in which Christy Mahon really does murder his da and the dirty deed takes over firmly from the gallus story, seems to provide O'Brien with a tonal stablity which is lacking in some of his other works. His hilarious satire on the Irish language revival, *An Béal Bocht*, is, for much of its short length, wildly funny but, rather like *At Swim*, it slumps at the end into a mood of quite another sort, when the central character, Bónapart Ó Cúnasa, briefly encounters his father for the very first time. The father, imprisoned for years, is now free. The son is on his way to prison. Their brief encounter has a Sisyphean horror which sorts oddly with the novel's earlier comic scenes. The two novels which O'Brien completed later in his career, *The Hard Life* and *The Dalkey Archive*, both leave one with a sense of dissatisfaction. In the former (*pace* Anthony Cronin who has described it as 'a little, late gem' and 'an astounding little success') the humour seems to have lost its early savour and to have deteriorated into schoolboy contrivance and heavy-handed improbability. The Emmett-like world of 'Cruiskeen Lawn' with its quaint mechanical devices and daft inventions, although an adequate basis for the newspaper sketches, proves an uneasy novelistic ploy. The tale of Mr Colloppy and the gravid water, and the visit to the Pope, is ultimately rather a stodgy sort of comedy, with the jokes proving almost as ponderous as Mr Colloppy himself. There is a failure here in the effort at blending the real and the fantastic. *The Dalkey Archive*, replete with bits cannibalised from the then unpublished novel, *The Third Policeman*, is a sad muddle. A brilliant comic opening is not sustained and the novelist's wilder fancies founder again in a muddled adventure into realism where his imagination loses its way. Best in the end, perhaps, to recall the triumphs rather than the failures. For a bilingual writer to have left us a brilliant comic masterpiece in each of our two languages is surely reason for gratitude.

SELECTED BIBLIOGRAPHY

RELATED WORKS

The Third Policeman, completed 1940, pub. London, 1967.
An Béal Bocht, Dublin, 1941. Trans., *The Poor Mouth* by Patrick C. Power, London, 1973.
The Hard Life, London, 1961.
The Dalkey Archive, London, 1964.

BIOGRAPHY

Ciarán Ó'Nualláin, *Óige an Dearthár*, Dublin, 1973.
Anne Clissmann, *Flann O'Brien: A Critical Introduction to His Writing*, Dublin, 1975.
Anthony Cronin, *No Laughing Matter: The Life and Times of Flann O'Brien*, London, 1989.

CRITICAL STUDIES

T. O'Keefe (ed.), *Myles*, London, 1973.
Ann Clissmann (see above).
Rudiger Imhof (ed.) *Alive-Alive O!: Flann O'Brien's, 'At Swim-Two-Birds'*, Dublin & Totowa, 1985.

CRITICAL ARTICLES

John Wain, 'To Write for My Own Race', *Encounter* XXIX 1 (July 1967), 71-85.
Del Ivan Janik, 'Flann O'Brien: The Novelist as Critic', *Eire-Ireland*, IV, 4 (Winter 1969), 64-72.
Ruth apRoberts, '*At Swim-Two-Birds* and the Novel as Self-Evident Sham', *Eire-Ireland*, VI, 2 (Summer 1971), 76-97.

Mary Power, 'Flann O'Brien and Classical Satire', *Eire-Ireland*, XIII, 1 (Spring 1978), 87-102.

Margaret Felter, 'Department of Interesting Authors: A Flash Through the Tunnel', *Journal of Irish Literature*, IX, 3 (Sept. 1980), 136-150.

Joseph Browne, 'Flann O'Brien: Post Joyce or Propter Joyce?', *Eire-Ireland*, XIX, 4 (Winter 1984), 148-157.

William M. Chace, 'Joyce and Flann O'Brien', *Eire-Ireland*, XXII, 4 (Winter 1987), 140-152.

XVI

Frank O'Connor (1903-1966)

DUTCH INTERIOR

He was born Michael Francis O'Donovan and later devised his well-known literary pseudonym by combining his second forename with the family name of his mother, Minnie O'Connor. The father had served with the Munster Fusiliers in South Africa. The mother worked as a charwoman. As is clear from autobiographical writings such as *An Only Child* and *My Father's Son*, the boy was passionately devoted to his mother and frankly terrified of his father, who tended to become violent and obstreperous during his not infrequent drinking bouts. Michael attended St Patrick's National School, where he had the good fortune to be taught by the novelist and short story writer, Daniel Corkery, who was to become his first literary mentor. Corkery introduced him to the Irish language and to Irish nationalism. The young O'Connor took the Republican side in the Civil War and was imprisoned at Gormanstown. After his release, he worked as a librarian in Sligo, Wicklow and his native Cork, and began to contribute both poetry and prose to the *Irish Statesman*. The journal's editor, George Russell, was to replace Corkery as his literary guide. O'Connor's first collection of short stories, *Guests of the Nation*, appeared in 1931. The celebrated title story and others also in the collection reflect the writer's early experience of Irish political turbulence and his changing attitudes to various aspects of political idealism and its effects on individuals. He soon became disenchanted with the new Ireland which emerged from the Civil War struggle and, in particular, developed an almost pathological hatred of DeValera, the most powerful of the major figures to survive the vicious conflict and play a leading part in the politics of a newly independent Free State. O'Connor was appointed librarian of the Pembroke Library in Dublin in 1928. His first novel, *The Saint and Mary Kate*, was published in 1932 and, in 1935, he was appointed to the Board of the Abbey Theatre, where he came into close contact with W. B. Yeats, for whom he developed an intense respect and admiration.

Although he wrote novels, biography, poetry, plays and criticism, O'Connor's finest work was done in two areas, the short story and translations from the Irish. He made himself expert in Old, Middle and Modern Irish and, as his distaste for the Ireland of his own day increased, he more and more turned to the task of preserving through his translations what was best in the Irish past. His most enduring work consists of the best of his short stories (e.g. classics such as 'Guests of the Nation', 'In The Train', 'Bridal Night', 'The Long Road to Ummera' and many more) and the translations contained in *Kings, Lords and Commons* (1961) and *The Little Monasteries* (1963). His version of Brian Merriman's famous comic satire, *The Midnight Court*, was published in 1945 and, free though the translation is, it remains the most satisfying of all the many Englishings of this much-translated comic masterpiece.

O'Connor married, in 1938, Evelyn Bowen Speaight, formerly the wife of the well-known actor Robert Speaight and, in 1939, after the death of Yeats, his turbulent connection with the Abbey Theatre was severed when he was forced to resign from the Board of Directors. His Dublin decade was now at an end and he and Evelyn went to live in Wicklow. For a few years, he was poetry editor of the newly launched magazine, *The Bell*, to which he also contributed short stories, essays and reviews. His second novel, *Dutch Interior* (1940), was promptly banned, as was his fine translation of *The Midnight Court*. The wartime period was a difficult time for Irish writers, with censorship at home and restricted markets abroad. O'Connor did some broadcasting for Radio Éireann and the BBC, reading his stories and translations. In 1948, he and his wife separated and their divorce was made final in 1952. Late in 1951, he accepted invitations to teach at Northwestern University and at Harvard, thus beginning a new phase of his career, as university teacher and writer-in-residence at various American colleges. The brilliant auto-didact, who had left school at fourteen, proved a tremendous success as a teacher of literature and his lectures were invariably thronged. Two of his critical works, *The Mirror in the Roadway: A Study of the Modern Novel* (1956) and his celebrated study of the short story, *The Lonely Voice* (1962), derived from his experience of teaching in America. In 1953, he married a young Harvard graduate student, Harriet Rich. For a time, he moved frequently between America and Ireland. In 1961, he published his autobiographical volume, *An Only Child*, a moving celebration of his enduring affection for his mother, who had died in 1952. In 1961, also, while lecturing at Stanford University, he suffered a stroke. He returned to Ireland and took up his final residence in Dublin. Trinity College awarded him a D. Litt. in 1962 and appointed him to a teaching post in the college, where he again enjoyed the kind of popular success with students which had been his in America. He died in Dublin in 1966. His historical survey of Irish literature, *The Backward Look*, was published in the following year.

DUTCH INTERIOR (1940)

Frank O'Connor's uncertainty about his capacities as a novelist were vividly conveyed in a series of letters which he wrote to his Cork friend, Nancy McCarthy, in 1931, at the time when he was bringing his first novel, *The Saint and Mary Kate*, to completion. At times he seemed confident that the book would be a great success and even volunteered the daring comment that 'it may be a masterpiece', but such moods did not endure for long and he later modified his view, simply stating that it would prove to be a 'readable bit of humorous writing'. Later again, he seemed to despair of the entire enterprise and, in June 1931, wrote to Nancy McCarthy:

> The truth is that I know nothing whatever of novel writing or didn't while I was writing it. A novel . . . is the smallest number of characters in the least number of situations necessary to precipitate a given crisis. But what use are definitions when my book is the greatest number of characters in the greatest number of situations leading up to a non-existent crisis. It's deplorable. A man with half my talent would have done it ten times better.

In the event, reviews were mixed. Yeats liked the novel and praised it in letters to friends but some of the Irish reviewers were frankly hostile. English critics were kinder to the book, on the whole, some of them remarking its poetic qualities which they saw as tempering the work's drab realism. This first novel is, in fact, derivative in its treatment of character and incident, showing clearly the influence of Dickens in its fondness for poignantly touching climaxes and of O'Casey in its handling of the varied inhabitants of the Cork tenement, the 'Doll's House', in which the novel's people all reside together. Towards the end of the book, O'Connor opens up the rather claustrophobic scene a little, sends his main character off to Dublin and embarks on a kind of brief venture into a James Stephens-like picaresque, as the two protagonists of the book's title, the 'Saint' (Phil Dinan) and Mary Kate, find their way home again from Dublin to Cork. Indeed, the entire novel frequently recalls *The Charwoman's Daughter*, with Kate as a Lee-side Mary Makebelieve, going forth in a cruel world to confront its terrors. The depiction of the tenement dwellers and the harshness of their poverty-stricken lives is competent enough. The good-hearted busybody nicknamed 'Dona Nobis' is a memorable creation and O'Connor sketches convincingly the sleazy existence of Kate's prostitute mother, Babe McCormick. The central opposition in the novel is between the simplistic goodness of the 'Saint' and 'the insane methodicalness with which he ruled his life' on the one hand, and Kate's tentative strivings after sexual fulfilment on the other. Phil, ravaged with grief after his beloved mother's death, embarks on an obsessive programme of religious perfectionism more suited to an anchorite in a desert cave than to a lusty young Cork carpenter. His attitudes to sex, along with his daily round of ascetic practices, make him seem a near simpleton but it is worth noting that Joyce had employed a similar tactic in *A Portrait of the Artist as a Young Man* when he had Stephen Dedalus embark on a programme of strict self-denial and prayer after his repentance for his sins of the flesh. Stephen's period of mortification is, however, brief and soon declines into an inevitable spiritual sterility, while Phil Dinan's pious practices continue throughout the entire novel and completely frustrate any possibility of meaningful union between him and the girl who loves him. He refuses to kiss Kate on the grounds that, if he did so, he would have to marry her and he characterises his feelings for her not as love which should be explored and developed but as lust which must be repressed. O'Connor indulges in frequent authorial intrusions of a rather self-conscious kind ('her chronicler, as a disciple of the realist school, feels bound to add' – 'It is right for an author to dwell . . .') and is much given to heavy-handed philosophical generalisations ('no man ever outgrows abstract interests and no woman ever grows into them') which recall the weaker aspects of James Stephens. He also lards his novel with frequent examples of Cork idiom and slang, a risk which Daniel Corkery carefully avoided but one which O'Connor's friend and contemporary, Sean O'Faolain, also seemed willing to run. All in all, Phil Dinan's obsessive innocence requires something other than the novel's sustained realism to make it at all convincing. As he is depicted, he soon becomes irritatingly improbable and poor Kate seems well rid of him when he wanders off in search of his identity and she is left behind in the dreary world of her mother and Dona Nobis. Phil's infuriating innocence cries aloud for some sort of tonal sophistication from the author which O'Connor, at this early stage of his career, simply cannot provide. One is left wondering whether he may have had his tongue in his cheek when he appended as epigraph to this novel the verses from St Teresa:

> Let nothing disturb thee
> Nothing affright thee,
> Everything passes,
> God is unchanging.
> He who has patience,
> Everything comes to him,
> He who has God,
> He lacks for nothing –
> God, only, suffices.

His second venture in the novel form came in the years after his frustrating experiences as a member of the Board of Directors of the Abbey Theatre. *Dutch Interior* began life under an earlier title, *The Provincials*, which makes its subject matter abundantly clear. O'Connor had never quite shaken off the powerful influence of his earliest literary mentor and his second novel invites comparison with *The Threshold of Quiet* at many points. The setting, in O'Connor's native city of Cork, is identical. This is the same claustrophobic, rain-swept, inward-looking town, inhabited by aspiring but frustrated young provincials. The gathering at Fr Lynott's house in Chapter XI ('Grania's Lullaby'), where dreams are briefly allowed to flower in an atmosphere of social warmth and cordiality, is indebted to similar encounters at Martin Cloyne's house by the Lough, in the earlier novel. Peter Devane, with his intense attachment to his wayward brother, Gus, recalls Corkery's Stevie Galvin. Nevertheless, *Dutch Interior* is, in a number of important respects, very different from his old teacher's austere and only novel. Where Corkery was content to present his provincial town with a calculatedly genial objectivity, O'Connor chooses to depict a damp, gossipy, mean-minded place in which ideals crumble and love rots. Young men age prematurely and, as Peter Devane tells Stevie Dalton in Chapter X, personality goes to seed and produces 'characters' like himself, bitter, disillusioned figures who never succeed in realising their youthful ideals. Corkery's 'quiet desperation' may leave his main protagonists lonely and near to despair, but the novel's ending insists that 'when such quiet souls quit our company, it is the sweetness of their quiet spirits that remains like a fragrance in the air'. *Dutch Interior* offers no such soothing reassurance at the end. No sweetness or fragrance here – instead, we have Donoghue, the cuckolded husband, coming inno-cently to Stevie Dalton, his wife's seducer, to announce delightedly the birth of the child which he thinks his own. As Donoghue goes back happily to his desecrated hearth, Stevie tells his friend, Peter Devane, that he sees around him only ghosts:

> 'Ghosts,' Stevie said softly. 'Nothing but ghosts. My own ghosts this time.' He looked round him : the bright room with its cheerful furniture seemed suddenly to have become empty.

Nor does O'Connor match Corkery's clarity of design. *Dutch Interior* begins very promisingly, but soon deteriorates into a string of impressionistic vignettes which, though often vividly realised in themselves, never cohere into a convincing novelistic whole. The opening chapter, in which Peter Devane rushes from school and hastens to the fine terrace house where his mother works as a charwoman, is splendidly evocative of the boy's suppressed aspirations and of his deep affection for the mother – familiar O'Connor territory this, perhaps, but realised here with an almost Lawrencian sensuousness. As Peter explores the upper rooms of the elegant house, takes tea in the cosy warmth of the basement kitchen, and walks homeward with his weary mother, one thinks of Paul and Mrs Morel on the loving little outings which bind them together at the beginning of *Sons and Lovers*. Unhappily, O'Connor fails to sustain or develop this strand of the novel. Peter Devane is set aside, to allow for the introduction of the other major figure, Stevie Dalton. Then, we must encounter 'the beautiful Miss Maddens', a trio who seem to have strayed out of some rambling O'Connor short story like 'The Holy Door'. Enter also Eileen, whose ruinous marriage to Donoghue is yet another aside in a novel which seems to consist mainly of such digressions from an abandoned central theme. Gus Devane, Peter's rackety brother, must depart for America, only to return later in the manner of George Moore's Bryden of 'Home Sickness', unable to settle happily either in Cork or out of it. Chunks of the novel precisely echo O'Connor's work in the shorter form for which he is better known. The visit paid by Gus Devane and Stevie Dalton to their old school and their old teacher, McCarthy, is obviously linked to the short story, 'Mac's Masterpiece', published in 1938. Inevitably, the author himself recognised his novel's many defects and enumerated them in a letter to Sean O'Faolain in the summer of 1939, the year before publication:

> You needn't be either terrified or envious of the novel – it's no good! Potentially, I still think, very good: a lovely design but I can't fill it. It's too ambitious – there are vast empty spaces where the implications elude me entirely, where they flap about like canvas unpegged in a high wind. That's why I say 'simplify' and reread the Workhouse Ward in despair. I too can make a story of two people chattering and create them with past and future out of one crude situation, riding them like a jockey, but a race that is all falls and running after a runaway horse – that's not a work of art but a bloody endurance test.

Later, he was to confess to another friend, Stan Stewart, that he was reluctant to attempt another novel, though his contracts with publishers required one of him:

> . . . my mind is small and intense, and to take it travelling through the thousand paragraphs of a novel is like embarking on a Siberian journey. I like short trips in fiction. Castlebar to Ennis is about my average; an excellent sprinter but why must I compete in a Marathon?

The novel's title has intrigued and puzzled many commentators. Benedict Kiely, who slates the work with unaccustomed severity, calls it 'a poor novel' and cannot decide whether the 'savage irony' of the title is deliberate or not:

Dutch Interior is a poor novel and frequently it forces the reader into thinking that O'Connor has strung together enough of his worst short stories to fill nearly three hundred pages. But the savage irony of the title, whether deliberate or not, gives the shapeless book a certain importance and all through it O'Connor is looking, not into clean and coloured domestic content, but out over a threshold of unquiet at badly-lighted streets where sodden figures move uncertainly in the rain.

Kiely's doubts about the possible ambiguity of the title recall a corresponding uncertainty about O'Connor's epigraph to his first novel. Years later, in his critical work on the Novel, *The Mirror in the Roadway* (1957), O'Connor himself, in commenting on the rise of the novel during the nineteenth century, referred to the solidly domestic nature of what he saw as an essentially middle-class form and referred once more to the notion of the 'Dutch interior':

> It was in the Lowlands rather than in England that the middle classes established themselves politically, and pictorially their attitude was fully expressed in Dutch genre painting. Except for the moral passion which is literature's main contribution to the arts, a Dutch interior might be chosen as the ideal of the nineteenth-century novelist. Dutch painting clarifies what we can already discern in the remains of the middle-class Elizabethan theatre. The novel, when it came, would be primarily domestic and civic, would concentrate on the study of society and the place of the individual in it, and on the structure of the classes, professions, and trades rather than on the mythological or historical past.

This suggests that the novel's title may be, at once, ironic and almost elegiac. On the one hand, O'Connor's often sleazy and penurious domestic settings are scarcely on a par with the solidly furnished dwellings of the comfortable burghers who gaze at us from Dutch genre paintings. The tatty homes of such as 'the beautiful Miss Maddens' scarcely accord with such standards. Yet, the novel does take us into homes which are at least aspiring to middle-class status – Eileen's home in the early days of her marriage, Fr Lynott's drawing-room with its piano and its creature comforts, even the shabby but comfortable apartment in which Peter Devane lives with his mother. The elegiac note enters, one feels, in the extent to which this novel fails, inevitably, to match up to O'Connor's notion of the novel as concerned with 'the structure of the classes, professions and trades'. His unmannerly town of Cork emerges as altogether too provincial, too introspective, too thinly constituted in a social sense, to allow of the kind of solid novelistic study which he seems to have most admired. Thomas Flanagan, who knew O'Connor well, describes *Dutch Interior* as 'a savage, tearing and lonely book, a chronicle of spirit wasted and wasting in a provincial backwater'. O'Connor himself had identified the work's central weakness in his letter to O'Faolain, when he confessed that the book contained 'vast empty spaces where the implications elude me entirely'. If he had been capable of pursuing that insight further, he might have succeeded in giving his novel some of the substance it lacks and might have saved it from becoming the kind of confused shadow play, the blurred pageant of futility that, sadly, it is. Shortly after its publication, O'Connor contributed an article on 'The Future of Irish Literature' to the January 1942 'Irish Number' of Cyril Connolly's *Horizon*. In it, he lumped together O'Faolain's *Bird Alone*, his own *Dutch Interior*, Gerald O'Donovan's *Father Ralph* and Joyce's *A Portrait of the Artist as a Young Man*, characterising each of them as 'the novel every Irish writer who isn't a rogue or an imbecile is doomed to write when the emptiness and horror of Irish life begins to dawn on him'. He went on to sound once again the kind of criticism of Irish society which his friend, O'Faolain, had also often voiced:

> In Ireland, the moment a writer raises his eyes from the slums and cabins, he finds nothing but a vicious and ignorant middle-class, and for aristocracy the remnants of an English garrison, alien in religion and education. From such material he finds it almost impossible to create a picture of life which, to quote Dumas' definition of the theatre, will embody 'a portrait, a judgement and an ideal'.

If read in these terms, *Dutch Interior* can be seen to offer portraits and judgements aplenty but to lack any sense of the ideal against which such portraits and judgements could be adequately assessed.

SELECTED BIBLIOGRAPHY

RELATED WORKS
The Saint and Mary Kate, London, New York, 1932.

AUTOBIOGRAPHY
An Only Child, London, 1961.
My Father's Son, London, 1968.

BIOGRAPHY
James Matthews, *Voices: A Life of Frank O'Connor*, Dublin, 1983.

CRITICAL STUDIES
Maurice Sheehy (ed.), *Michael/Frank*, Dublin, London, 1969.
Maurice Wohlgelernter, *Frank O'Connor: An Introduction*, New York, 1977.

William M. Tomory, *Frank O'Connor*, Boston, 1981.

CRITICAL ARTICLES

Ruth Sherry, 'Frank O'Connor As Novelist', *Canadian Journal of Irish Studies*, 9, 1 (June 1983), 23-44.

READING LIST

HISTORY

Ernest A. Boyd, *Ireland's Literary Renaissance*, Dublin & London, 1916, rev. ed. 1922.

Lloyd R. Morris, *The Celtic Dawn: A Survey of the Renaissance in Ireland*, New York, 1917.

Stephen Gwynn, *Irish Literature and Drama in the English Language: A Short History*, London, 1936.

Alan Warner, *A Guide to Anglo-Irish Literature*, Dublin, 1981.

Roger McHugh & Maurice Harmon, *Short History of Anglo-Irish Literature*, Dublin, 1982.

A. Norman Jeffares, *Anglo-Irish Literature*, Dublin, 1982.

A. C. Partridge, *Language and Society in Anglo-Irish Literature*, Dublin 1984.

Seamus Deane, *A Short History of Irish Literature*, London, 1986.

CRITICISM

Benedict Kiely, *Modern Irish Fiction – A Critique,* Dublin, 1950.

Estella Ruth Taylor, *The Modern Irish Writers*, New York, 1954.

Herbert Howarth, *The Irish Writers 1880-1940: Literature Under Parnell's Star*, London, 1958.

Vivian Mercier, *The Irish Comic Tradition*, London, 1962.

Francis MacManus, *The Years of the Great Test 1926-39*, Cork, 1967.

Patrick Rafroidi & Maurice Harmon (eds.), *The Irish Novel in Our Time*, Lille, 1976.

Peter Costello, *The Heart Grown Brutal*, Dublin, 1977.

Richard Fallis, *The Irish Literary Renaissance*, Dublin, 1978.

George Watson, *Irish Identity and the Literary Revival*, London, 1979.

Ronald Schleifer (ed.), *The Genres of the Irish Literary Revival*, Dublin,1980.

Terence Brown, *Ireland: A Social and Cultural History 1922-1979*, Glasgow, 1981.

Anthony Cronin, *Heritage Now: Irish Literature in the English Language*, Dingle, 1982.

James M. Cahalan, *Great Hatred, Little Room: The Irish Historical Novel*, Dublin, 1983.

Augustine Martin (ed.), *The Genius of Irish Prose*, Cork, 1985.

Seamus Deane, *Celtic Revivals: Essays in Modern Irish Literature*, London, 1985.

W. J. McCormack, *Ascendancy and Tradition in Anglo-Irish Literary History from 1789-1939*, Oxford, 1985.

John Wilson Foster, *Fictions of the Irish Literary Revival: A Changeling Art*, Dublin, 1987.

David Cairns & Shaun Richards, *Writing Ireland: Colonialism, Nationalism and Culture*, Manchester, 1988.

INDEX